PRAISE FOR *Menstruation Matters*

"*Menstruation Matters* is a must-read for anyone who wants to live in a world where everyone can manage their period with dignity. We still have a long way to go to eradicate stigma and menstrual inequality; however, as the Member of the Scottish Parliament who introduced the bill to make menstrual products available to all who need them in Scotland, I know that progress is possible. Momentum is with the changemakers within the menstrual equality movement. *Menstruation Matters* contains thoughtful suggestions for lawmakers and advocates worldwide to consider. It's a welcome addition to the literature for those who don't want to find themselves on the wrong side of history."
—Monica Lennon, Member of the Scottish Parliament and Sponsor of the Period Products (Free Provision) (Scotland) Act

"Menstruation is an issue of basic human rights and equality. Menstruation is not a reason to deny anyone the right to participate in education, religious worship, politics, or family life. This book brings new insight to a discussion of a topic that has too long been treated as the source of stigma and shame, when menstruation is a reality for half the world's population."
—Indira Jaisring, former Additional Solicitor General of India and Attorney for the plaintiffs in *Indian Young Lawyers Association v. Kerala*

"Periods have become a vital matter of law and policy, in the US and around the globe. *Menstruation Matters* deftly melds scholarship and jurisprudence with on-the-ground advocacy, providing a vital resource for the next generation of feminist legal leaders."
—Jennifer Weiss-Wolf, author of *Periods Gone Public: Taking a Stand for Menstrual Equity*

"Access to period products is not a privilege, it is a right. It means women, girls, and people who menstruate having access to basic activities, capacity to take part in work and in community. *Menstruation Matters* is a brilliant resource and addition to a conversation we need to have — because ultimately all women and girls and people who menstruate are entitled to respect, dignity, and bodily autonomy, and a belief in the integrity of their bodies. It's why, at the City of Melbourne local government, I put forward an Australian first motion to make menstrual products available for free in select council facilities. It's time to end the shame—because menstruation matters."
—Jamal Hakim, Councillor at the City of Melbourne

MENSTRUATION MATTERS

Menstruation Matters

Challenging the Law's Silence on Periods

Bridget J. Crawford *and* Emily Gold Waldman

NEW YORK UNIVERSITY PRESS
New York

NEW YORK UNIVERSITY PRESS
New York
www.nyupress.org

© 2022 by New York University
All rights reserved

References to Internet websites (URLs) were accurate at the time of writing. Neither of the authors nor New York University Press is responsible for URLs that may have expired or changed since the manuscript was prepared.

Library of Congress Cataloging-in-Publication Data
Names: Crawford, Bridget J., author. | Waldman, Emily Gold, author.
Title: Menstruation matters : challenging the law's silence on periods / Bridget J. Crawford and Emily Gold Waldman.
Description: New York : New York University, [2022] |
Includes bibliographical references and index.
Identifiers: LCCN 2021039796 | ISBN 9781479809677 (hardback) | ISBN 9781479809691 (ebook) | ISBN 9781479809684 (ebook other)
Subjects: LCSH: Women—Legal status, laws, etc.—United States. | Menstruation—Social aspects.
Classification: LCC KF478 .C739 2022 | DDC 342.7308/78—dc23
LC record available at https://lccn.loc.gov/2021039796

New York University Press books are printed on acid-free paper, and their binding materials are chosen for strength and durability. We strive to use environmentally responsible suppliers and materials to the greatest extent possible in publishing our books.

Manufactured in the United States of America

10 9 8 7 6 5 4 3 2 1

Also available as an ebook

For Benjamin, Arielle, and Aurora

CONTENTS

Preface	ix
Introduction	1
1 Menstrual Stigma, Shame, and Period Poverty	13
2 The Tampon Tax	34
3 Schools and Menstruation	59
4 Periods in Public	86
5 Periods at Work	109
6 Menstruating While Male	130
7 Menstruation, Health, and the Environment	146
8 Menstrual Capitalism	172
9 Menstruation around the Globe	188
Conclusion	207
Acknowledgments	213
Notes	215
Index	263
About the Authors	275

PREFACE

We embarked on writing this book in 2020 after closely following the state-by-state campaign to repeal the sales tax on menstrual products—commonly called the "tampon tax"—for four years. Gender discrimination, at the cash register and otherwise, flourishes in a culture of silence, stigma, and shame associated with menstruation. As law professors, we were struck by the fact that the law is mostly silent about menstruation, even though approximately half the population menstruates for a large portion of their lives. Until recently, most people would have said that periods are private matters not to be discussed in public. To a certain extent, that culture of silence is changing. "Period poverty" is becoming more visible both in the United States and elsewhere. In many corners, menstrual products like tampons and pads are now understood as the essential products that they are. Indeed, the importance of being able to address the involuntary biological process of menstruation in a reliable, safe, and affordable way has become more obvious than ever, in large part because of the reach of social media.

Inspired by the work of advocates of all ages, we set out to explore the many ways that menstruation matters in law and life in the United States. Our topics include cultural attitudes toward menstruation, the tampon tax, the need for accessible products in schools, prisons, and other public buildings, employment discrimination matters, health and environmental concerns, the complex market for menstrual products, and similar issues in other countries. Our book asks what the law says about menstruation (spoiler alert: not much) and lays out a course of action for legal reform aimed at eliminating menstruation-related barriers to full participation in all aspects of public life.

With this book, we imagine law and society transformed to take into account the biological needs of all people. We invite you to consider the many ways that menstruation matters.

Introduction

"Are you there, law? It's me, menstruation."

These sentences could be the subtitle of this book. The phrasing immediately conjures Judy Blume's beloved book *Are You There God? It's Me, Margaret*—itself a landmark in the cultural acknowledgment of menstruation—and also served as the title we developed for the first-ever law review symposium on menstruation held in 2021.[1] The query is also a real one. Approximately half the world's population menstruates for a significant portion of their lives, and yet the law is remarkably silent about this common human experience.

At first, silence about menstruation may seem unsurprising. After all, menstruation is often viewed as a purely private matter, and indeed many people treat it that way. But menstruation actually implicates a striking number of legal questions that cut across American law, from constitutional law to tax law to education law to employment law and more. For example, if states tax menstrual products while exempting other necessities, does that violate the Equal Protection Clause of the Constitution? If schools do not provide menstrual products to students who need them, does that undermine Title IX's goal of providing "equal access to education" regardless of sex? What obligations do employers have to accommodate the needs of menstruating employees?

These questions are not just hypothetical. A growing menstrual advocacy movement has begun to raise such issues and press for reforms—and these efforts have already yielded tangible results. The law is becoming less silent than before. Since 2016, numerous states have enacted laws eliminating their sales tax on menstrual products, requiring public school districts to provide free menstrual products in school restrooms, and mandating that their prisons provide free menstrual products to inmates. Terms like "tampon tax" and "period poverty" have entered the public discourse, as has the broader concept of "menstrual equity." The menstrual advocacy movement has become a worldwide effort, reaching a recent milestone with Scotland's 2020 passage of the Period Products (Free Provision) (Scotland) Bill—a law that requires local authorities to ensure that period products are obtainable free of charge by all who need them.

This book explores the actual and potential intersections of law and menstruation. It analyzes why the law has historically been so silent about menstruation, why and how a movement has recently gathered steam to raise and address menstruation-related issues, what the existing law can be interpreted to say about these issues, and—perhaps most importantly—what the law *should* say. A common theme underlies our inquiry: law and society should become more responsive to human needs by reducing the barriers that menstruation can impose on full participation in public life.

A Brief History of the Menstrual Advocacy Movement in the United States

Today's menstrual advocacy movement has strong roots in the women's health movement that first developed in the 1970s. Informed by parallel developments in the areas of consumer rights and environmentalism, the women's health movement was spurred by a group of Boston-area women who organized as the Boston Women's Health Book Collective. They sought to remedy a general lack of knowledge about women's health by publishing their own informative booklet, *Women and Their Bodies*, in 1970. The booklet developed into the first edition of *Our Bodies, Ourselves*,[2] which became a foundational resource about women's health in general and about menstruation in particular. Prior to the publication of *Our Bodies, Ourselves*, most educational materials about menstrual products and their use had been written by employees of the same companies that manufactured them.[3] The Boston Women's Health Book Collective provided a very different perspective. The group critiqued the conventional menstrual-products industry, showing how companies promoted a one-size-fits-all approach to menstruation and contributed to myths about menstrual blood as being disgusting or shameful. For example, the group questioned the utility of products like scented tampons, when menstrual blood actually has no odor before it is expelled and comes into contact with the air.[4] The group also helped sound the alarm about toxic shock syndrome, a potentially fatal condition believed to be caused by a toxin-producing bacteria associated with high-absorbency tampons on the market at the time.

In 1980 alone, twenty-eight women died from menstruation-related toxic shock syndrome. Activists from the Boston Women's Health Book Collective and elsewhere pressed the Food and Drug Administration (FDA) to develop warning labels about the importance of using the lowest-absorbency products required and to institute standardized absorbency ratings for tampons.[5] Even though the Boston Women's Health Book Collective no longer publishes *Our Bodies, Ourselves*,[6] the book had an immeasurably important influence, both in developing and amplifying women's voices on matters related to their own health and, as University of Massachusetts professor Chris Bobel explains, by "calling the menstrual product industry to account."[7] These signature achievements helped generations of people to better understand menstruation.

Law in Early Menstrual Activism

It was not easy to get the FDA to respond to the public health crisis of toxic shock syndrome. The Public Citizen Health Research Group, the nonprofit consumer-advocacy group founded by Ralph Nader, had to sue in federal court to get the agency to act.[8] The United States District Court for the District of Columbia ultimately found that the agency had been "unreasonable" in its failure to promulgate final regulations standardizing tampon absorbency. The agency's delay, the court said, "reflects an insensitivity to a long-existing and clearly identifiable problem. [The FDA's] delay is particularly disturbing since the public health and human lives are at stake."[9] The government finally promulgated such regulations almost nine years after the press first widely reported problems of toxic shock syndrome.

Early menstrual activists also pursued legal remedies in another key area: the so-called tampon tax. In the mid-1980s, three Chicago women brought a lawsuit on behalf of themselves and a class of similarly situated individuals seeking an injunction against the Illinois state, city, and local taxes imposed on tampons and pads. In that case, *Geary v. Dominick's Finer Foods, Inc.*,[10] the plaintiffs sued individual retailers of menstrual-hygiene products, the city of Chicago, and state, city, and local taxing authorities, arguing that tampons and pads fell within the relevant state and city tax classification of "medical appliances," which were tax exempt. (Diapers and absorbent pads had already been included in that statutory definition.) Their claim was successful, leading Illinois and Chicago to stop imposing the sales tax on menstrual-hygiene products until 2009, when the regulatory definitions changed and the tax was restored.[11] In 2015, a new generation of menstrual advocates would pick up the mantle of the tampon tax fight in the United States.

Menstrual Activism in the Twenty-First Century

The November 2015 issue of *Cosmopolitan* magazine proclaimed 2015 "the year the period went public."[12] It highlighted "8 Greatest Menstrual Moments of 2015," from musician Kiran Gandhi's running the London marathon without a tampon (becoming a "free-bleeding, stigma-busting sensation") to Apple's updating the iPhone Health app to include period tracking. In addition to these cultural moments, law was also in the mix: the article noted that in July 2015, Canada ended its tax on menstrual products.[13] *Cosmopolitan* also joined forces with advocate Jennifer Weiss-Wolf to launch a Change.org petition calling for the repeal of the tampon tax across the country.[14]

Today's menstrual advocacy draws not only from the women's health movement of the 1970s but also from the third-wave feminist sensibilities and commitments that emerged in the 1990s. The "third wave" mantle was adopted by writers, scholars, artists, and activists as a generational marker and to signify a departure from the feminism of preceding generations.[15] Along with an embrace of a more expansive, fun-loving, and liberating brand of feminism, hallmarks of third-wave feminist activism include engagement with broad social-justice issues, interest in structural economic inequality, and a nuanced understanding of the social and cultural power of media and technology.[16] Chris Bobel has chronicled a variety of activist and artistic third-wave feminist work that includes menstruation themes and concerns.[17] Such work has direct antecedents in Judy Chicago's 1971 photograph "Red Flag," showing the artist removing a bloody tampon, and her 1972 installation "Menstruation Bathroom," featuring a trash can overflowing with bloody menstrual pads and bloody tampons strewn on the floor.[18]

The metaphor of feminism's "waves" and the label "third-wave feminism" are not universally embraced. Nevertheless, as a descriptive label—to frame the sensibilities, experiences, and priorities of those who came to political consciousness in the 1980s and 1990s—the term "third-wave feminism" has utility. In some ways, the current interest in and popularity of menstruation-related work might be understood as a uniquely third-wave feminist engagement with law.[19] At the same time, contemporary menstrual activism extends well beyond the third-wave frame in multiple ways. Looking through the lens of the experience of Jennifer Weiss-Wolf, the US movement's most vocal proponent, is illuminating.

Weiss-Wolf describes coming to menstrual activism in uniquely personal terms: after a New Year's Day polar bear swim with friends, Weiss-Wolf went onto Facebook, where she saw a neighbor's posts for a tampon and pad collection drive for a local food pantry. That led Weiss-Wolf to do more research and write an opinion piece for the *New York Times*; that work in turn snowballed into even more research and policy proposals, which were shared via extensive media outreach.[20]

Weiss-Wolf, who is an attorney, then joined forces with attorney Laura Strausfeld to found in 2016 the nation's first menstruation-related law and policy organization, Period Equity, with a focus on "ensuring that menstrual products are safe, accessible, and affordable for all who need them."[21] Weiss-Wolf has explained, "A central component of my advocacy strategy has been to elevate the national discourse around menstrual equity policy—not only as a way to eradicate stigma and educate the public about the plight of those who lack access, but also to motivate legislators to act and ensure they know the public will is on the side of these laws."[22] Weiss-Wolf keenly understands that changes in cultural attitudes can influence and support legal change.

It is no coincidence that Weiss-Wolf, born in 1967, falls squarely within the third-wave feminist demographic.[23] Her work—and menstrual activism in the United States in general—bears four significant hallmarks of third-wave feminism: building coalitions; embracing a "leaderless" movement; harnessing the media; and recognizing complex individual identities.[24] Consider, for example, Weiss-Wolf's framing of menstruation as a common ground for social-justice movements as well as bipartisan change. "Our issues aren't all the same, but whether you're dissecting it by poverty or gender or any issues that affect things like access, participation, equality, justice, democracy—[menstrual equity touches] all those things. This is why we can't leave it out,"[25] she has reflected. In other words, menstruation is not a single-axis issue that affects a small number of people; it impacts approximately half of the population in numerous ways for a large portion of their lives.

Although Weiss-Wolf is one of the most prominent advocates for menstruation-related issues in the United States, the menstrual advocacy movement has countless "leaders" of all ages. The London Marathon runner featured in *Cosmopolitan*'s November 2015 issue—who was twenty-four years old at the time—explained that "I ran with blood dripping down my legs for sisters who don't have access to tampons and sisters who, despite cramping and pain, hide it away and pretend like it doesn't exist. I ran to say, it does exist, and we overcome it every day."[26] In 2018, a group of Girl Scouts in Brooklyn undertook a project monitoring New York City's compliance with the law to make menstrual products available in public schools.[27] Separate from the efforts of the Brooklyn Girl Scouts, in 2019, three seventh-grade girls (whose school or location was not revealed) staged a "cookie protest" with tampon-shaped cookies when the school principal denied their request that their school make free menstrual products available in school bathrooms.[28] When images of the cookies went viral, they created their own website to further spread their message. What those cookie-baking seventh graders and others understand is that social media is a highly effective way of normalizing conversations about menstruation in order to effect change. Such conversations are particularly important, as chapter 1 discusses, because longstanding silence about menstruation helped lay the groundwork for the law's failure to address it. Recent menstrual activism has also begun increasingly emphasizing that not all who menstruate identify as female, consistent with both third-wave feminist and contemporary sensibilities that personal identity is complex.[29]

The current menstrual-activism movement explicitly and directly engages with law in ways that would be familiar to feminists of the "second wave" in the 1970s. The efforts to eliminate the tampon tax have included lawsuits, as well as legislative and public advocacy. These strategies are mutually reinforcing. Just a few months after a group of plaintiffs filed a class-action lawsuit seeking a refund of all New York State sales tax paid on menstrual products,[30] the New York state legislature voted in 2016 to exempt menstrual products from taxation. The attorneys reflected, "There's no question that the lawsuit brought a lot of attention to this issue and was a powerful catalyst for change."[31] Engagement with the law is thus a hallmark of the contemporary menstrual advocacy movement. This book takes up the challenge of envisioning how law and society can be better adapted to the needs of the approximately one-half of the population that menstruates for a large portion of their lives. An involuntary biological process like menstruation should never be an obstacle to full participation in public life.

Organization and Structure of This Book

Chapter 1 sets the backdrop for contemporary conversations about law and menstruation. For years, menstruation has been treated as a largely "private" matter that is not within the realm of polite public discourse. A general cultural squeamishness in talking about the biology of menstruation, and of female bodies in particular, has paved the way for the law's general silence about menstruation. That silence is closely connected to what is known internationally as "period poverty," which includes, among other issues, the lack of access to affordable menstrual products and the lack of access to sanitation and other supplies for menstrual hygiene. Period poverty can become more visible during economic downturns, and is exacerbated by multiple governmental policies.[32] For example, even though menstrual products are a necessity, certain governmental benefits cannot be used to purchase them. These policies have resulted not necessarily from an overt intent to discriminate against those who menstruate but rather from the historic stigma surrounding open and frank discussion of women's biological needs. These policies both perpetuate that stigma and impose tangible financial harms.

One of those financial harms is the tampon tax, to which chapter 2 turns. There are still many states that impose a sales tax on menstrual products, often while exempting numerous other items that are deemed necessities rather than luxuries. Some states even go further, exempting items like tattoos and cowboy boots while still taxing tampons and pads. In recent years, states including New York, Florida, and others have repealed the tampon tax, and there is now a state-by-state campaign coordinated by Period Equity to repeal the sales tax on menstrual products in all states that retain it. Chapter 2 argues that exempting other products from state sales tax, while continuing to tax menstrual products, is an unconstitutional form of sex discrimination.[33]

Chapter 3 considers ways that menstruation can hold students back from fully participating in school—including a lack of access to menstrual products, strict "bathroom break" policies that limit students' ability to attend to their menstrual needs, and more—and explores legal remedies for addressing this issue. Within the past few years, awareness has grown about these challenges, and some lawmakers have already taken action at the state and local levels, as have individual school districts. We analyze the successful advocacy and political efforts that have yielded such reforms, explore where existing law fits in, and consider what more is necessary.[34]

Chapter 4 provides an overview of efforts to make menstrual products available in public spaces, with a particular focus on prisons. Since 2017, Federal Bureau of Prisons policy has suggested that federal prisons should provide free menstrual products to inmates. The First Step Act, enacted at the end of 2018, made this a legal requirement for federal facilities.[35] Some states followed suit, but the majority of states still allow prisons to charge inmates—often at exorbitant rates—for the menstrual products they need. Other menstruation-related abuses in prisons include shaming and harassment; some prisons have even limited the menstrual products that prison visitors can use or wear when they enter. Outside the prison context, some municipalities have started initiatives to provide free menstrual products in other public spaces; this chapter explores those as well.

Chapter 5 considers challenges that employees face while menstruating. These can include limited access to restrooms, strict restrictions on breaks and leaves, and even extreme situations like being terminated for menstruating at work. This chapter explores various ways that existing law—and possible clarifications and expansions of it—can better ensure that menstruation does not prevent people from fully participating in the workplace. It also analyzes menstrual-leave laws, which have never been pursued in the United States but do exist in several other countries, including Japan and parts of China.

Chapter 6 brings to the forefront a discussion of the fact that not all who menstruate identify as cis girls and women. In 2019, in response to criticism from transgender advocates, Procter & Gamble agreed to eliminate the "Venus" or woman symbol from the packaging of Always pads. Some advocates hailed the change as making the products more accessible to trans and gender-nonbinary consumers. Others critiqued the company for erasing women from its advertising.[36] This chapter explores how that tension plays out within the law itself. Because a male/female sex binary is embedded in key areas of antidiscrimination doctrine, the most straightforward legal strategy often may be to characterize unfavorable treatment of menstruation as a form of discrimination against women. But that language runs the risk of underinclusivity. We suggest a way of navigating this tension: emphasizing that the negative treatment of menstruation reflects a form of sex discrimination that harms all who menstruate.

Chapter 7 addresses both health and environmental aspects of menstrual products. These products are put close to—or inside—human bodies, and yet their safety has never been studied systematically, even though they contain potentially dangerous chemicals. To address the unknown risks associated with tampons and pads, this chapter argues for the necessity of legal reform. There are a variety of public-law changes and private-governance initiatives that, combined with better testing and disclosure laws, could lead to a more sustainable menstrual-product industry. In this context, part of what "sustainable" means is human health and safety; it also means legal reform that seeks to preserve the earth's resources and environment. Tampons and pads generate a tremendous amount of waste and contribute to pollution in ways that the law is well equipped to address, in tandem with other public and private legal reforms.

Chapter 8 turns to a consideration of menstruation as big business. Increasingly, companies are using messages of female empowerment and gender equality in order to sell products. Menstruation-related apps for smart phones have also become increasingly common. The companies that sell—or more commonly, give away—period-tracking and fertility apps typically require users to enter their name, email address, age, and gender, along with the highly personal data about their menstrual cycles.[37] That aggregated data then becomes a commodity for advertisers as well as hackers. United States data-privacy laws, which are notoriously less rigorous than the laws of the European Union, need to be revised to provide robust protection for sensitive health information such as this. Relatedly, in the elite sports context, coaches of organizations like the US Women's National Soccer Team have begun monitoring their athletes' menstrual cycles in order to optimize their performance. The team's former fitness coach, Dawn Scott, adjusted each player's diet, sleep, and training schedule in response to this individual menstrual-cycle information, later saying that period tracking was one of the many strategies that "helped us win" the 2019 World Cup.[38] Sports, too, is a big business, and menstrual monitoring is now part of the business strategy.

Chapter 9 broadens the lens even further to explore the menstrual advocacy movement in the global context. Almost all of the topics covered by this book are important issues in other countries as well. Indeed, menstruation—as a common experience of approximately half the world's population for multiple decades of their lives—is a sort of unifier, cutting across other divisions like race, class, and national origin. And the menstrual advocacy movements in different countries have drawn from and built upon each other. For example, efforts to repeal the tampon tax coevolved (with different levels of success) in Canada, India, Australia, Germany, and the UK, after Kenya led the way in 2004. This chapter focuses on several specific menstrual reforms in other countries: India's elimination of the menstruation-based ban on girls and women ages ten to fifty from visiting the Lord Ayyapppa Temple, as well as its classification of menstrual products as tax exempt; Kenya's program to distribute menstrual products to all students; Australia's elimination of the tampon tax and New Zealand's program to provide free menstrual products in numerous schools; and, finally, Scotland's landmark passage of a law guaranteeing free menstrual products to all who need them.

What each chapter shows, in distinct but related ways, is that *menstruation matters*—and that it matters in ways that the law can and should address. In order to make sure that all people can be full participants in every aspect of public life, law and society need to take into account the biological fact of menstruation. The recent salience of menstruation in public discourse has shone a spotlight on the ways that ignoring biological difference—such as assuming nonmenstruating people as the norm and treating menstruation as an aberration—can lead to rules and structures that perpetuate inequality. Addressing these issues will help all members of society become equal participants in the public life that is necessary to a flourishing economy, democracy, and cultural landscape.

Notes on Language

Throughout this book, we seek to use inclusive language that recognizes that biology, sex, and gender are not coextensive terms, and that not all who menstruate identify as female. A photo posted to Facebook in 2017 by transgender artist and advocate Cass Clemmer is a striking visual reminder that menstruating bodies come in all shapes, sizes, and gender presentations, representing the full spectrum of humanity. Clemmer is shown sitting in an open-legged position on a bench wearing light-colored trousers that have a period stain, holding a sign saying "Periods are NOT Just for Women #bleedingwhiletrans."[39]

Throughout the book, we use a variety of terms to describe diverse human experiences of gender identity, recognizing that terms and language are constantly changing.[40] Some terms we use may be familiar to readers. "Sex assigned at birth" refers to the label given at that time, typically by doctors, based on external genitalia. "Gender identity" refers to a person's internal sense of themselves as a gendered being. "Gender expression" is a person's outward gender presentation. "Transgender" (frequently shortened to "trans") refers to someone whose gender identity, gender expression, or both are different from that "typically associated" with the sex they were assigned at birth.[41] "Cisgender" (frequently shortened to "cis") refers to someone who is not trans. A "gender-nonbinary" individual has a gender expression that is perceived as inconsistent with the either/or cultural stereotypes of masculinity or femininity. A "genderqueer" person has a gender identity that is neither male nor female; the identity may be a combination of gender identities or outside any gender-based categories at all.[42]

That said, we do refer to "women and girls" in various places throughout the book, and this happens for several reasons. Sometimes we are doing so because particular researchers or projects did, and we are attempting to describe the work of others. At other times, we use this language in an analysis of historic views and treatment of menstruation. A particularly complex linguistic issue comes up in the context of developing effective legal claims within the existing jurisprudence, as we discuss in chapter 6. We take to heart the writings of Trina Grillo, who argued that "essentialism is not always a bad thing; however, unconscious, self-protective, self-advancing essentialism is. The question is whether the essentialism, which is sometimes unavoidable, is explicit, is considered temporary, and is contingent."[43] We seek to make ours temporary and contingent, following Grillo's model.

In the effort to combat stigma, shame, and discrimination, the voices of all people who menstruate should be amplified. Any tentative and contingent embrace of essentialism in the context of legal advocacy must be distinguished from a lack of awareness or a desire to exclude. When it comes to talking about the complexity of the human experience, the English language is impoverished in many respects, but we who seek a truly inclusive society must represent, include, value, and honor the full range of human experience. Too long have law and society been organized around the needs of those whose voices, bodies, and experiences are presumed to be the norm. This book seeks to change that.

1

Menstrual Stigma, Shame, and Period Poverty

Every month during menstruation, Rachel Krengel, a young London mother of two, had three strategies to manage on her limited budget: wearing a single pad for twenty hours; wearing a diaphragm to catch the blood; or wearing nothing at all and bleeding through her clothes. Krengel did not even tell her partner about her lack of menstrual supplies. Her silence, Krengel explained, was linked to deep feelings of stigma and shame. In later reflecting on the experience, Krengel astutely connected silence around menstruation and silence around poverty. Observing that taboos about discussing menstruation can lead women to "hand off tampons to each other like we're doing a drug deal," Krengel reflected that "[t]wo massively stigmatized experiences—menstruation and poverty—intersect to create this bizarre and horrible form of poverty." She added that, as between purchasing menstrual products and buying food for the family, the choice was clear: "You can make dinner for four people for [a small amount of money].... That seemed so much more important than something that was only for me. [Menstrual products] are the first thing that goes under the bus when you're poor."[1]

A homeless woman named Nancy described similar sentiments in a podcast interview at the Women's Free Homeless Clinic in Santa Barbara, California. Nancy recounted that when she could not afford tampons or pads, she would "[s]tick rags up in there. Maybe find an old shirt alongside a road and stick it up in there. I've done that." Echoing Krengel's observations, the clinic's medical director, Jorie Nilson, described how she consistently saw women prioritizing food over menstrual supplies. "They spend their money on food because that's the basic necessity," Nilson explained. "Any money they have goes to food." The clinic has thus started providing women with free menstrual products because, as Nilson put it, those are "part of basic healthcare for a woman."[2]

Worldwide, the inability to manage one's menstruation in a safe, affordable, and clean way—free of stigma or shame—remains a persistent issue. In the United States, where approximately 10.5% of the population lives in poverty, that poverty is not distributed equally. Approximately 11.5% of all women live in poverty, whereas for men the figure is 9.4%.[3] One study of low-income women in St. Louis, Missouri, by researcher Anne Sebert Kuhlmann, found that nearly two-thirds of those surveyed had been unable to afford menstrual products at some point in the previous year.[4] Menstrual products are not covered by government grocery-assistance programs like the Supplemental Nutrition Assistance Program (known as SNAP or "food stamps") and the Special Supplemental Nutrition Program for Women, Infants, and Children (known as WIC), both of which are limited to food. Indeed, Kuhlman's study found that some of her survey participants had needed to sell their food stamps (at a discount) in order to be able to afford tampons.[5]

Temporary Assistance to Needy Families (TANF), introduced as part of the 1996 government overhaul of the welfare system, provides some limited help in this regard.[6] TANF is a cash benefit for families with children, and this cash can be used for many things, including menstrual products. But TANF is time limited. The federal government sets a lifetime limit of sixty months of benefits, and states are free to set their own lower limits. In Connecticut, for example, a TANF recipient can receive benefits for only twenty-one months (with six-month extensions allowed in some cases).[7] In Mississippi, the monthly TANF benefit for a family of three is $179.[8] Given that the average American woman spends about $18,000 on menstrual products over the course of a lifetime,[9] and given the wide range of other expenses faced by TANF recipients, TANF alone does not keep menstrual products within reach for many people.

For younger people, the lack of access to menstrual products is linked to school absenteeism, as discussed more fully in chapter 3. In the United States, the Harris Poll (commissioned by Thinx, Inc., and a nonprofit entity called PERIOD) recently conducted a study entitled "State of the Period," surveying one thousand teens who menstruate. The results clearly demonstrate the connection between product access and absenteeism. A full 20% of the respondents reported struggling to afford period products (or not being able to afford them at all), 25% said they had missed class because of a lack of access to products, and 84% said that they had either missed class time or known someone who missed class time because of a lack of access to products. Two-thirds also said that they had felt stress due to a lack of access to products, and 61% reported wearing a tampon or pad for more than four hours because they did not have enough access to products.[10] Law professor Christopher Cotropia recently conducted a survey of 693 females and reached roughly similar findings.[11] In addition to these findings about affordability and access, the State of the Period study also suggests that today's teenagers are internalizing the norms of stigma and silence that Rachel Krengel, the London mother of two, described: 66% did not want to be at school when they were menstruating; and 83% thought that the lack of access to menstrual products was an issue that is not talked about enough.[12]

Indeed, "period poverty"—along with the underlying menstrual stigma and silence that help give rise to it in the first place—is an obstacle to full participation in school, work, and other aspects of public life. Period poverty is defined in multiple ways, including not being able to afford commercial menstrual products; inadequate access to supplies and services needed for menstrual hygiene; lack of adequate menstrual education; menstruation-associated stigma and shame; and all of the foregoing.[13] Until recently, the primary actors around issues of period poverty have been community organizations, nongovernmental organizations, and professionals in the fields of water, sanitation, and hygiene and sexual reproductive health rights.[14] Representatives of these groups have been active around menstruation issues for years.[15] Some for-profit companies primarily in the business of manufacturing menstrual products, as well as some from outside the menstrual sector—such as Lidl grocery stores in Ireland and Morrisons stores in the United Kingdom—have newly undertaken charitable efforts designed to address period poverty through product giveaways or other corporate donations.[16] And, as described throughout this book, leaders in government have also begun paying more attention to this issue, prompted in significant part by public awareness campaigns.

Culturally speaking, issues of period poverty crossed over to popular consciousness in Australia, New Zealand, Europe, and North America in 2015, when news of local and national efforts to repeal the tampon tax and otherwise transform the culture of silence around menstruation spread from country to country, facilitated by public awareness campaigns that skillfully deployed social media and the internet. In

Australia, for example, tampon-tax activists used an online campaign to draw attention to their cause, an idea that was picked up in Canada, the United States, and many parts of Europe.[17] The continuing efforts to eliminate the tampon tax throughout the United States are the subject of further discussion in chapter 2.

The underlying goals of the menstrual advocacy movement have been described in overlapping but distinct ways. Jennifer Weiss-Wolf, one of the leaders in the US campaign to repeal the tampon tax, coined the term "menstrual equity" as a way of capturing the larger vision. In one early formulation, she characterized menstrual equity as focused on effectuating "laws and policies that ensure menstrual products are safe and affordable and available to those who need them," explaining that the "ability to access these items affects a person's freedom to work and study, to be healthy, and to participate in daily life with basic dignity."[18] The website of Period Equity, the nonprofit entity she cofounded, similarly describes menstrual equity as encompassing three issues: "the [tampon] tax, access, and safety." The website explains, "We believe that in order to have a fully participatory society, we must have laws and policies that . . . ensur[e] menstrual products are safe, accessible, and affordable for all who need them."[19]

Others have expanded the menstrual-equity concept even further. Women's Voices for the Earth, a nonprofit advocacy group, explains it this way:

> The most commonly recognized definition [of menstrual equity] refers to the affordability, accessibility and safety of menstrual products. But menstrual equity is not just defined by products—it is also about education and reproductive care. It's about making sure that people have the needs [sic], support, and choices to decide how they want to take care of their menstrual health. And it's about finally ending the stigma around periods that has prevented not only decision-makers, but also healthcare providers, educators and individuals from ensuring that menstrual health is a priority.[20]

Margaret Johnson, a professor at the University of Baltimore School of Law, takes a similarly capacious approach to law-related menstrual-equity efforts, which she calls "menstrual justice." As she puts it, menstrual justice focuses on ending "oppression of menstruators simply because they menstruate," with that oppression also taking the form of harassment and stigmas in the workplace or at school, failure to provide for the dignity of vulnerable people like incarcerated persons and the homeless, and failure to recognize the needs of trans and nonbinary individuals who menstruate.[21]

With growing international public awareness, advocates in the United States and elsewhere have begun considering the ways that the law can be harnessed to achieve menstrual equity. Jyoti Sanghera, chief of the UN Human Rights Office on Economic and Social Issues, has called period poverty "a violation of several human rights, most importantly of the right to human dignity."[22] On International Women's Day in 2019, a group of UN Human Rights experts issued a statement about the importance of breaking taboos around menstruation:

> The stigma and shame generated by stereotypes around menstruation have severe impacts on all aspects of women's and girls' human rights, including their human rights to equality, health, housing, water, sanitation, education, freedom of religion or belief, safe and healthy working conditions, and to take part in cultural life and public life without discrimination.[23]

Period poverty is a complex system fueled by interlocking forces of menstrual myths, ignorance, stigma, shame, and silence. It is important to understand each of these elements.

Menstrual Myths and Ignorance

Misunderstandings about menstruation are alive and well in the twenty-first century, even in the United States. In 2020, the Harris Poll (the same organization that performed the State of the Period study of teenagers) conducted the Tampax Period Education Survey of adults, and found "a significant knowledge gap when it comes to periods and tampons." Seventy-seven percent of adults believed that a tampon could get lost inside a woman's body, 62% of women could not locate a vagina on a diagram, and 7% of adults believed that the use of a tampon would mean that a woman was no longer a virgin.[24]

None of this is surprising, given the uneven state of menstrual education throughout the United States, described further in chapter 3. Popular culture sometimes plays a role in filling this gap. For instance, Tampax later partnered with comedian and actress Amy Schumer to create a series of humorous instructional videos—entitled "Time to Tampax"—for its YouTube channel.[25] Magazines including *Teen Vogue*, *Seventeen*, and *Cosmopolitan* have engaged in similar education efforts. In 2019, *Teen Vogue* published an article addressing six "period myths," including the factually incorrect beliefs that people should not swim while menstruating and can never get pregnant during their periods, as well as the stigma-based notions that "[p]eriods are dirty" and that "[p]eriods are shameful and shouldn't be talked about."[26]

Periods Are Stigmatized and Shamed

Lack of accurate information about menstruation contributes to unnecessary fear, shame, and stigma. The Harris Poll's State of the Period survey not only showed that a significant percentage of adolescents lack access to menstrual products but also revealed that even larger percentages "reported feelings of shame, self-consciousness, and/or embarrassment" about the overall process of menstruation. Sixty-four percent of respondents agreed that society teaches people to be ashamed of their periods, 69% said that they felt embarrassed when they had to bring their menstrual products to the bathroom, 71% felt self-conscious when they had their periods, and a full 80% felt that "there is a negative association with periods, that they are gross or unsanitary."[27]

Psychological research also suggests that the average person views menstruating women less favorably than it views nonmenstruating women. In a study conducted at a Colorado university in 2002, researchers recruited individuals (ranging in age from seventeen to thirty-six) to participate in an experiment on "group productivity." Each individual had a separate session with a female "partner"—ostensibly another study participant, but actually a lab confederate. During the experiment, the confederate "accidentally" dropped either a tampon or a hair clip. Shortly after that intervention occurred, the actual participant had the opportunity to rate the partner's competence and likeability, and to choose how close to sit to her.

The results were striking. The participants who were with the confederate when she dropped a tampon rated their partner as less competent and likeable than the participants who were with the same confederate when she dropped a hair clip. Participants were also less likely to choose a chair right next to a tampon-dropping partner than a hair clip–dropping partner. As the researchers put it, the tampon-dropping confederate was viewed as "less competent, less likeable, and tended to be both psychologically and physically avoided relative to a woman who dropped a less 'offensive' but nonetheless highly feminine item—a hair clip."[28]

Other research shows similar results. In a survey of over three hundred college students in Mexico and the United States, for example, participants were asked to complete the phrases, "A menstruating woman is . . ." and "A premenstrual woman is . . ." Of the 180 words found in at least half of the respondents' answers, 51% were negative words like "whining," "moody," and "incapable." Just over 30.5% of the words were neutral, like "cyclical," and only 18.3% of the words were positive, like "active."[29]

Menstrual stigma is not new, to be sure. In many cultures, going back millennia and continuing to the present day, menstruation has been treated as something that is unclean, suspect, or both. The Irish epic *Táin Bó Cúailng*, written down in the Middle Ages and set in the first century, recounts the defeat of a woman warrior whose battle loss is caused by her menstruation, which "made three great trenches in each of which a household can fit."[30] In the Torah, according to Leviticus, "Whenever a woman has her menstrual period, she will be ceremonially unclean for seven days. Anyone who touches her during that time will be unclean until evening. . . . If you touch any object she has sat on, you must wash your clothes and bathe yourself in water, and you will remain unclean until evening."[31] Misperceptions and myths about menstruation are intertwined.

Taboos seep into daily behavior and cultural attitudes. In Orthodox Judaism, those who are menstruating are considered *niddah*, or separate, and it is customary for menstruating wives to observe a ritual separation from their husbands.[32] In an essay adapted from her memoir about leaving Orthodox Judaism, writer Tova Mirvis recounts the rules that she had been taught, shortly before her marriage, about Jewish family purity:

When we had our periods and for the seven days following, we were in a state of impurity: we couldn't touch our husbands—no sex, not a hug, not a handshake. Once our periods had ceased, we were to check ourselves for any remaining smudges or stains. When we believed ourselves to be clean, we were to leave the cloths inside us for thirty minutes, just to be sure, and then start counting seven clean days. Only at the end of these could we immerse in the mikvah and once again be permissible.[33]

Customs surrounding the separation of menstruating females exist throughout the world. In some parts of present-day India, for example, those who are menstruating are expected to sleep in a different part of the house (or at least shielded from others by a curtain), and to use separate dishes and wear the same clothes until their period ends, because of the association of menstrual bleeding with uncleanliness and the possibility of "contaminating" the household's food.[34] In parts of Ethiopia, it is customary to exile from the home anyone who is menstruating, postpartum, or giving birth.[35] In parts of Afghanistan, it is customary to refrain from washing one's body during menstruation, for fear of becoming infertile.[36] In Bangladesh, some women bury their menstrual cloths in order to prevent evil spirits from using them.[37]

These stigmas and taboos often manifest in teasing and mistreatment by others; these may be peers, family members, or authority figures.[38] This behavior may be particularly prevalent in schools, as described further in chapter 3. In Kenya, some students have reported being teased about menstruation by their male teachers after being absent for a few days, although their teachers deny it.[39] In northeastern Ethiopia, some menstruating girls have described not even wanting to avail themselves of school-provided pads, for fear of being followed and teased.[40] Nor did some of these students want to buy menstrual products from stores, for fear of being the subject of gossip. Thus, on many days during their periods, even girls who had access to menstrual products in school would not come to class, choosing to stay home instead.[41]

Silence Surrounding Menstruation

Even in cultures that do not prescribe or expect the physical separation of menstruating women, silence surrounding menstruation is common.

Maureen C. McHugh, a women's studies professor, writes that throughout society, "[g]irls are taught to maintain a silence about menstruation; there is a taboo that makes it socially unacceptable to talk about menstruation."[42] People who menstruate often themselves contribute to taboos around menstruation, by using euphemisms to describe it. According to the International Women's Health Collective and the period app Clue, there are more than five thousand words and phrases used worldwide to describe menstruation, including "*Ederbeerwoch*" (strawberry week) in Germany, "the blob" in the United Kingdom, "*les Anglais debarqué*" (the English have landed) in France, and "*Красная армия*" (the Red Army) in Russia.[43] In the United States, common phrases are "on the rag," "the curse," "Aunt Flo," "the crimson tide," "shark week," and "that time of the month."[44]

Such terms signal to the listener and the speaker alike that discussions of menstruation should remain secretive. As writer Alma Gottlieb has explained, "[Using] euphemisms that often involve shame and/or censure has deep roots in patriarchal ideology" inherent in Judaism, Christianity, and Islam.[45] Those who violate the taboos may incur "emotional, sociological, spiritual, and/or political risks."[46] Indeed, silence can be an act of self-preservation, given the myths, stigma, and even unconscious stereotypes that surround menstruation. The ultimate conclusion of the researchers in the Colorado study (involving the female confederate who "accidentally" dropped a tampon) was that menstrual concealment is, unfortunately, rational. As they put it,

> [T]he great lengths to which many women go to avoid revelation of menstrual status and discussion of related issues may indeed be well-founded, for reminders of menstruation do appear to lead to negative judgments of women. Although women are not confined to menstrual huts in this culture, norms of secrecy and concealment surrounding menstruation nevertheless serve the function of keeping women's corporeal bodies out of the public eye.[47]

This wide-scale concealment creates its own reinforcing cycle: "[T]he sanitized, deodorized, and idealized images of women's bodies become the only ones we encounter and accept."[48]

All of these observations give new resonance to Gloria Steinem's famous "If Men Could Menstruate" essay from 1978, in which she imagined an alternate universe where "suddenly, magically, men could menstruate and women could not." Her essay imagined that in such a universe, the longstanding silence surrounding menstruation would instantly dissolve. Indeed, it would reverse itself: "[M]enstruation would become an enviable, boast-worthy" event. Steinem elaborated: "Men would brag about how long and how much"; "Young boys would talk about it as the envied beginning of manhood"; "Street guys would invent slang ('He's a three-pad man')"; and "TV shows would treat the subject openly. . . . So would newspapers. . . . And so would movies."[49] Steinem's emphasis on the lack of silence that might accompany male menstruation provides a new angle on the longstanding cultural and legal silence surrounding menstruation. She vividly illustrates how silence and powerlessness are related; they draw from and reinforce each other.

Echoes of Steinem's essay reverberated in two social media campaigns that occurred during the course of the 2016 presidential campaign. During a Republican presidential primary debate in 2015, after Fox News host Megyn Kelly questioned then-candidate Donald Trump about negative comments he had made about women in the past, he retaliated in the press, saying,

> Certainly, I don't have a lot of respect for Megyn Kelly. She's a lightweight and y'know, she came out there reading her little script and trying to be tough and be sharp. And when you meet her you realize she's not very tough and she's not very sharp. . . . She gets out there and she starts asking me all sorts of ridiculous questions, and you could see there was blood coming out of her eyes, blood coming out of her . . . wherever.[50]

Taking Trump's comments as a thinly veiled reference to menstruation, numerous women began to tweet at Trump about their periods, using the hashtag #periodsarenotaninsult. One illustrative tweet read, "@realDonaldTrump been bleeding 3 days now, flow is slowing down a bit. soon the blood will take on a brownish hue. #periodsarenotaninsult."[51] An even more pointed connection (whether knowing or not) to Steinem's essay appeared in another tweet: "Meanwhile, if men got periods, you just know that @realDonaldTrump would brag his was the heaviest in history #periodsarenotaninsult."[52]

A subsequent campaign with the #periodsforpence hashtag had similar undercurrents. Women began calling and tweeting at then-governor Mike Pence about their periods, in order to protest an Indiana law that required all miscarried fetuses (of any gestational age) to be interred or cremated. As the leader of the campaign, Laura Shanley, explained on Facebook,

> Fertilized eggs can be expelled during a woman's period without a woman even knowing that she might have had the potential blastocyst in her. Therefore, any period could potentially be a miscarriage without knowledge. I would certainly hate for any of my fellow Hoosier women to be at risk of penalty if they do not "properly dispose" of this or report it. Just to cover our bases, perhaps we should make sure to contact Governor Pence's office to report our periods. We wouldn't want him thinking that THOUSANDS OF HOOSIER WOMEN A DAY are trying to hide anything, would we?[53]

The Facebook page ultimately garnered nearly eighty thousand likes; it morphed into a "Tampons for Trump" campaign after Trump selected Pence as his running mate.[54]

In these social media efforts, women intentionally and explicitly defied conventions about menstrual silence. Indeed, they put a new, more serious twist on Steinem's musings about men jokingly bragging about menstrual prowess. The message was twofold: women would not remain silent about their periods, and would not be silent in response to negative rhetoric and policies connected to the female body. The breaking of the silence around menstruation—and these women's insistence on describing theirs in detail—reflected a more general attempt to assert cultural power.

US Media Messages about Menstruation

For many years, messages in the media and popular culture about menstruation also helped perpetuate silence about menstruation. Judy Blume's young adult book *Are You There God? It's Me, Margaret*, published in 1970, became a counterpoint. The book frankly discusses menstruation, puberty, and the human body. Margaret longs to get her period and develop breasts, as do her friends. Finally, in the concluding pages of the book, Margaret gets her period and shares the news with both her mother and God.[55] In a letter to her readers on the fiftieth anniversary of the book in 2020, Judy Blume reflected, "I remember thinking I'm going to be honest. I'm going to tell the truth."[56]

Notwithstanding the openness of Blume's book, most popular culture references to menstruation at that time remained covert. Menstrual products could not even be advertised on television until 1972. And the 1970s ads for the Modess line of Johnson & Johnson sanitary napkins, for example, featured women dressed in ball gowns and bridal gowns, with no mention of the product at all—just the tag-line "Modess . . . Because." Modess touted its discreet brown paper packaging that allowed users to "save embarrassment."[57] These ads signaled that menstruation was something so undignified that it could not even be mentioned by name. Indeed, Johnson & Johnson's chief historian, Margaret Gurowitz, commented that "[t]hese two words ['Modess . . . Because.'] helped spare the reader of any self-consciousness around the topic of feminine hygiene, providing dignity around what was not an easily discussed subject in society at that time."[58]

Even when later advertisements began to mention the specific menstrual products being sold, they still contained mixed messages. A 1982 ad for Stayfree pads, for example, featured national gymnastics champion Cathy Rigby in a split-leg handstand pose on a balance beam with the line, "Right now I need all the comfort I can get," and the gymnast's autograph. Scrutiny of Rigby's leotard, however, makes it quite clear that she was not wearing a Stayfree (or any other) pad for the shot.[59] It was not until 1985 that actress Courtney Cox made television history by becoming the first person to say "period" on television in an ad for Tampax.[60] Even today, most United States television advertisements use blue liquid (rather than simulated red blood) as a way of demonstrating menstrual pads' absorbency. In early 2020, the US-based brand Kotex ran a social media advertisement for its Security Extra Thin pad with that featured red liquid being poured on the pad and the phrase, "Can your pad keep up?" Consumers' reactions to the ad, which had been posted on Instagram, were mixed: some commentators expressed gratitude for the more realistic approach, but others expressed a desire not to see even simulated body fluids.[61] The ad did not enjoy widespread distribution, suggesting the persistence of consumer squeamishness.

Turning to Law: The Case for Menstrual Equity

Stigma and silence surrounding menstruation have long contributed to legal silence about menstruation as well. Indeed, until recently, the law has been an unexplored tool for preventing menstruation from serving as an obstacle to full participation in public life. But a new group of scholars and activists—trained and grounded in law—is now pursuing effective and lasting change through legislative and policy reform. This book seeks to more fully conceptualize a robust role for law in eliminating period poverty and achieving menstrual equity. While each subsequent chapter focuses on a particular aspect of this vision, this chapter concludes by using the COVID-19 pandemic as a case study of the role that law can play in the service of human needs related to menstruation.

Law as a Tool of Menstrual Activism: The COVID-19 Pandemic as a Case Study

For many people worldwide, the COVID-19 pandemic exacerbated the challenges of managing menstruation. Not only did it make period poverty more acute, but it also created general scarcity of menstrual products, presented new hygiene- and sanitation-related obstacles in attending to menstrual needs, reduced access to toilets, made it difficult for some to maintain personal or cultural standards about privacy surrounding menstruation, cut students off from the menstrual education and support they had been receiving from their schools, and limited people's ability to see healthcare providers for menstruation-related conditions. That said, the extreme nature of the crisis also brought menstruation-related issues more squarely into public discourse, due to the efforts of menstrual advocates, grassroots citizens' groups, nongovernmental organizations, and the popular press. Some lawmakers, too, took notice—to the point that 2020 became a year of several notable legal reforms connected to menstruation.

Perhaps the most broadly shared menstruation-related challenge wrought by COVID-19 was the fear—and, for many people, the reality—of running out of menstrual products. In the first weeks of the pandemic in the United States, the news was full of stories of consumers rushing to the store to buy toilet paper and paper towels in bulk, resulting in bare shelves that made for dramatic press coverage. Garnering less notice were reports that both stores and online retailers had run out of several major brands of menstrual products.[62] Dana Marlowe, the founder of the Maryland-based organization I Support the Girls (a nonprofit entity that collects menstrual products and bras for shelters, prisons, and people in need), recounted receiving a panicked call from her friend, who wondered if she could give Marlowe homemade matzoh balls in exchange for a box of tampons.[63] The desperate friend reported that she had scoured all of the local pharmacies for menstrual products, but the shelves had been picked clean. On March 21, 2020, I Support the Girls tweeted, "Stop hoarding menstrual products! Our requests have spiked the past week from not just homeless and DV [domestic violence] shelters in need, but everyone in need. Periods don't stop for pandemics. Don't hoard tampons. Please be kind."[64] Marlowe's organization ended up donating nine hundred thousand menstrual products in March 2020, compared to two hundred thousand in March 2019.[65]

The shortage was worldwide. A young woman in Indonesia reported that "[t]he [menstrual] products is [sic] rare and hard to find. Many people buy too much for themselves," alluding to the problem of hoarding by others who could afford to stockpile supplies.[66] An Australian woman had the same observation, saying that "[d]ue to bulk buying it has been extremely hard to find any products at all, and when you do find them, they are quite expensive."[67] Indeed, in a survey conducted by the nongovernmental humanitarian organization Plan International of professionals who work in the fields of water, sanitation and hygiene, and sexual-reproductive health rights in twenty-four countries, 74% of respondents agreed that the COVID-19 pandemic had reduced access to menstrual products.[68]

The scarcity of menstrual products stemmed not only from hoarding but also from the pandemic-induced disruptions to supply and delivery chains. In March 2020, for instance, Prime Minister Narendra Modi of India issued "a total ban of coming out of your homes";[69] as a result of this lockdown, all commercial and private businesses were shut by government decree. Initially, menstrual products were not on the list of "essential goods" whose deliveries were exempt from the shutdown orders, although they were later added. In the meantime, some people took matters into their own hands, literally, by making their own pads.[70] On top of the official lockdown orders that impaired the delivery of menstrual products, other disruptions resulted from the closure of factories, the grounding of flights, and the partial shutdown of ports.[71]

The scarcity of menstrual products created conditions in which vendors could raise prices. A public health specialist in Zimbabwe, for example, noted that "most retail shops have taken advantage of the [lockdown] situation and hiked prices" of menstrual products.[72] A young woman in Fiji reported that "[p]rices went up as soon as there was a confirmed case of COVID19 in Fiji. Sometimes I have to forgo buying hygiene products as money will have to be used on food and bills."[73] Meanwhile, in some countries, places that ordinarily made menstrual products available for free, including shelters and schools, either ran out of them, did not provide them while focused on food insecurity, or closed entirely.[74] It was a perfect storm for period poverty.

Even though issues of period poverty are not new, the pandemic made them much more salient. As many middle-class and affluent people in North America, Europe, Australia, and New Zealand experienced for the first time potential or actual short-term disruptions in regular access to menstrual products, they became more conscious of similar experiences of others during nonpandemic times.[75] This, in turn, spurred some people to action. In the United States, for example, local news outlets carried stories of citizen-organized drives for menstrual products.[76] At an international level, organizations such as UNICEF and Plan International also worked to draw attention to menstruation-related needs heightened by the pandemic.[77]

For similar reasons why it became difficult to access menstrual products, it also became challenging for some to access soap and other materials needed for basic hygiene. Like menstrual products, soap and shampoo were not initially on the list of "essential products" that were exempt from numerous governments' mandatory shutdown rules, causing delays in the manufacture and transport of these goods. Washing and toileting are essential to menstrual management; without access to soap, it is difficult to keep oneself clean. For people in refugee camps or poor communities where water, sanitation, and hygiene services are already scarce in nonpandemic times, shortages of soap became more acute. UNICEF, for example, urged humanitarian organizations to monitor access to water and sanitation, water distribution, sewer overflow, and supply shortages or price increase in soap and cleaning supplies.[78] The problems were especially acute for those with disabilities who rely on community-based services or caregivers for daily assistance with personal hygiene, including menstrual management.[79]

The pandemic reduced access to water, too. In countries like Ethiopia[80] and the Solomon Islands,[81] water shutdowns are not uncommon. Responding to a Plan International survey examining conditions in seven countries, a young woman in the Solomon Islands said that water shortages made managing her period more difficult: "We sometimes have water cuts. So menstrual hygiene is sometimes tedious."[82] A woman in Fiji, where there were isolation rules in place during the coronavirus pandemic, took the approach of going to a nearby spring or river when there was a problem with the water supply.[83] The feasibility of that option, however, depends on both the availability and cleanliness of natural resources. "Some adolescent girls and young women in rural areas may resort to unclean sources of water as a result of the lockdown," noted a health professional in Zimbabwe.[84]

Access to toilets also became a pandemic issue, particularly in light of stay-at-home orders. In one area of the city of Jaipur, India, for example, a study found that only 51.27% of all households have access to a toilet in their own homes.[85] Therefore prohibitions on leaving one's home during a lockdown made toileting more difficult. Additionally, even for those who do have a toilet at home, the suddenly reduced availability of public restrooms presented a challenge. The comments of two Australian women in response to Plan International's survey were illuminating. One of them observed that "[w]ith public restrooms closed almost everywhere changing tampons or emptying cups became quite difficult."[86] If one could find public toilets, the other explained, they were not necessarily usable: "I work outside and use public toilets often but with COVID-19 a lot of the toilets are closed and also a lot of them do not have soap available to wash your hands."[87]

In some parts of the world, the standard approaches to disposing of menstrual products were also disrupted by the coronavirus pandemic. In some places, it is conventional to bury menstrual waste far from home.[88] If traditional methods are not possible, individuals may engage in disposal practices that are either unhygienic, inconsistent with cultural beliefs, or both.[89] A young woman in Papua New Guinea, for example, reported that during the coronavirus pandemic, "We were not allowed to move around to dispose [products] and it was really uncomfortable."[90] Almost half of all health officials surveyed by Plan International said that "there had been issues with disruptions to hygienic management of periods" caused by the pandemic virus.[91] One in three surveyed girls and women in the Pacific said that they "had trouble knowing where they could comfortably dispose of period products" during this time.[92] In these places, the customary strategies for concealing menstruation had suddenly become impracticable.

Another pandemic-induced challenge to menstrual management was the loss of access to schools and healthcare providers. With the abrupt closure of schools, students were cut off from what, for some of them, had been a primary source of menstrual education and menstrual products. In Kenya, for instance, just prior to the pandemic, the government had approved a National Menstrual Hygiene Management policy, which contemplated expanded distribution of menstrual products in schools as well as more programming for students. Similarly, as discussed further in chapter 3, several states in the United States had recently required school districts to begin providing menstrual products free of charge. The pandemic, however, rendered those developments temporarily moot.

Meanwhile, as the healthcare system had to divert its attention to dealing with COVID-19, many nonurgent medical appointments and procedures were canceled or delayed, either by healthcare providers or by patients who did not want to risk exposure. In a survey of 290 Turkish patients suffering from endometriosis (a chronic condition related to menstruation, in which endometrial tissue grows outside the uterine cavity and becomes painful and inflamed as hormones fluctuate during the menstrual cycle), 83.36% reported that they were afraid of having endometriosis-related problems during the pandemic, and 53.63%

thought that the pandemic was affecting management of their endometriosis.[93] A much smaller percentage (8.57%), however, reported having a planned endometriosis surgery that was postponed, suggesting that the most severe cases still received medical attention.[94]

Experiences of the pandemic suggest both the potential and the limitations of law. For example, menstrual products and soap, as well as businesses involved in their production and sale, should be legally classified as essential businesses from the beginning of any crisis. Otherwise, when pandemics or other crises disrupt access to menstrual products, individuals may resort to managing menstruation by using materials that are uncomfortable, unreliable, or unsafe. It is also important to recognize that stores' ability to stock menstrual products is only helpful if people can leave their homes in order to procure them. Similarly, online retailers are not accessible to those without effective internet connections or mail delivery.

Sanitation issues and access to water, essential for maintaining personal hygiene after changing menstrual products, might also be the proper subject for further lawmaking. Water shortages and inadequate government efforts in response to them, particularly outside the United States and Europe, are longstanding challenges.[95] Monitoring compliance with existing laws and developing and implementing new ones where necessary should be priorities during both pandemic and nonpandemic times. In Kenya, for example, the government has programs designed both to provide menstrual products more broadly to those in need and to improve access to water in low-income areas.[96] According to local commentators, the COVID-19 pandemic has made clear that the government needs to accelerate its efforts on both fronts.[97]

In terms of access to medical care during a pandemic, there may be very little that law itself can do. When healthcare providers and hospitals are devoted entirely to the serious needs of COVID-19 patients at the height of a crisis, it is not realistic to divert those efforts for anything other than life-or-death care. Even so, health-enhancing regulations should make available clear information about what types of health issues, including menstrual health, are appropriate for medical attention at what point, perhaps borrowing from the model of "red zones," "orange zones," or the staged reopening of cities. Such a system, if developed with expert medical input, would communicate more clearly to members of the general public about when it is safe and appropriate to seek medical care, what doctors and other providers are available to provide that care, and what safety precautions patients should take when availing themselves of healthcare services.

Menstrual Products Reclassified during the Pandemic

Over the course of the pandemic, several notable legal and policy developments related to menstruation occurred. First, in the United States, the bipartisan Coronavirus Aid, Relief, and Economic Security (CARES) Act, enacted on March 27, 2020, contained a variety of provisions designed to help individuals and businesses respond to the economic crisis caused by the virus.[98] One of the lesser known aspects of the CARES Act was a provision allowing funds from tax-advantaged health savings accounts to be used for purchasing any "menstrual care product," defined as a "tampon, pad, liner, cup, sponge, or similar product used by individuals with respect to menstruation or other genital-tract secretions."[99] The change is applicable to Flexible Spending Accounts (employer-owned and funded by the employer and/or employee), Health Savings Accounts (for those who self-insure), and Health Reimbursement Arrangements (employer owned and funded). The CARES Act provision drew from previous proposals by Representative Grace Meng (D-NY), as discussed further in chapter 4, that were never taken up for a vote.

In commenting on the CARES Act provision, attorney Jennifer Berman described the change as a victory for advocates who wanted "for a lot of years to be able to add [menstrual products] to the list of reimbursable expenses."[100] Indeed, the change mattered for several reasons. First, it improved the affordability of menstrual products, although it is important to note that flexible spending accounts, health savings accounts, and health reimbursement arrangements do not tend to be available to the nation's lowest-income earners. Second, as Jennifer Weiss-Wolf noted, the change laid "the groundwork for additional and more expansive policy reform."[101] She explained, "The particular wording in the stimulus bill acknowledges the medical necessity of these products. That will be an important bedrock for future policy advocacy." For example, the explicit recognition of menstrual products as necessities strengthens the argument, discussed further in chapter 2, that they should receive the same state sales tax exemptions as other necessities. It also opens the door for further conversations about how to reduce the burdens that menstruation places on full participation in public life. This type of signaling at the governmental level thus has both expressive and functional value.

The #Bloodybarpocalypse

In the United States, pandemic-era heightened sensitivity to menstruation-related issues on the part of lawyers particularly coalesced at the end of July 2020, around publicity that several state boards of bar examiners had rules preventing test takers from bringing their own menstrual products with them to the bar exam.[102] For example, Arizona sent to July bar exam candidates a list of items "strictly prohibited" in the exam room.[103] The list included predictable items, such as cell phones and backpacks, but also "feminine hygiene products," explaining that these "will be made available in women's restrooms."[104] While such a rule would be problematic even in normal times, it was particularly troubling in a pandemic, when the last thing test takers wanted to do was reach into a communal bowl in a restroom.

Social media pressure, some of it expressed using the hashtag #bloodybarpocalypse, caused Arizona to change its policy.[105] A group of over twenty-eight hundred lawyers and law professors signed an open letter to the National Conference of Bar Examiners, urging the group to establish policies that prohibit these bans on menstrual products.[106] In response, the National Conference sent states a communication to "strongly discourage" the bans.[107] This letter, along with further social media pressure, prompted Texas to change its policy, at least for the September 2020 exam. West Virginia retained its written policy of telling applicants that they could not bring their own menstrual products and that the "WVBLE [West Virginia Board of Law Examiners] will provide exam items as well as, ear plugs, tissues, and first aid and feminine hygiene products,"[108] although a spokesperson for the West Virginia courts told the press that applicants could bring their own menstrual products, thus creating ambiguity for test takers.[109] Going forward, bar examiners will need to rethink their policies and more clearly communicate them to bar candidates.

Scotland's Passage of the Period Products (Free Provision) (Scotland) Act

On an international level, the most dramatic menstrual-equity development that occurred during the COVID-19 pandemic was Scotland's November 24, 2020, passage of the Period Products (Free Provision) (Scotland) Act, which requires local authorities to ensure that period products are obtainable free of charge by all who need them.[110] This law, described further in chapter 9, passed unanimously in the Scottish Parliament. Although it had been in the works even before the pandemic began—a draft bill had received initial approval in February 2020—the pandemic heightened its urgency. The lawmaker who had submitted the bill, Monica Lennon, explicitly linked its final passage to the pandemic, telling her fellow lawmakers right before the vote that "[i]n these dark times, we can bring light and hope to the world this evening." Lennon further reflected that the bill "matters now more than ever, because periods don't stop in a pandemic."[111]

Looking Ahead

The increasing salience of period poverty during the COVID-19 crisis has raised public awareness in a way that can be carried forward into nonpandemic times. If period poverty encompasses the lack of access to menstrual products, supplies, and services for health and sanitation, and information and treatment from educators and health professionals—as well as the stigma and shame that can accompany menstruation—then the *absence* of period poverty should be the hallmark of an equitable and just society. Menstrual equity is, after all, a subset of the larger project of gender equity. For gender equity to be achieved, law and society must account for biological functions such as menstruation (along with pregnancy, breastfeeding, and menopause) and take steps to ensure that these natural biological processes are not limiting people's ability to participate fully in any aspect of society. The stage is set to consider more broadly how law can achieve this goal.

2

The Tampon Tax

When Laura Coryton was a twenty-one-year-old student at the University of London in 2014, she was surprised and upset to learn that menstrual products were being taxed at a rate of 5%, while luxury items like crocodile meat and cake decorations were tax exempt[1]—and she decided to take action. She launched a petition at Change.org to urge UK lawmakers to "[s]top taxing periods. Period."[2] "If you value the functioning of those who menstruate at least as much as you enjoy your flying crocodile Fridays then sign our petition and join our campaign," the petition urged. "Help to put an end to the marginalisation of issues traditionally associated with women by demanding a zero tax rate for sanitary products. Periods are no luxury."[3] Overnight, Coryton's petition received five hundred signatures; in just a few weeks, over twenty-five thousand individuals had added their names.[4] Little did Coryton know at the time that the publicity generated by her petition would spark a global movement—still ongoing—for repeal of consumer-based taxes on menstrual products, commonly called the "tampon tax."

There was plenty of dry tinder onto which the spark of Coryton's petition fell, including some earlier tampon-tax litigation in the United States in the mid-1980s, several unsuccessful legislative initiatives in Canada, and the repeal of tampon taxes by Kenya in 2004. What made Coryton's petition unique was that it launched at a time when the internet made possible near-instantaneous communication with more people than ever before.[5] Thus, in ways that were unimaginable even ten years before, Coryton's petition drew international media attention and helped to spread awareness of the fundamental unfairness of a tax that had largely remained under the radar.

What Is the Tampon Tax?

Technically speaking, the "tampon tax" is not strictly a tax on tampons themselves; it is not a tax merely on tampons, either. The phrase describes any one or more of national or local taxes that different countries and jurisdictions impose on the sale, manufacture, and/or production of a range of menstrual products, including pads, tampons, and menstrual cups. Depending on the particular country and even on the jurisdiction within the country, tampon taxes may take the form of (or go by the name of) (1) a national value-added tax (VAT), as in most European countries, as well as Senegal, Lebanon, and China, for example; (2) a national goods and services tax (GST) that is redistributed to the country's states, such as in Australia, Canada, and India, for example; or (3) a state-level sales tax, as in the approximately twenty-seven US states that have some form of tax on menstrual products. Each tax system—whether GST, VAT, or sales tax—has unique details and complexity. But what all of the systems have in common is that they are consumption taxes, meaning that the end purchaser pays a tax at the point of sale.

In every country and state, in every VAT, GST, or sales-tax system, some products have favored status. In the European Union, for example, the average standard VAT rate in 2021 is approximately 21%.[6] Reduced rates (not lower than 5%) apply to items listed in an EU directive as eligible for this special classification; these items include infant car seats, theater tickets, and admission to sporting events.[7] There is an even more favorable category—the "zero rate"—that includes most groceries and children's clothing. Presumably, the zero rate is meant to capture items that are clearly necessities, while other items are subject to a 5% (or higher) rate because they are considered luxuries. Coryton's petition took aim at the seeming illogic of the UK's tax laws at the time. Menstrual products, which are necessities in any common sense of the word, were subject to a 5% tax, but edible cake decorations and exotic meats like crocodile, kangaroo, and ostrich were in the "zero rate" category.[8] Coryton's petition got the attention of ordinary consumers, activists, and lawmakers with a simple message: "Stop taxing periods. Period."

In response to new public attention to the existence and unfairness of the UK's tampon tax, then–UK prime minister David Cameron pledged in spring 2015 to look into the issue. He ultimately responded that although he supported eliminating the tax, the UK's ability to unilaterally eliminate the tax was hampered by European Union rules at the time requiring a VAT of at least 5% on such products. Indeed, only after Brexit took effect on January 1, 2021, did Britain ultimately eliminate the tax.[9]

Precursors to the Contemporary Tampon-Tax Debate

Historically speaking, Coryton's petition was not the first effort to rally public opinion against the tampon tax. As noted in the book's introduction, in 1986, three Chicago women sued the state and city taxing authorities, seeking an injunction against the taxes imposed on the sale of tampons and pads.[10] The plaintiffs argued that tampons and pads should be included in the category of "medical appliances" that were exempt from taxation, and the Illinois Supreme Court ruled in their favor.[11] When the Illinois law changed in 2009 in a way that made menstrual products subject to taxation again, it did so without much publicity or opposition. The next class-action lawsuit in the United States challenging the validity of a state's tampon tax was not filed until 2016, as discussed further below.

Meanwhile, since the early 1980s, Canadian women had been active in campaigning against the tampon tax. In 1982, the Ontario finance minister created several new exemptions to the province's sales tax, but did not include menstrual products among the newly exempt items. Sheila Copps, a member of Provincial Parliament at that time, recalled that angry women mailed blood-filled tampons to the minister's office in protest, but the tax law did not change, despite continued (if gradually muted) opposition.[12] In 2004, a new generation of Canadian lawmakers again took up the cause and introduced a motion to eliminate the national GST on menstrual products. That action languished for several years. Meanwhile, in 2004, Kenya became the first country in the world to eliminate its VAT on menstrual products in an effort to make menstrual products more affordable to consumers.[13]

The effort to repeal the Canadian tampon tax was revitalized by an internet petition posted by twenty-nine-year-old Toronto activist Jill Piebiak to Change.org on January 15, 2015.[14] Like Coryton's petition, Piebiak's emphasized that some products like "incontinence products, cocktail cherries, human sperm, and wedding cakes are not subject to GST [goods and services tax]," while menstrual products still carried a 5% tax because "[a]ccording to the Government of Canada all menstrual hygiene products are considered a non-essential item or luxury." And also like Coryton's petition, the Canadian petition included the simple plea: "Don't tax periods—period."[15] On May 11, 2015, Canada's House of Commons unanimously passed a motion to eliminate the country's GST on menstrual products. On May 28, 2015, Canada's prime minister announced the elimination of the country's tampon tax as of July 1 that same year.[16] "To what do you owe such quick success?" an interviewer later asked Jill Piebiak, the Canadian petition's author. "Social media," she answered. "Our campaign went from zero to 74,000 supporters in just a few months. It was hard for government to ignore."[17] Internet advocacy played a key role in spreading public awareness that in turn facilitated legislative change.

In Australia, similar success eventually met a petition begun by Sydney University student Subeta Vimalarajah. Posted in 2015 around the same time as Piebiak's Canadian petition, Vimalarajah's internet petition urged Australia's eight state and territory treasurers to "Stop Taxing My Period!"[18] Over ninety-three thousand people signed the petition within a few weeks, building on a history of tampon-tax activism in Australia that had been ongoing since the country first introduced its GST in 2000. On May 25, 2015, Australia's federal treasurer, Joe Hockey, stated publicly that he agreed with the petition signers that the 10% GST on menstrual products should be eliminated, and that he would raise the issue with the state and territory treasurers. Hockey's state and territorial counterparts (whose consent was required for tax repeal) opposed the elimination of the tampon tax on the grounds that they could not afford to lose the revenue.[19] Only in 2018, after increased public pressure, did both major political parties in Australia come to support the elimination of the tampon tax, with the state and territorial leaders agreeing to the change.[20]

The UK, Canadian, and Australian internet petitions, along with Kenya's elimination of the tampon tax, caught the eye of Jennifer Weiss-Wolf, the New York attorney who had turned her attention at the start of 2015 toward what she would later call "menstrual equity," as described in the introduction. As Weiss-Wolf began researching and writing about issues of period poverty and menstruation-related issues, and connecting with other advocates, she "became convinced that the tampon tax was an ideal starting place for policy advocacy here at home."[21] At that time, forty US states imposed sales tax on menstrual products, including her home state of New York.

Weiss-Wolf was struck by the way that the tampon tax implicates both discrimination and tax concerns, raising the potential for "cross-party appeal" across the political spectrum.[22] Sure enough, in May 2015, New York State Assembly member Linda Rosenthal, a Democrat from Manhattan, introduced into the assembly a tampon-tax-repeal bill, with Republican state senator Sue Serino sponsoring the Senate version. But even with support from both major political parties, the bill proceeded slowly through the New York legislature.[23]

While New York State's legislative mechanisms worked in the background, in October 2015, Weiss-Wolf and *Cosmopolitan* magazine together launched a petition calling for the elimination of the tampon tax throughout the United States.[24] Their petition featured a color-coded map of the United States, depicting the tampon-tax landscape at the time: forty states imposed a sales tax on menstrual products, five states (Alaska, Delaware, Montana, New Hampshire, and Oregon) had no sales tax at all, and five states (Maryland, Massachusetts, Minnesota, New Jersey, and Pennsylvania) had specifically exempted menstrual products from the tax. "Change is possible!" the US petition proclaimed. "This summer, Canada made history when its Parliament voted unanimously to eliminate a national tax on menstrual products. Across the pond and down under, women in the U.K. and Australia are insisting their governments do the same. A global movement is underway!"[25]

At the surface level, the tampon tax may seem like a relatively minor issue. On any one purchase, the tax represents a small portion of the total out-of-pocket expense. But over the years, expenses add up. In the United States, the average consumer of menstrual products might spend between $700 and $2,000 over the course of a lifetime for menstrual products themselves, and an additional $20 to $145 in state sales taxes, depending on the rate.[26] Multiplied by the number of consumers in the jurisdiction, the tampon tax is not trivial. In many states, the sales tax is the most significant source of state revenue, and the tampon tax certainly contributes to that.[27] Many states are therefore reluctant to forego tampon-tax revenue, even though its collection means that approximately half the population pays a sales tax to manage an involuntary biological function, while the other half does not.

In her writings for the popular press, Weiss-Wolf framed the tampon tax as a form of gender discrimination. She soon joined forces with Laura Strausfeld, another New York lawyer who had long been interested in challenging unfavorable tax treatment of menstrual products.

"In early 2016, I began to see articles in the media about the unfairness of the tax," Strausfeld later recalled. "I reached out to Jennifer Weiss-Wolf . . . and asked if she thought a class action could help the cause."[28] Together, they formed a nonprofit policy organization, Period Equity, and persuaded New York civil rights law firm Emery Celli Brinckerhoff Abady Ward & Maazel LLP to represent five women in a class-action lawsuit challenging the tampon tax in New York. The complaint was filed on March 3, 2016, making it the first US legal challenge to the tampon tax in this new wave of twenty-first-century menstrual activism.[29]

Turning to the Courthouse

Because sales tax is imposed in the United States on a state-by-state basis, each state has its own approach for precisely which goods get taxed and which are exempt. The nature of New York's tax laws made that state the perfect place for a test case challenging the tampon tax. New York collects a sales tax of 4% on "every sale of tangible personal property," unless the item fits within a statutory exemption.[30] And New York has many such exemptions. The division between taxable and exempt products roughly, but not precisely, tracks the division between "necessities" and "luxuries." For example, in New York, almost all foods and drinks are exempt, as are drugs and medicines. Particularly notable, though, was the fact that at the time of the filing of the tampon-tax class action, many products that were roughly analogous to menstrual products were on the tax-exempt list, and yet menstrual products were not. Most strikingly, bandages, incontinence liners and pads, dressings, and gauze were all in the tax-exempt category of "medical equipment and supplies," but so-called feminine hygiene products, including "douches, sanitary napkins, tampons, and vaginal creams," were taxable, except for products "used to treat vaginal infection(s)." Essentially, tampons and pads had been lumped in with taxable nonnecessities related to female genitalia (such as douches), rather than with tax-exempt unisex necessities used to absorb blood and other bodily fluids (such as bandages and incontinence pads).

From its first allegations, the New York lawsuit emphasized the illogic and unfairness of this treatment. The New York State "Department [of Taxation and Finance] imposes a double standard when defining medical items for women and men," the complaint asserted. "Medical products exclusively for women are taxed. Medical products also used by men are not.... For example, the Department considers Rogaine, foot powder, dandruff shampoo, chapstick, facial wash, adult diapers, and incontinence pads to be medical items.... But medical items used *only* by women—tampons and sanitary pads—are taxed."[31] The complaint went on to point out that tampons and pads were "not luxury items, but a necessity for women's health," and that if anything, they were "far more necessary to the preservation of health" than many of the products that New York had classified as medical (and therefore tax exempt).[32] The complaint alleged in particular that New York's unfavorable tax treatment of menstrual products violated the Equal Protection Clause of the United States Constitution and the New York Constitution, because it was a form of sex discrimination. "Justice Scalia once wrote for the Supreme Court that 'A tax on wearing yarmulkes is a tax on Jews,'" the complaint argued. "A tax on tampons and sanitary pads is a tax on women. The Tampon Tax is irrational. It is discrimination. It is wrong."[33]

On May 25, 2016—less than three months after the filing of the lawsuit—the New York legislature finally approved the tampon-tax-repeal legislation. Governor Andrew Cuomo signed the bill into law on July 21, 2016. "We just axed the tax! Good riddance to sexist tax," tweeted Assemblymember Rosenthal that day, tagging Jennifer Weiss-Wolf in the tweet.[34] Governor Andrew Cuomo was similarly enthusiastic. "This is a regressive tax on essential products that women have had to pay for far too long and lifting it is a matter of social and economic justice," he stated in a press release. The release also noted that in total, the change was expected to save purchasers roughly $10 million a year.[35] The plaintiffs in the class action voluntarily withdrew their suit after the change in the law. The combination of legal action and public advocacy had been remarkably speedy and effective.

Just as New York was in the process of repealing its tampon tax, on July 6, 2016, a parallel class-action suit was filed in Florida challenging that state's tampon tax. As in New York, Florida presented a relatively straightforward case. Products classified as "common household remedies," including bandages and gauze, were tax exempt, but tampons and pads were not. Instead, menstrual products were in the category of taxable toilet articles used for grooming purposes, such as perfume and shampoo. The Florida complaint pointed out that "[t]ampons and pads serve an absorbent function similar to that of band-aids, bandages, and gauze." It added that they were necessary for women's health, because their medically recommended uses include "[s]topping and absorbing the flow of menstrual blood to prevent encrustation and detritus. . . . [d]ecreasing the risk of bacterial infections," and more.[36]

Within a year of the case's filing but before a final decision in the case, Florida's legislature repealed the tampon tax as part of a larger tax-cut package. As in New York, the Florida plaintiffs then voluntarily withdrew their suit.

Because of quick action by the New York and Florida state legislatures, the plaintiffs' substantive legal claims were never fully fleshed out in briefs and other filings. But what if these cases had gone forward? Would the plaintiffs have prevailed in striking down the tampon tax on equal protection grounds? Any predictions must take into account rulings in two other class-action challenges to the tampon tax. A California tampon-tax lawsuit filed in 2018 was dismissed on grounds that the plaintiffs—individual customers as opposed to the retailers who had paid the tax to the state—were not procedurally entitled to sue under California law. The court also briefly discussed and rejected the substantive equal protection challenge, but without fully exploring the issues—and in any case, this aspect of the ruling is not binding.[37] Another California case is not likely in the immediate future, because the California governor repealed the state's tampon tax temporarily through a budget measure. (That change is not permanent.)[38]

In Ohio, a class-action lawsuit filed in 2016 ended up in a complex procedural posture that ultimately became moot when, on April 1, 2020, Ohio legislatively repealed its tampon tax with bipartisan support.[39] Even so, in an opinion issued almost two months after repeal of the tampon tax, the Ohio Court of Appeals, Tenth District, affirmed the decision of the Board of Tax Appeals to dismiss the class-action challenge to the state's tampon tax, reasoning that the plaintiffs had failed to show that the tax significantly interfered with the exercise of any fundamental rights of women, and that the plaintiffs had failed to demonstrate any discriminatory intent on the part of the legislature in taxing menstrual products.[40] A dissent by Judge Jennifer Brunner, since elected to the Ohio Supreme Court, reasoned that the tampon tax lacked rational basis and that the majority had misapplied the applicable standards relevant to gender-based classifications in law.[41] In any event, the constitutionality of the tampon tax very much remains a live issue—one that raises complex and important legal questions—in the many states that still tax menstrual products.

Is the Tampon Tax Unconstitutional?

The idea that the tampon tax—or, more specifically, taxing menstrual products while exempting other necessities—amounts to sex discrimination seems intuitively obvious to many people. But the argument does not neatly map onto existing equal protection doctrine. There are two different categories of sex-discrimination claims that can be brought under the Equal Protection Clause of the United States Constitution: (1) challenges to facial sex-based classifications, meaning classifications that are written into the law or policy in question; and (2) challenges to rules that are facially neutral but still have a disparate impact as to sex, meaning women are affected more than men (or vice versa). The tampon tax cuts across those two categories.

As background, the Equal Protection Clause of the Fourteenth Amendment provides that no state shall "deny to any person within its jurisdiction the equal protection of the laws."[42] The Supreme Court has interpreted that to mean that when the government draws classifications or distinctions, it needs a sufficient justification for doing so. What counts as "sufficient" depends on the nature and type of the distinction. When the government is facially classifying on the basis of race, religion, national origin, or alienage, the classification must pass "strict scrutiny," meaning that it must be narrowly tailored to achieve a compelling purpose. Facial sex-based classifications must pass "intermediate scrutiny," which means that they must be substantially related to an important governmental purpose. By contrast, when the government is not making a distinction based on a suspect classification like race, religion, national origin, alienage, or sex, courts use the lowest level of review—known as "rational basis." This test merely looks at whether the distinction is rationally related to a legitimate governmental purpose, and is very easy to meet.

If a court is evaluating a statute or policy that is facially neutral but has a proven disparate impact on a suspect class, a heightened analysis applies, but only if the government's discriminatory intent can be shown. For example, in the 1979 case of *Personnel Administrator v. Feeney*,[43] Massachusetts had a statute that gave preference to veterans for state civil service positions. At the time, veterans made up over 25% of the Massachusetts population, and over 98% of them were male. Thus, even though the veterans' preference statute did not facially distinguish as to sex (or any other suspect class), it clearly had a disparate impact on women. Men were far more likely than women to benefit from the veterans' preference in hiring. But the Supreme Court held that for equal protection purposes, a showing of disparate impact as to sex was not enough to trigger intermediate scrutiny. In the absence of a facial sex-based classification, the only way to get to intermediate scrutiny (as opposed to rational basis) was to show disparate impact plus discriminatory intent on the government's part. Moreover, the Supreme Court defined discriminatory intent very narrowly in *Feeney*, stating that it was not enough to show that the government had been aware that the statute would disparately impact women. Instead, the plaintiffs had to demonstrate that this was the Massachusetts government's goal. As the *Feeney* Court put it, the required showing was that the legislature adopted the rule "at least in part 'because of,' not merely 'in spite of,' its adverse effects upon an identifiable group." Since the *Feeney* plaintiffs could not prove that, the Court applied only rational-basis review, and upheld the veterans' preference statute.[44] The standard announced in *Feeney* remains good law today.

The tampon tax sits right on the divide between the "facial classification" and "facial neutrality" scenarios. A tax on menstrual products is not an explicitly facial sex-based classification in the way that, say, an all-girls public school or an all-male military draft is. But given the connection between menstrual products and female biology, it comes very close. Indeed, as the New York complaint noted, the tampon tax calls to mind Justice Scalia's famous statement that "[a] tax on wearing yarmulkes is a tax on Jews."[45] A sales tax on yarmulkes probably would not stand out if every single wearable item, religious and otherwise, were taxed the same way. But if a state sales-tax law exempted most items of religious clothing, while still imposing the tax on yarmulkes, that would likely be viewed by courts as an unconstitutional tax on Jews. Similarly, sales tax systems that exempt analogous unisex necessities but not menstrual products are the functional equivalent of a tax on women.

To be sure, not everyone who menstruates identifies as a woman, as we discuss further in chapter 7. But everyone who menstruates does have a uterus and at least one ovary. Moreover, menstruation has long been linked, socially and culturally, to female biology. Given the relationship between menstruation and the female reproductive system, it is logical to view the tampon tax as a facially sex-based classification. The tampon tax does not have a mere disparate impact on women in the way that, for example, veterans' preference statutes do. The need for menstrual products is linked to reproductive biology in a way that veteran status is not.

Although there is a strong argument that the tampon tax is an unconstitutional tax on women, there is one Supreme Court case that points the other way: a 1974 case called *Geduldig v. Aiello*.[46] *Geduldig* involved an equal protection challenge to California's short-term disability insurance system, which covered most disabilities, but excluded those resulting from alcoholism, drug addiction, sexual psychopathy, and normal pregnancies. The Supreme Court rejected the argument that the exclusion of normal pregnancies amounted to sex discrimination under the Equal Protection Clause.[47] "While it is true that only women can become pregnant it does not follow that every legislative classification concerning pregnancy is a sex-based classification," the Court wrote. "The program divides potential recipients into two groups—pregnant women and nonpregnant persons. While the first group is exclusively female, the second includes members of both sexes."[48]

Geduldig was roundly criticized at the time, and when the Supreme Court construed Title VII's sex discrimination the same way in *General Electric v. Gilbert* in 1976,[49] Congress quickly took action. In 1978, Congress amended Title VII by passing the Pregnancy Discrimination Act (PDA).[50] The PDA states that Title VII's statutory prohibition of employment discrimination based on sex includes discrimination based on pregnancy. It further specifies that pregnancy discrimination includes treating pregnancy worse than other conditions that similarly affect the ability to work.[51] But Congress can only amend statutes; it cannot amend the Supreme Court's interpretations of the Constitution. Thus, notwithstanding Title VII's inclusion of pregnancy discrimination as a form of sex discrimination, *Geduldig* technically remains good law for equal protection purposes. And *Geduldig*'s reasoning is in tension with the idea that the tampon tax is a sex-based classification under the Equal

Protection Clause. After all, if pregnancy did not count as a proxy for female sex, why should menstruation or menstrual products?

This argument is weaker than it first seems, however. First, *Geduldig* dates back to 1974, which was before the Supreme Court even fleshed out its modern approach to sex-discrimination cases brought under the Equal Protection Clause. It was not until the end of 1976, for example, that the Supreme Court held in *Craig v. Boren* that intermediate scrutiny applied to facial sex-based classifications.[52] (Notably, the Supreme Court's *Gilbert* decision, which blessed *Geduldig* and extended it to the Title VII context, was also issued before *Boren*.) Of course, even as of 1974, some Supreme Court justices had suggested that certain instances of governmental sex discrimination should trigger heightened review.[53] But the lack of clarity on when heightened review should occur, and what the standard should be—not decided until the very end of 1976—arguably muddled the analysis of the Court in both *Geduldig* and *Gilbert*.

Geduldig's overly formalistic approach is also anachronistic. As legal scholars Holning Lau and Hillary Li have pointed out, the Supreme Court's 2015 decision in the landmark marriage-equality case of *Obergefell v. Hodges*[54] contrasts in interesting ways with *Geduldig*. Although *Geduldig* "concluded that there was no sex discrimination because not all women are, or will ever be, pregnant. . . . *Obergefell* was much less concerned about the fact that some gays and lesbians are neither interested nor ever will be interested in getting married," they observe.[55] Indeed, whereas *Geduldig* focused on whether every single woman was tangibly affected by the unfavorable treatment of pregnancy, *Obergefell* focused much more on the symbolic and aggregate effects of discrimination in the form of bans on same-sex marriage. This shift to focusing on symbolic and aggregate harms is entirely consistent with the idea that taxes on menstrual products should be viewed as sex based.

Finally, *Geduldig* only said that not "*every* legislative classification concerning pregnancy is a sex-based classification."[56] This left the door open for some governmental classifications concerning pregnancy to count as sex-based classifications. Arguably, there is an even stronger case that classifications surrounding menstruation are sex-based compared to pregnancy-based classifications. *Geduldig* stated that "pregnancy is an objectively identifiable physical condition with unique characteristics," with most women falling, at any given time, into the category of "nonpregnant persons."[57] With declining fertility rates, that is even truer today than it was in *Geduldig*'s time. Menstruation, by contrast, is a regular occurrence in the lives of approximately half the population from, on average, the ages of thirteen to fifty-one. *Geduldig*'s approach of dividing women into "pregnant women" and "nonpregnant persons" therefore makes even less sense in the context of menstruation. Most women at any given time fall into the category of those who menstruate. In sum, the nearly fifty-year-old *Geduldig* decision should not be seen as foreclosing the current argument that the tampon tax represents a facial sex-based classification. The state's interest in raising revenue, while "important" in the colloquial sense of the term, is not an important enough constitutional interest to justify a distinction in the tax law based on sex.[58]

Although the facial-classification model does most of the work to invalidate the tampon tax, analysis under the facial-neutrality model shows that the tax should trigger and fail intermediate scrutiny as well. In the case of a facially neutral statute, to get to intermediate scrutiny, the tampon tax must be shown both to have a disparate impact and to stem from discriminatory intent. The disparate impact here is clear: the vast majority of users of menstrual products identify as girls or women, and even those users who do not so identify nevertheless possess the same reproductive organs that effectuate menstruation. That men sometimes purchase these products for women does not change the analysis either, as a federal appellate court recently explained in a case involving higher tariffs for men's leather gloves than for other gloves. It may be true that "women buy men's gloves for men and men buy women's gloves for women," the court said. "But this comparison entirely misses the point. The claimed discrimination is based on the sex of the glove *users*, not the sex of the glove *purchasers*."[59] Thus, the key fact is that *users* of menstrual products typically are girls and women.

The bigger challenge within the facial-neutrality model is proving discriminatory intent. There is no "smoking gun" evidence that proves that the tampon tax resulted from a conscious, intentional desire to harm women. However, as chapter 1 described, there are longstanding taboos surrounding menstruation, leading to shame, stigma, and—importantly—silence surrounding menstruation. The failure to include menstrual products on the list of exempted necessities is a foreseeable result of the desire not to see, consider, or think about menstruation at all. And without an affirmative discussion of what menstrual products are used for and why they are necessary, they run the risk of getting grouped with products like vaginal douches, rather than with the other tax-exempt necessities with which they truly belong. This result is unsurprising given that most state legislators have historically been men. Indeed, when a popular YouTube personality asked then-president Barack Obama about the tampon tax, he responded, "I have to tell you, I have no idea why states would tax these as luxury items. I suspect it's because men were making the laws when those taxes were passed."[60]

Notably, in the case involving the disparity in how men's and women's leather gloves were taxed, the court ultimately concluded that there was no discriminatory intent, reasoning that although "'[a] tax on wearing yarmulkes is a tax on Jews.' . . . [m]en's gloves are hardly an irrational object of disfavor, and a tax on them creates no compelling inference that Congress intended to discriminate against men."[61] By contrast, menstruation and its related products *have* long been an irrational object of disfavor. Like a tax on yarmulkes vis-à-vis Jews, a tax on menstrual products should give rise to an inference of discriminatory intent against women.

The facial-classification and facial-neutrality models thus work together to show why the tampon tax should trigger intermediate scrutiny. And because it cannot pass intermediate scrutiny, it is unconstitutional. In *United States v. Virginia*, Justice Ginsburg not only described intermediate scrutiny as "skeptical scrutiny" but also added that it requires an "exceedingly persuasive justification."[62] There is no exceedingly persuasive justification for taxing menstrual products more heavily than analogous necessities. Indeed, doing so runs counter to the type of justifications for sex-based differentiation that the *Virginia* Court said could pass intermediate scrutiny: "to compensate women 'for particular economic disabilities [they have] suffered,' to 'promot[e] equal employment opportunity,' [or] to advance full development of the talent and capacities of our Nation's people."[63] Chapter 1 described how period poverty keeps girls and women from fully participating in school, work, and other aspects of public life. The tampon tax exacerbates that problem. The differential tax treatment also sends the message that products enabling people to leave their homes while menstruating are not necessities, but luxuries. It constitutes invidious discrimination when the tax law, or any other law, makes full participation in public life more difficult because of an involuntary biological process such as menstruation.

Although the tampon tax should be viewed as a sex-based classification that triggers (and fails) intermediate scrutiny, even if it were not, the tax arguably cannot pass even the lowest level of review: rational basis. To be sure, very few governmental classifications are struck down on this level of review, which is extremely deferential. But in the few cases where governmental distinctions have failed rational-basis review, it was because the distinction was connected to animus toward a disfavored group. For example, in *United States Department of Agriculture v. Moreno*,[64] the Supreme Court struck down a congressional amendment to the Food Stamp Act that excluded households containing unrelated individuals. The *Moreno* Court explained that the change failed rational-basis review because the legislative history indicated that the change stemmed from a desire to prevent people in "hippie communes" from receiving benefits. It is worth noting that even though the United States government was obviously going to save money from the change, that was not enough of a legitimate purpose to justify it.[65] By the same token, the tax revenue from the tampon tax is not a sufficient legitimate purpose to justify it, given its connection to menstrual stigma and its exclusive use by people who possess what is traditionally called "female" biology.

The Ongoing Legal and Legislative Push to Eliminate the Tampon Tax

For all of these reasons, there is a strong case that the tampon tax is unconstitutional. But no court has yet reached this conclusion. In addition to pressure through class-action litigation such as in New York, Florida, California, and Ohio, public advocacy efforts have persuaded numerous other states to act on their own. In 2016, Connecticut, Illinois, and Washington, DC (in addition to New York) all repealed their tampon taxes. Florida joined the group in 2017, as noted above. In 2018, Nevada became the first (and still only) state to repeal its tampon tax by popular vote. In an Election Day referendum, 56.5% of Nevada voters voted in favor of repealing the tax on tampons and pads, while 43.5% voted against.[66] In 2019, both Rhode Island and Utah repealed their tampon taxes. In 2020, Washington State joined California and Ohio in doing so. Most recently, Louisiana, Vermont, Maine, and Michigan have followed suit, with other states expected to do the same.

Internationally, the movement continues to progress as well. Australia and India officially removed their tampon taxes in 2018.[67] That same year, Colombia's Constitutional Court struck down the country's tampon tax, ruling that it reflected discrimination against women.[68] Rwanda eliminated its tampon tax in 2019, citing concerns about the affordability of menstrual products.[69] The United Kingdom repealed its tax after its withdrawal from the European Union at the end of 2020, as described above.

Within the United States, the rhetoric surrounding the elimination of the tampon tax consistently frames it as an issue of gender equality. Elected officials repeatedly describe the tampon tax as a tax on women. "Women should not be taxed because they are women," said DC councilmember Anita Bonds.[70] Rhode Island state representative Edith Ajello echoed these sentiments, explaining that the tampon tax "amounts to a tax on being a woman, and I'm so glad that Rhode Island is joining the growing ranks of states that recognize that they should not be imposing a tax on a woman every time she needs to buy menstrual products."[71]

Notably, several lawmakers also have linked their success in achieving tampon-tax repeals to breaking the traditional silence surrounding menstruation. Ohio state representative Brigid Kelly, who had sponsored the tampon-tax repeal there, commented that her male colleagues had been professional in discussions about the issue, but even so, "it's definitely not something they are eager to discuss over the lunch table."[72] The implication—which other legislators have also noted in the context of diverse menstrual-equity issues, as discussed in chapter 4—is that sometimes these changes are agreed to as a way of cutting short any further discussion about menstruation. Utah state representative Robert Spendlove put a more positive spin on the dynamics. Spendlove acknowledged that before menstrual-equity advocate Emily Bell McCormick had spoken with him about the tampon tax, he "didn't know the issue very well." He reflected, "It was honestly because of Emily. . . . She did a really good job of kind of explaining the issue to me, helping me understand the inequity that existed in our existing tax system. And once she explained it to me, it was easy for me to support it."[73] McCormick similarly observed that, in the past, menstrual equity had been "seen as a pretty extreme movement," and many people were uncomfortable with public discussions of menstruation. To address the awkwardness, McCormick and others "reframed this as, 'Oh, no, this is totally normal. It's completely appropriate to talk about. It needs to be talked about.'"[74] These types of anecdotes illuminate the culture of silence about menstrual products, and some people's discomfort when they are discussed. All of this, of course, provides further insight about why menstrual products did not end up on tax-exempt lists in the first place.

In the meantime, though, the majority of US states still impose the tampon tax, and Period Equity is pushing ahead with its lawsuits. Depending on the particularities of any state's tax law, the discrepancy between taxable and exempted products may be less glaring than it was in New York and Florida. In those states, there was an obvious close comparator: other blood-absorbent products, like bandages and dressings, were tax-exempt while menstrual products remained in the taxable category. By contrast, in many of the remaining states (apart from Texas, which follows New York's and Florida's old approach of exempting bandages but not menstrual products), the exempted products are not quite as analogous.

Ironically, part of the reason why these exempted products are less analogous is that they are blatantly *less* "necessary" than menstrual products. For example, the website for Tax Free. Period.—a joint effort of Period Equity and the menstrual-product company LOLA—points out that Arizona exempts licorice; Georgia exempts tattoos; Kentucky exempts pixie sticks; and the list goes on. "Bingo supplies? Doughnuts? Seriously? Click around the country to see some of the items that are tax-exempt in states that tax tampons," the site marvels.[75] This type of information makes for compelling advocacy—but how will the argument fare legally?

The Complexities of Comparison

In states that do not have tax exemptions for any blood-absorbing products, whether bandages or menstrual products, advocates face a particular challenge in framing their arguments. This is not purely a matter of strategy; it is also a theoretical question that implicates some of the most challenging and profound issues in sex-discrimination law. Discrimination claims are usually based on comparisons—proof that one person, or one group, receives worse treatment than another. But with sex-discrimination claims, particularly those related to female biology, there is often no perfect comparison because of inherent biological differences between men and women (to use the traditional jurisprudential binaries). This is certainly true for menstruation and menstrual products. The comparison challenges also arise in the contexts of pregnancy, breastfeeding, and menopause. Feminist legal theorists have debated for decades how to approach this question, which is sometimes referred to as the sameness/difference debate: should advocates emphasize the need for equal treatment of men and women, or should they emphasize the need for law to accommodate differences between the sexes, particularly in the case of biological differences?

In the courts, the sameness/difference debate has played out most fully so far with respect to pregnancy. We have already seen that the Supreme Court held in *Geduldig*, decided in 1974, that treating pregnancy less favorably than other medical conditions did not necessarily amount to sex discrimination. The *Geduldig* Court oddly concluded that the relevant comparison was not between men and women, but rather between "pregnant women" and "nonpregnant" men and women. Since women were in both groups, the Court reasoned that there was no sex discrimination. The Pregnancy Discrimination Act (PDA) rejected that reasoning, shifting the comparative frame (at least in the Title VII context) to pregnant employees versus nonpregnant employees who were also limited in their ability to work. But the PDA kept intact the underlying comparative structure. To win a pregnancy-accommodation claim, for instance, it is not enough for a plaintiff to show that her pregnancy-related needs were not accommodated. She must also show that she was treated differently from "other persons not so affected [by pregnancy] but similar in their ability or inability to work."[76] That means, unfortunately, that if an employer does not accommodate anyone at all (outside of separate requirements under the Americans with Disabilities Act), the pregnant worker is out of luck; she has no remedy at all. The Pregnant Workers Fairness Act, which was passed in the House of Representatives in May 2021, would change that, by giving pregnant workers an independent entitlement to accommodations. However, that act has not yet been passed by the Senate.

Not surprisingly, the PDA's language has generated disputes about which employees count as sufficiently "similar" for purposes of the comparison. One case that took up that question, *UPS v. Young*, made it to the Supreme Court in 2014.[77] The *Young* case, as we explain, may inform the comparison question for menstrual products as well.

Peggy Young was a part-time UPS driver who became pregnant after suffering several miscarriages. Young's doctor told her not to lift more than twenty pounds during the first twenty weeks of her pregnancy, and not more than ten pounds after that point. But her job required her to lift up to seventy pounds (and up to 150 pounds with assistance). UPS denied Young's request for a "light-duty" accommodation, telling her that she could not work at all while subject to a lifting restriction. That meant that Young was required to stay home without pay during most of her pregnancy, losing not only her salary but also her health insurance coverage.[78]

Young's subsequent PDA lawsuit presented a puzzle: had she been treated differently from "similar" employees? The PDA states that "women affected by pregnancy, childbirth, or related medical conditions shall be treated the same for all employment-related purposes . . . as other persons not so affected but similar in their ability or inability to work."[79] At the time when Young brought her case, UPS's policy was to grant accommodations to three categories of employees: (1) drivers who had become disabled on the job, (2) those who had lost their Department of Transportation certifications, and (3) those who suffered from a disability covered by the Americans with Disabilities Act. UPS argued that it had not violated the PDA because it accommodated only those employees who fell into one of the three specific categories, which Young did not. As the Supreme Court put it, "UPS said that, since Young did not fall within any of those categories, it had not discriminated against Young on the basis of pregnancy but had treated her just as it treated all 'other' relevant 'persons.'" Young countered that once an employer was accommodating any subset of workers with disabling conditions, "pregnant workers who are similar in the ability to work [must] receive the same treatment even if still other nonpregnant workers do not receive accommodations."[80]

The Supreme Court rejected both sides' arguments. First, the Court stated that Young was claiming a sort of "'most-favored-nation' status" for pregnancy, summarizing her argument as follows:

> As long as an employer provides one or two workers with an accommodation—say, those with particularly hazardous jobs, or those whose workplace presence is particularly needed, or those who have worked at the company for many years, or those who are over the age of 55—then it must provide similar accommodations to *all* pregnant workers (with comparable physical limitations), irrespective of the nature of their jobs, the employer's need to keep them working, their ages, or any other criteria.[81]

This argument proved too much, the Court concluded: "We doubt that Congress intended to grant pregnant workers an unconditional most-favored-nation status." Second, the Court reasoned that UPS's argument went too far in the other direction. Giving employers unfettered rein to create categories that operated to exclude pregnant workers, noted the Court, would undermine the very purpose of the PDA.[82]

So the *Young* Court adopted a compromise approach. It outlined a three-step process for PDA claims, drawn from a landmark employment-discrimination case called *McDonnell Douglas Corp. v. Green*.[83] First, a PDA plaintiff can establish a prima facie case of pregnancy discrimination by showing that she sought an accommodation, that the employer did not accommodate her, and that the employer did accommodate other employees "similar in their ability or inability to work." Second, the employer may respond by articulating a "legitimate, nondiscriminatory" reason for denying the accommodation. The Court warned, though, that this reason cannot merely be that "it is more expensive or less convenient to add pregnant women to the category" of accommodated employees. Finally, at step three, the plaintiff can reach a jury by "providing sufficient evidence that the employer's policies impose a significant burden on pregnant workers, and that the employer's 'legitimate, nondiscriminatory' reasons are not sufficiently strong to justify the burden." One way—but not the only way—for the plaintiff to prove that the policies are imposing a significant burden is to show that the employer's policy is "accommodat[ing] a large percentage of nonpregnant workers while failing to accommodate a large percentage of pregnant workers."[84]

It is true that *Young* arose under Title VII (as amended by the PDA), while the tampon-tax cases arise under the Equal Protection Clause. But *Young*'s approach to ascertaining an appropriate comparator is relevant and adaptable for use by courts in other contexts. In particular, *Young* offers insights for how courts might think about tampon-tax cases in states where some products—say, doughnuts or dandruff shampoo—are tax exempt, but blood-absorbing products like bandages or gauze are taxable. To be sure, the fact that a state grants a tax exemption to just one product—such as prescription medicines, for example—is probably not enough to mean that the state must exempt menstrual products as well. *Young* explicitly rejected a "most-favored-nation" approach, and that will probably make it difficult to argue that any tampon tax automatically violates equal protection principles, even if there are policy reasons for exempting menstrual products. But once a state provides tax exemptions to numerous products, the case that the tampon tax is discriminatory becomes stronger. Here, *Young* provides a possible path forward.

Borrowing from *Young*, in any state that taxes menstrual products but exempts several other products from taxation, the first step would be for a plaintiff to show that menstrual products are being taxed by the state while other "similar" products are not. Just as *Young* did not prescribe exactly which employees count as "similar," tampon-tax plaintiffs should likewise have some latitude in identifying "similar" products with tax-exempt status. Clearly, products like bandages and gauze are similar to menstrual products because they have a similar function (absorbing blood or other bodily fluids), as emphasized in the New York and Florida lawsuits. The fact that Texas likewise taxes menstrual products while exempting bandages, gauze, and dressings (under the heading of "wound care dressings and supplies") also makes that state's law particularly ripe for challenge. In other states, tampon-tax challenges might point to sales-tax exemptions for over-the-counter personal care products (e.g., antiperspirants)[85] or for products used in the urogenital or perineal areas (e.g., condoms or hemorrhoid products), given that menstrual products are used in or near female genitalia. The specific arguments likely will vary from state to state, depending on the details of the state's particular tax exemptions. What is important, though, is *Young*'s clear message that "similar" does not have to mean identical.

If a plaintiff can advance to step two of the *Young* analysis by pointing to similar products that are exempt, a state would then need to respond by articulating a "legitimate, nondiscriminatory" reason for exempting other similar products while taxing menstrual products. And, as *Young* puts it, that reason cannot simply be that "it is more expensive or less convenient to add [menstrual products] to the [tax-exempt] category." This is an important point, given some states' arguments that they would lose too much money by eliminating the sales tax on menstrual products. California, for example, made this argument for years before agreeing to a temporary repeal of the tampon tax, and it (and other states) may deploy that argument again in the future.[86]

If the state is able to articulate "legitimate, nondiscriminatory" reasons for taxing menstrual products while exempting other similar products, the analysis advances to step three under *Young*. The tampon-tax plaintiffs would respond by providing "sufficient evidence" that the state's tax rules impose a "significant burden" in connection with menstruation, and that the state's "legitimate, nondiscriminatory" reasons are not "sufficiently strong to justify the burden." Given the amount of revenue generated by the tampon tax, it should not be difficult to show that the tax is a significant burden on users of menstrual products in aggregate. Moreover, per *Young*, a tampon-tax plaintiff could prove that the sales tax is a significant burden by showing that the state's policy has the effect of exempting a "large percentage" of similar products but not menstrual products. Here, too, comparisons to similar products—and explanations of why they are indeed similar—will be a key aspect of proving the case. So, too, will the aggregate number of exemptions and their aggregate tax expenditures (i.e., lost revenue), especially relative to the revenue generated by the state's tampon tax.

To be sure, *Young*'s approach, which stemmed from the PDA, is not binding in an equal protection challenge. But the fact that the Supreme Court has adopted this standard in the context of pregnancy-accommodation claims is encouraging for other sex-discrimination claims that are similarly intertwined with female biology, in that it provides a possible road map for how to think through comparison-based claims. Indeed, *Young*'s reasoning shows the wisdom of menstrual-equity advocates' comparison-based strategy for challenging the tampon tax. From the way that the various petitions highlight humorous (and frustrating) comparisons like tax-exempt crocodile meat and cocktail cherries to the way that the lawsuits analogize to similar products like bandages, the comparisons are effective both rhetorically and legally.

The Limits of Comparison

Given how entrenched the comparison framework is within discrimination law generally, it makes sense that menstrual-equity advocates have adopted it as a starting point in their public communications and court filings. But the framework also comes with costs. It implies that finding a similar analogue—a similar employee for a pregnancy-accommodation claim; a similar product for a tampon-tax challenge—is the only way to prevail. Indeed, the underlying premise that similar comparators are required relates back to the sameness/difference debate that continues to complicate advocacy for gender equality.

Young is certainly helpful in sending the message that "similar," rather than perfect, comparators can be sufficient. But in some cases involving reproductive biology, identifying even a similar (let alone perfect) comparator is impossible. For example, menstruating and breastfeeding candidates for professional licensing exams or other long tests often need to bring their own personal products (tampons, pads, pumps, ice packs, and so on) with them into testing spaces, and may also need regular breaks during long examinations like the multistate bar exam.[87] Similarly, as discussed more fully in chapter 3, menstruating students also have specific needs—including access to menstrual products, private bathroom stalls, and the assurance of knowing that they can take a bathroom break if necessary—that are sui generis. To be sure, certain disabilities also require periodic breaks in the way that menstruation and breastfeeding do, and menstrual products can be analogized to toilet paper, to a certain extent. But the need to fit every discrimination claim into the comparative box can be artificial, strained, and limiting.

Indeed, regardless of whether there is a similar comparator, it is clear that certain biological processes impose real costs and needs—unequally borne across the sexes—that require consideration and accommodation in order to achieve true societal equality. This is why the menstrual-equity movement's dual strategies—litigation and public policy/legislative advocacy—are both important. While some advocates are focused on using existing law to challenge menstrual inequities, others can focus on repealing problematic laws or passing new ones. The increasingly strong prospects for the passage of the Pregnant Workers Fairness Act are a hopeful sign here.

The Tampon Tax as the Gateway to Broader Menstrual Equity

The tampon-tax movement has already notched considerable successes. That it has prompted several US states—as well as Britain, Australia, Canada, Colombia, India, the United Kingdom, and Rwanda—to eliminate their tampon taxes in just a handful of years is remarkable. While the tax on each individual purchase is small, the aggregate savings are considerable, amounting to many millions of dollars a year in the United States alone. When New York repealed its tampon tax in 2016, Governor Andrew Cuomo's press release estimated that it would save purchasers $10 million a year.[88] More recently, when Washington repealed its tampon tax in 2020, state senator Lynda Wilson, who had sponsored the bill, noted that it would save purchasers more than $3 million a year.[89] "Besides being the biggest tax reduction passed by the Legislature, it's probably the best example of fairness and equity to come out of Olympia this year," Wilson observed.[90] Representative Brigid Kelly of Ohio, meanwhile, emphasized the individual impact of Ohio's repeal of the tax. "The sales tax on these items does not amount to much," she acknowledged to National Public Radio. "But when you're trying to figure out if you can give your kid milk money or if you have enough to get your own lunch then it is impactful in a very significant way."[91]

Of equal importance, the tampon-tax movement has sparked a larger cultural conversation that continues to evolve and gain momentum. Tax has a way of showing discrimination in a dollars-and-cents way that is easy to understand. Recall that it was a 2013 decision in a tax case, *United States v. Windsor*, that paved the way for the Supreme Court's recognition of same-sex marriage three years later in *Obergefell v. Hodges*.[92] Critics of the tampon tax thus focus on not only the fiscal burden itself but also its expressive function. The tampon tax both symbolizes and perpetuates existing gender-based inequalities. The movement to abolish it, therefore, has a broader aim than solely state tax reform. It also challenges the silence about menstruation, prompting new conversations about how law can help eliminate some of the menstruation-related structural obstacles to full participation in public life. Indeed, tampon-tax reform efforts have been the catalyst for the growing movement toward all forms of menstrual equity.

3

Schools and Menstruation

Elena Kagan is a trailblazer. Before becoming the fourth woman ever to serve on the Supreme Court, she was the first female solicitor general of the United States—and, before that, the first female dean of Harvard Law School. When Kagan assumed leadership of the school in 2003, many of her initiatives focused on improving student life, such as providing free coffee for students and creating a makeshift ice-skating rink on campus. One of her early notable enhancements was arranging for free tampons in all of the women's restrooms. Justice (then Dean) Kagan later explained that she had gotten the idea from attending a conference where she noticed a supply of tampons neatly stacked in a basket in the restroom. "It's such a small thing, but it says a lot about whether a place cares about its women," she later told an interviewer.[1]

That "small thing" in 2003 has since been replicated at many colleges and universities. There also is a growing movement to make menstrual products freely available at public schools throughout the country. Just as Justice Kagan did, advocates point to the significant expressive value of making menstrual products available. But they also emphasize period poverty and real student need. (Indeed, approximately half of all US public school students are eligible for free or reduced-price lunch, based on low household income.)[2] The need for free menstrual products in schools has thus emerged as another core aspect of the menstrual-equity movement. As with the tampon-tax movement, there has been a remarkable amount of progress since 2015.

New York Becomes First City to Require Free Menstrual
Products in Schools

In large part, the dialogue about menstrual products in schools has grown from and alongside the momentum surrounding efforts to repeal the tampon tax. For example, early in 2015—months before the October launch of the Change.org petition to repeal the tampon tax throughout the United States—menstrual-equity advocate Jennifer Weiss-Wolf met with New York City councilmember Julissa Ferreras-Copeland to discuss a broad agenda.[3] Ferreras-Copeland, a Democrat representing Queens, had been first elected to the city council in 2009; she was reelected in 2014 and became the first woman and first person of color to chair the city council's Finance Committee. In this role, Ferreras-Copeland had a powerful responsibility: overseeing New York City's $78.3 billion budget, a large portion of which is allocated each year to the operation of the New York City school system.[4]

The first 2015 meeting between Weiss-Wolf and Ferreras-Copeland was a success. "Ours was an immediate synergy," Weiss-Wolf later wrote. Weiss-Wolf had brought a list of proposals for Ferreras-Copeland to consider, and Ferreras-Copeland "needed no convincing that menstrual access was an issue she wanted to tackle." The two women soon convened a panel of community leaders and organizers from New York City's shelters, food pantries, after-school programs, and similar groups, hoping to learn more about the most pressing period-poverty issues throughout the city. Consistently, panel members emphasized the challenges faced by low-income students who lacked access to menstrual products.[5]

Weiss-Wolf and Ferreras-Copeland also organized a focus group with teenage girls. Those students shared their concerns about being unable afford menstrual products and not having access to them at school. The discussions particularly resonated with Ferreras-Copeland because of her past work experience: "I was the director of an after-school program in Queens, New York, and I came to learn that young girls would skip out and go home because they were on their periods," she told an online publication in the summer of 2015. "Sometimes it was due to the discomfort, but other times they'd run out of pads and were too embarrassed to ask a teacher or nurse. They preferred to lose learning time in order to save face."[6]

To begin tackling the problem of availability of menstrual products in schools, Ferreras-Copeland arranged a pilot program at the High School for Arts and Business in Corona, Queens. In the girls' bathroom there, a dispenser stocked with free pads and tampons was installed for the 2015–16 school year. The program was an unqualified success. School attendance increased, albeit slightly (from 90% to 92.4%),[7] and the students expressed great appreciation. "Now that we have this in the bathroom it just makes life 100 times better," commented the student body president. "It is kind of annoying to carry around and ask someone for a pad, and you have to slip it out of class.... It can be embarrassing," added another student. The school principal, Ana Zambrano-Byrakov, was as enthusiastic as students about the menstrual-products pilot program, noting that it reduced student stress because, for the students, "[i]t's one thing on your mind that you don't have to worry about."[8]

In addition to focusing on the practical need for menstrual products in schools, Ferreras-Copeland and others also linked providing such products to combating menstrual stigma and silence. "It's important to de-stigmatize feminine hygiene products, which help us carry out our daily functions without interruption," Ferreras-Copeland said, in public statements about the Queens pilot program. "It's also a matter of giving young girls dignity throughout the process—they shouldn't feel ashamed of being women."[9] These reflections echoed the comments of Kiran Gandhi, the athlete who ran the 2015 London Marathon while "free-bleeding" and who participated as a guest in one of the focus groups for New York City teens. Gandhi explained to the students, "The reason why being able to talk about your own body matters is that then you can actually innovate solutions around problems of stigma."[10]

Building on the momentum of the successful menstrual-products pilot program, Ferreras-Copeland announced in January 2016 that she was working on a package of city council initiatives related to menstrual equity. One initiative was a resolution calling on New York State to repeal the tampon tax; those efforts were already picking up steam in the New York state legislature, as described in chapter 2. The other initiative consisted of three proposed bills to make menstrual products freely available in New York City public schools, homeless shelters, and prisons. (The bills regarding shelters and prisons are discussed further in chapter 4.) Shortly thereafter, Ferreras-Copeland and the New York City Department of Education (DOE) announced an expansion of the school pilot program to twenty-five public middle schools and high schools in Queens and the Bronx.[11] "Having easy access to feminine care products is essential to ensuring that girls in our schools have the supports they need to focus on learning and feel comfortable during classes," DOE deputy chancellor Elizabeth Rose said at the time.[12] The DOE also announced plans to provide more menstrual education in health classes and additional information on posters, in brochures, and at assemblies.

The extraordinary efforts of Ferreras-Copeland and many others culminated in positive action by the New York City Council in late June 2016. By this point, the New York City Council resolution encouraging New York State to repeal the tampon tax was (happily) moot: the New York state legislature had voted on May 25, 2016, to repeal the tax, and Governor Cuomo conveyed his support for repeal. But the issue of freely providing menstrual products in schools, homeless shelters, and prisons was still very much alive. On June 21, 2016, the New York City Council voted forty-nine to zero in favor of doing so, making New York City the first city in the nation to guarantee access to such products.[13] Mayor Bill de Blasio immediately conveyed his support on social media.[14] Chirlane McCray, Mayor de Blasio's wife, even composed a poem entitled "Tampons for ALL" to mark the event. "This is one small step for NYC / And one giant leap for womankind," the poem concluded. "When it comes to menstruation / We all deserve peace of mind."[15] In June 2016, Weiss-Wolf reflected on the changes that had taken place in New York City and New York State within the previous year: "It has been lightning speed for the democratic process," she observed.[16] In the months and years following this innovative legislation in New York City, momentum began to build in other jurisdictions to provide menstrual products in schools, jails, homeless shelters, and other public facilities.

The Growing Push for Schools to Provide Free Menstrual Products

News of New York City's schools initiative spread throughout the United States, spurring more action. In early 2017, California assemblywoman Cristina Garcia proposed that California provide free menstrual products in schools, specifically citing New York City as an example.[17] Like Ferreras-Copeland, Garcia had relevant past experience. Having previously worked as a teacher, she commented that "[t]here's a real need, and this is a real problem. When I was a teacher, I always had a box of menstrual products that was there."[18]

In October 2017, California passed Garcia's proposed law, which requires all public schools with grades six through twelve that also meet a 40% pupil-poverty threshold to stock 50% of the school's restrooms with free menstrual products. Leading up to the vote on the bill, Garcia had overtly challenged the silence and stigma around menstruation, so much so that she earned the nickname "Tampon Queen." She carried a "Tampon Barbie" doll (a smiling Barbie holding a tampon) on the assembly floor and even posted a picture of a bloody tampon in her office window. "It's about taking a topic that's taboo, that we're told not to talk about—and when we do talk about, we're made fun of, we're ridiculed about it," she explained. "I just wanted to have a little bit of fun with it. I felt that was the way to take the rhetoric back and make it mine."[19] In California, as in New York, menstrual-product accessibility efforts occurred in tandem with tampon-tax advocacy. Assemblywoman Garcia's parallel push to eliminate California's tampon tax did not progress as quickly as the school measure, however; recently California temporarily eliminated its tampon tax through a budgetary measure that is set to expire automatically after a period of years, unless further reform occurs.

In 2017, the Illinois state legislature passed a menstrual-products school bill to take effect at the start of 2018. Its law went even further than California's. The Indiana law requires *all* grade six through twelve public schools—not just those meeting a poverty threshold—to provide free menstrual products in their bathrooms. The Illinois law, known as the Learn with Dignity Act, states in its "findings" that menstrual products are a "necessity" and that "[w]hen students have access to quality feminine hygiene products, they are able to continue with their daily lives with minimal interruption."[20] Notably, Illinois had repealed its tampon tax the prior year. Indeed, there is considerable—but not total—overlap in the way many states treat these two issues.

Building on the successes in making menstrual products available in schools in New York City, California, and Illinois, in 2018 New York State enacted a law that requires all public schools in the state serving students in grades six through twelve to provide free menstrual products in the restrooms. New York's leaders emphasized both the practical and the expressive effects of the law, noting its value in improving access and reducing stigma. For example, Governor Andrew Cuomo commented that "this legislation is a critical step forward in ensuring every girl in

New York has the same opportunities to grow into a confident, successful woman."[21] New Hampshire, which has no sales tax at all (and thus no tampon tax), followed suit in 2019. In June 2019, the Boston Public Schools announced that free menstrual products would likewise be provided to students in grades six to twelve. And on the federal level, Representative Grace Meng of New York proposed a bill—the Menstrual Equity for All Act of 2019—that would, among other things, give states the option of using federal grant funds to provide students with free menstrual products in schools. Her proposed bill did not move forward at the time, but one piece of it (treating menstrual products as qualified medical expenses for reimbursement from health flexible spending arrangements) did make it into the CARES Act in March 2020. This bodes well for possible future enactment of other parts of the original Menstrual Equity for All Act.

Meanwhile, in 2019, the state of Georgia took up the issue of menstrual products in schools, but with more mixed implications for the larger menstrual-equity movement. Georgia legislators explicitly rejected a bill to repeal Georgia's tampon tax, instead moving to redirect some tampon-tax revenue to provide menstrual products to low-income students.[22] This approach—essentially pitting the tax issue and the access issue against each other in a zero-sum relationship—was an idea proposed by House speaker pro tem Jan Jones, who expressed skepticism that the tampon tax was a form of gender discrimination. "I think the [real] problem is [access for] low-income folks, whether it's accessing diapers or feminine hygiene products—things that we would consider, in a modern society, to be a necessity," she said.[23] "And I would rather use that [tax] funding to solve a problem than to satisfy someone's definition of what's fair."[24] State representative Kim Schofield, who had advocated repealing the tampon tax, was wary of the trade-off. "Yes, let's address this basic issue for students so they can have what they need so it doesn't disrupt learning," Schofield countered. "But for adults, we need to take the tax off, just plain and simple."[25]

Georgia's example shows that progress on these two menstrual-equity issues—eliminating the tampon tax and making menstrual products freely available in schools—does not always occur in tandem. Ironically, the two issues can end up being inversely linked. Georgia's approach has echoes of a similar debate that occurred in the United Kingdom before

Brexit. Leaders there attempted to quiet tampon-tax critics by allocating tampon-tax revenue to so-called women's health and support charities, such as shelters for survivors of domestic violence. As a practical matter, the UK's trade-off strategy essentially forced purchasers of menstrual products to bear a disproportionate burden in paying for services that should have been funded by all taxpayers equally.[26] Jones's proposal had the same effect in Georgia, essentially making consumers of menstrual products shoulder the cost of making tampons and pads available to students in schools for free.

In 2020, Virginia—which also reduced (but did not outright repeal) its tampon tax in 2019—passed legislation that requires all public schools to make menstrual products freely available to students. More progress is likely to come as other states follow suit.

It is important to acknowledge that providing students with free menstrual products comes with a financial cost. But the cost may not be as great as school districts expect. When New York State first passed its law, for instance, school officials in Yonkers, New York—a city of approximately two hundred thousand people located adjacent to New York City's northern border—estimated that it would spend $37,000 to install menstrual product dispensers in 175 restrooms in the school district, and between $125,000 and $200,000 each year thereafter to continue to provide menstrual products to students, at an annual cost of approximately $29 per student.[27] Actual data from the Cambridge (Massachusetts) Public Schools, however, suggest that the true cost per student is in fact much lower. Over a period of three calendar years (2017, 2018, and 2019), the Cambridge Public Schools had a one-time expense of approximately $33,000 for dispensers and waste receptacles. For the same time period, the district spent a cumulative total of $12,666 for pads, tampons, and waste wrappers. To be sure, Cambridge has a smaller population (approximately 115,000 people) than does Yonkers, but taking all expenses into account, the actual average cost of providing menstrual products to students in the Cambridge Public Schools came out to only approximately $2.48 per student per year.[28]

Students Speaking Out

Increasingly, students themselves have emerged as important advocates in the movement for free menstrual products at schools. This is true from the university level on down. For example, in 2016, motivated by both the tampon-tax repeal efforts and New York City's new law making menstrual products available in public schools, Brown University's student government leaders began a campus-wide initiative to put free menstrual products in campus restrooms.[29] "We thought we could be the tipping point . . . pushing conversation to action," said Brown's student government president, Viet Nguyen, at the time. Nguyen also expressed hope that the university would ultimately take on this responsibility itself.[30] Two years later, Brown did.[31] Other universities, including Harvard, Texas A&M, and Purdue, followed in Brown's footsteps, often after being spurred by their own student governments.

Meanwhile, younger students have been increasingly speaking out about the need for menstrual products in schools. During the 2019 hearings on New Hampshire's bill, for instance, seventeen-year-old Caroline Dillon—who also had worked with state senator Martha Hennessey in drafting the bill—testified before the legislature about the bill's importance. "It's very difficult to go to the nurse multiple times every single day for a week every month," Dillon explained.[32] Many students also have organized successfully to effectuate change in their districts or schools. In Eugene, Oregon, for example, a group of four students testified several times before the Eugene School Board, eventually convincing the board to place free products in all middle school and high school girls' and gender-neutral bathrooms in 2019.[33] "By providing free pads and tampons in our school bathrooms we're ensuring that menstruating students spend more time in class and less time worrying about where they're going to find these products," said Posey Chiddix, a high school sophomore in the group.[34] In Dallas, Texas, a group of high schoolers at Skyline High School spent years pushing for the installation of dispensers of free products in their bathrooms; they ultimately succeeded in 2019.[35]

Like legislators, students have identified and articulated the link between providing free products and reducing menstrual stigma. An article in the *New York Times*, for instance, described the reaction of Vienna

Vernose, a private high school senior in Newtown, Pennsylvania, when a tampon fell out of her backpack and a male classmate reacted with "*ew*."[36] Upset by the incident, Vernose discussed it with classmates in her Women's History Seminar, and together those students decided to start a "Menstrual Product Equality" campaign. They put out bowls filled with tampons during a school open house, with signs next to the bowls reading, "These are here for anyone who needs them. Never be ashamed of your body and what it needs."[37]

Similar to other menstrual-equity advocates, students are adept at using social media to draw attention to their cause. In 2019, for example, a group of seventh graders held a "cookie protest" featuring tampon-shaped cookies after school administrators declined to make menstrual products available for free in the school restrooms. Although the location of the school was not specified in the media (whether because of the age of the students or in response to requests by the students or their families), pictures of the cookies circulated widely on social media. Free menstrual products became available in the school bathrooms soon thereafter.[38]

The Role of Law in the Push for Menstrual Products in Schools

In timing, methods, and concept, efforts to repeal the tampon tax and to provide free menstrual products in schools have been, and continue to be, intertwined in many ways. On a theoretical level, both goals fall squarely under the menstrual-equity umbrella. On the ground, the goals are pursued—often in tandem—by many of the same advocates, such as Weiss-Wolf, Ferreras-Copeland, and Garcia. Both efforts have also harnessed the power of social media to draw attention to their goals. But the campaigns represent different approaches to law. The tampon-tax movement's initiatives have been two-pronged, with advocates simultaneously pursuing litigation and legislation. By contrast, the push for free products in schools has relied exclusively on legislative reform, as well as more informal initiatives for rule changes at the school district level.

This difference in legal strategies makes sense. With the tampon tax, there is a robust equal protection argument to be made in court, particularly in the states that already provide numerous tax exemptions for roughly comparable products. Indeed, as discussed in chapter 2, a comparison-focused strategy works well with tampon-tax lawsuits. But challenging the lack of free menstrual products in schools is trickier under existing law. To be sure, in rhetoric, advocates have identified some comparisons in advocating for menstrual products in schools. They identify in particular the universal availability of toilet paper in school restrooms, as well as the fact that some schools provide free condoms. "Just like we've been able to demystify, take the taboo out of condoms, then we should do the same for tampons," Ferreras-Copeland noted, for example, in speaking to a local television station about the initial menstrual-product pilot program in Queens.[39] However, advocates for menstrual products in schools have not turned to lawsuits to claim that once schools provide students with toilet paper and condoms, the schools are required under the Equal Protection Clause to provide free menstrual products as well. Practically speaking, it is unlikely that such an argument would succeed. The argument would be too close to the "most-favored-nation" type of argument that the Supreme Court rejected in *UPS v. Young*, as described in chapter 2. Recall that in *Young*, the plaintiff unsuccessfully asserted that once an employer accommodates *any* employee, it must accommodate pregnant employees as well. If that argument did not work under the Pregnancy Discrimination Act, which explicitly protects pregnancy, it is even less likely to work in the constitutional context. Pushing for new laws and policy changes thus has been the more practical legal strategy for bringing free menstrual products to schools. And, as the flurry of publicity and new laws shows, that strategy has been increasingly successful.

Turning to Title IX

Notwithstanding the emphasis on informal efforts or legislative change, one potentially useful source of existing law that could push schools toward providing free menstrual products is Title IX. This is the federal law that prohibits sex discrimination in federally funded schools (i.e., all public schools, colleges, and universities, as well as nearly all private colleges and universities). Title IX provides that "[n]o person in the United States shall, on the basis of sex, be excluded from participation in, be denied the benefits of, or be subjected to discrimination under any education program or activity receiving Federal financial assistance."[40]

However, no part of the statute, its regulations, or any related guidance mentions the issue of menstrual products. Thus, it would be difficult to argue that Title IX *clearly* requires schools to provide these products for free. But it is nevertheless notable that Title IX's underlying goal, in the words of the United States Department of Justice, is to ensure "equal access to education"—that is, to "ensure that no educational opportunity is denied to women on the basis of sex and that women are granted 'equal opportunity to aspire, achieve, participate in and contribute to society based on their individual talents and capacities.'"[41] With that goal as a guiding principle, there is a strong argument that Title IX should not remain silent about menstruation.

Research has made increasingly clear that a lack of access to menstrual products deprives many students of educational opportunities. The Society for Women's Health Research recently surveyed 362 school nurses from a mix of rural, suburban, and urban areas. Seventy-five percent of those nurses said that their school bathrooms were not well stocked with menstrual products. The director of the society's scientific programs, Rebecca Nebel, reflected, "Female students are distinctly disadvantaged by restrictive bathroom policies and the lack of free and easily available menstrual products in school bathrooms."[42]

This assessment is backed up by students' own accounts. The State of the Period report discussed in chapter 1—which summarized the survey responses of one thousand menstruating teens—found that lack of access was a widespread problem with significant educational implications. Of all respondents, 20% had struggled to afford period products (or were not able to afford them at all), 25% had missed class due to a lack of access to products, 61% had worn a tampon or pad for more than the recommended four hours due to a lack of access to products, 66.6% had felt stress due to a lack of access to products, and an overwhelming 84% had missed class time or known someone who missed class time because of a lack of access to products.[43]

Adding to this body of knowledge is law professor Christopher Cotropia's survey of 693 females between eighteen and twenty-five years of age, all of whom attended high schools in the United States.[44] Cotropia found "statistically significant correlations between not providing [menstrual products] at school and missing school, leaving school early, and negative impacts on learning."[45] In particular, he found that students who could not afford menstrual products were 5.89 times more likely to miss school, 5.82 times more likely to be late for school, and 4.14 times more likely to leave school early than were students who could afford menstrual products.

Cotropia also found that making menstrual products available in the office of a nurse or school administrator was far less effective than putting them directly in the restroom. A large majority of respondents (73.6%) described being embarrassed to ask school personnel for such products, and many explained why by referring to the stigma and silence that have long surrounded menstruation. "It's socially taboo to talk about periods," said one respondent. Another explained that "you had to get a hall pass to go to the nurse, and if you didn't look sick then everyone would guess why." A third echoed, "[I]t was always something I was embarrassed to ask, even though it's normal."[46] These responses from the participants in Cotropia's study affirm Professor Jill Wood's related observation that "[m]enstruation is considered inappropriate public conversation to the extent that girls and women are often too uncomfortable to discuss the topic even with each other, healthcare providers, or family members."[47] This shame overlaps with shame about being unable to afford products. "Now that I'm an adult I realize how ridiculous it sounds but I was worried that if I didn't bring my own it made me low class. Like we couldn't afford them," said one respondent to Cotropia's study.[48] On top of the embarrassment that many students feel about having to go to the nurse's office and request a pad or tampon, it is also logistically challenging. If a student starts menstruating while in the bathroom, walking over to the nurse's office for a tampon or pad raises the risk of bleeding through clothes on the way.

In addition to highlighting the pressing need for free and accessible menstrual products among low-income students, Cotropia's results also demonstrate the need for products in *all* schools. In particular, Cotropia found that the vast majority of survey respondents had experienced being unprepared when their periods started at school. A remarkable 80% of respondents described having resorted to using toilet paper or paper towels because they did not have menstrual products with them that day at school, even though many of them *did* bring products to school on days when their periods had already started at home. This makes sense: menstrual cycles, particularly in adolescence, are often irregular. Months can go by between periods, so students often do not know when their next one is coming. Additionally, middle and high schoolers are often on closed campuses, without the ability to leave to buy a box of tampons or pads at a store. Once they are at school, they are stuck. Indeed, Cotropia found that respondents whose schools did not provide menstrual products were 2.7 times more likely to respond "yes" to the question of whether the lack of access to a pad or tampon had "ever affect[ed] your ability to learn in high school," such as by causing them to underperform on a test or be unable to focus in class. And the students who could not afford the own menstrual products suffered even more: they were 3.75 times more likely to respond affirmatively to the same question.[49]

Action Steps under Title IX

Given the ways that lack of access to menstrual products at school interferes with students' education—and given the close connection between menstruation and what has historically been called "female" biology—regulations and guidance under Title IX should be developed to address this issue. A Department of Education action requiring *all* school districts to provide free menstrual products to *all* students, as a mandate under schools' existing Title IX obligations, would be the most aggressive approach. But such an action likely would be challenged in court, on grounds that it crosses the line into new federal lawmaking without congressional involvement.

There are other options short of an unfunded Title IX mandate, though. At the very least, it would be consistent with Title IX's mandate for the Department of Education to provide *guidance* to schools about "best practices" in this area, such as making menstrual products freely available in restrooms, rather than in nurses' offices only. The Department of Education's Office of Civil Rights (OCR) already provides analogous Title IX guidance as to how schools might choose to support pregnant and parenting students, and it could issue similar suggestions here.[50] For example, just as OCR has implied that schools "might be *required* to provide a larger desk" for pregnant students,[51] OCR could strongly suggest that, at a minimum, schools *should* provide free menstrual products to students whose household incomes are low enough to make them eligible for free or reduced-priced lunches. These sorts of federal interventions would help fulfill Title IX's mission of ensuring equal access to education, regardless of sex, and would complement the current state-by-state lawmaking efforts. The interventions also would combine well with any new federal legislation, such as the Menstrual Equity for All Act proposed by Representative Grace Meng.

Reaching All Menstruating Students

So far, most of the rhetoric surrounding the efforts to provide free menstrual products in schools has centered explicitly on the needs of "girls." Ferreras-Copeland, for example, began her efforts by setting up a focus group with teenage girls and then setting up a pilot program in a girls' restroom; she also frequently referred to the needs of "young girls" in her conversations with the media about the topic. Just as New York governor Andrew Cuomo commented that his state's legislation would ensure that "every girl" had the opportunity to become "a confident, successful woman," New Hampshire governor Chris Sununu described his state's new law as helping to "ensure young women in New Hampshire public schools will have the freedom to learn without disruption—and free of shame, or fear of stigma."[52]

This language is not surprising, as it is consistent with the image many people have when imagining a young student who might need access to menstrual products. But not all menstruating students are cisgender girls or women. As chapter 6 explores in more depth, the universe of people who menstruate also includes trans boys and men, as well as gender-nonbinary and genderqueer people. University students have been particularly attentive to this issue. For example, from the start, Brown University's student government leaders put menstrual products in women's, men's, and gender-neutral bathrooms. "We wanted people to recognize that this issue affects trans students as well and that menstruation is experienced by more than just those who identify as women and that not all people who identify as women menstruate," explained student-government leader Nguyen.[53]

Scotland's example is also helpful here. In 2017, Scotland announced a plan to provide free menstrual products to all students in schools at both the secondary and university levels. In connection with that goal, the Scottish government created a broad working group that included, among others, local government leaders, university representatives, and students. That group produced a document that set forth guiding principles for the delivery of such products, including "[g]ender equality, ensuring anyone who menstruates can access products, including transgender men and non-binary individuals, and that language is gender neutral." The document added that "[t]he roll out of gender neutral toilets should also be taken account of."[54]

The state laws requiring free menstrual products in schools have not yet specifically addressed the need to make products available to all students who menstruate. The law that comes the closest to doing so is New Hampshire's, which refers to "menstrual hygiene products" (as opposed to the "feminine hygiene products" terminology used by New York, California, and Illinois). New Hampshire's law further specifies that the products should be placed in both "all gender neutral bathrooms and bathrooms designated for females located in public middle and high schools."[55] Other states' laws generally refer to making the products available in "school" bathrooms, without specifying which bathrooms. Illinois's law, for example, refers to making the products available in "the bathrooms in school buildings";[56] California's law refers to placing them in "at least 50 percent of the school's restrooms";[57] New York's law refers to placing them "in the restrooms of [each elementary and secondary public] school building or buildings";[58] and Virginia's law requires that the products be placed "in the bathrooms of each middle school and high school in the local school division."[59] In 2019, an Illinois legislator, state representative Barbara Hernandez, proposed an amendment to the Illinois Learn with Dignity Act that would require schools to make free menstrual products available in "*each* bathroom of every school building,"[60] rather than just in "the bathrooms of school buildings." She explained that she was promoting the bill because "[d]enying access to feminine hygiene products to anyone who needs them is denying a basic human right."[61] Although Hernandez herself used the gendered "feminine hygiene products" terminology in explaining her reasoning, her goal was clearly inclusive. That particular Illinois bill did not become law, however.

Recent legal developments make the issue of gender inclusivity even more salient. Since 2016, there have been many twists and turns regarding federal protection for students' use of the bathrooms that accord with their gender identity. During the Obama era, the Department of Education issued guidance that Title IX's prohibition of sex discrimination covered gender identity–based discrimination as well. In particular, on May 13, 2016, the Department's OCR issued a "Dear Colleague" letter that explicitly stated, under the subheading "Restrooms and Locker Rooms," "A school may provide separate facilities on the basis of sex, but must allow transgender students access to such facilities consistent with their gender identity."[62] The Trump administration, however, withdrew that guidance on February 22, 2017, justifying the switch by explaining that "in this context, there must be due regard for the primary role of the States and local school districts in establishing educational policy."[63] During the Trump administration, some states such as New York continued to require school districts to let students use the bathrooms that matched their gender identity,[64] but other states did not and instead left the issue up to individual school districts.

Against this shifting backdrop, a high-profile lawsuit that had been filed during the Obama presidency continued to play out. In 2015, a transgender boy, Gavin Grimm, had sued his Virginia school district, challenging its policy of prohibiting transgender students from using the restrooms that matched their gender identity.[65] Under his school district's policy, transgender students had to use either the restrooms that matched their sex assigned at birth, the restroom in the nurse's office, or one of several newly constructed single-stall bathrooms. Grimm alleged that the school district's policy discriminated against him and other transgender students in violation of Title IX and the Equal Protection Clause. He lost in the Eastern District of Virginia, but the United States Court of Appeals for the Fourth Circuit then reversed, ruling in Grimm's favor in 2016, based on the Obama administration's "Dear Colleague" guidance document.[66] The school district filed a petition for a writ of certiorari, and the Supreme Court agreed to hear the case. Once the Trump administration withdrew the guidance in 2017, however, the Supreme Court remanded for reconsideration in light of the policy shift.

By the time Grimm's case made its way back to the Fourth Circuit for a decision, the Supreme Court had decided *Bostock v. Clayton County*.[67] In June 2020, the Supreme Court ruled in that case that Title VII's prohibition of employment discrimination "because of sex" encompasses discrimination on the basis of sexual orientation or gender identity. In its August 2020 decision, the Fourth Circuit then applied *Bostock* to Grimm's case, and found that *Bostock*'s reasoning strongly supported Grimm's claim of discrimination. "[W]e have little difficulty holding that a bathroom policy precluding Grimm from using the boys restrooms discriminated against him 'on the basis of sex,'" the court stated.[68] The court noted that Title IX interpretation generally tracks Title VII interpretation, and that *Bostock*'s reasoning was equally applicable in Grimm's case. The court thus ruled that the school district's application of its restroom policy against Grimm—i.e., not letting him use the boys' restroom because his sex assigned at birth was female—violated Title IX.[69]

Still two more twists followed. First, in its final days, the Trump administration issued a memo suggesting that *Bostock* should not apply to the school restroom context. Second, the Biden administration took the opposite approach very shortly thereafter. On the very day of his inauguration (January 20, 2021), President Biden issued an executive order titled "Preventing and Combating Discrimination on the Basis of Gender Identity or Sexual Orientation," stating, among other things, that "[c]hildren should be able to learn without worrying about whether they will be denied access to the restroom."[70] Two days later, the Trump administration's *Bostock* memo was removed from the Department of Justice's website. And on March 26, 2021, Principal Deputy Assistant Attorney General Pamela Karlan issued a detailed memo concluding that "the best reading of Title IX's prohibition on discrimination 'on the basis of sex' is that it includes discrimination on the basis of gender identity and sexual orientation."[71] Her memo approvingly cited the Fourth Circuit's *Grimm* decision. Therefore, at this point, federal policy is clearly back in favor of requiring schools to allow students to use the restrooms that accord with their gender identity—underscoring the need to provide menstrual products in all restrooms.

Addressing Burdensome Policies

Lack of access to menstrual products is perhaps the most significant obstacle that menstruating students face—but it is not the only one. School policies that limit students' ability to take bathroom breaks, or require them to wear light-colored pants as part of school uniforms, also impose special burdens on menstruating students.

Many schools restrict students' ability to leave class for the bathroom, generally out of concerns that students will misbehave there, miss what is being covered in class, or perhaps use the break as an opportunity to sneak off somewhere else instead. Results from the survey of 362 school nurses conducted by the Society for Women's Health Research show how common these restrictions are.[72] Roughly half of the schools surveyed did not allow their students to freely access the school bathrooms, instead imposing various limitations on whether and when they could do so. Most critiques of such school bathroom restrictions understandably have focused on their negative effects on all students' bladders, but such policies also disproportionately burden menstruating students. Indeed, in the spring of 2018, National Public Radio reported that a Chicago charter school network had such a strict bathroom break policy that some menstruating students were bleeding through their clothes.[73] A similar story was reported about KIPP DC Northeast Academy, a charter school in Washington, DC.[74]

In addition to school-wide restrictive policies, individual teachers often impose their own ad hoc limitations. A group of eighth graders at Bronx Prep Middle School created a podcast series, aptly entitled "*Sssh! Periods!*" in which they discussed various aspects of menstruating at school. In the beginning of the first episode, one student recounted,

> One time, during lunch, I realized that I had my period, and I was raising my hand to go to the bathroom and the teacher didn't let me go. Then at the end of the period, I went up to her . . . and said "I'm on my period." And she was like, "Oh! Why didn't you tell me earlier?" And I'm just like, "Because we were in the middle of class and you said I couldn't go to the bathroom!"[75]

Another joined in: "When you tell the teacher, their whole mood changes when you say, 'I'm on my period.'" A different student commented, "I'm literally the queen of bleeding out. It's not usually my fault; it's because I can't go to the bathroom during class."[76] Separately, an article posted on a parenting website highlights the issue of "period shaming," giving an example of a student whose period suddenly started during a volleyball match.⁷⁷ "My instant reaction was running towards my coach and saying I needed to go to the bathroom," she recalled. Her coach responded, "[W]hat are you doing, get back on the court and wait until the game is over[!]" Distracted and upset by the prospect of blood streaming down her leg, she made it through the game, but never played volleyball again.⁷⁸

Notably, in none of these stories do the menstruating students seem to have explicitly told their teachers or coaches in the moment *why* they needed to use the bathroom. Either they never did, or they only did so after the fact. Given the power differentials between students and teachers, as well as many stigmas surrounding menstruation, it is not surprising that students may feel uncomfortable speaking up. Indeed, as Cotropia's findings demonstrate, many menstruating students do not feel comfortable asking even the school nurse for a tampon or pad, let alone announcing their menstruation status to a teacher or coach.

For menstruating students, dress codes or uniform rules that require all students to wear khaki or other light-colored pants are also particularly challenging. Students frequently worry about visible leaks and stains. Interestingly, the same Chicago charter school network that had a strict bathroom-break policy also required all students to wear khaki pants. The combined effect of the two rules prompted some schools within the network to add a *third* rule: students who bled through their pants could tie a sweater around their waist to hide the stain, and an administrator would send an email to the staff to let them know that the student should not receive a demerit for being outside the dress code.⁷⁹ "[I]magine being a menstruating teenager and having an email being sent out to the school's entire staff about that fact," reflected an NPR commentator on Twitter.⁸⁰ At one of the schools within the network, female students—with the support of teachers—were able to get the dress code changed to black pants,⁸¹ but the policy apparently remained unchanged elsewhere.

The school uniform issue has also received international focus. In 2016, UNICEF released guidance recommending that "the skirt/trouser part of a girls' uniform should ideally be a dark colour that does not show stains," noting that "[j]ust changing the colour of the bottom part of a girls' uniform from a light colour to a dark colour could provide girls with another layer of protection against embarrassment from having a leak."[82] This sort of simple change can make a real difference in whether the student can continue to focus and learn at school.

A key step in combating both restrictive bathroom-break and problematic dress-code policies is raising awareness about how they affect menstruating students, with the hope that doing so will yield policy changes. To a certain extent, traditional media coverage and social media communication can generate that public awareness. But law has a particular role to play, too. One path is for advocates to continue to push for the passage of new local, state, or even federal laws that address these issues, perhaps alongside the passage of laws that require schools to provide access to menstrual products. A second, and even tandem, path is to address these issues through new Title IX regulations and guidance. Indeed, school bathroom and uniform policies arguably implicate Title IX's prohibition on depriving students of educational opportunities on the basis of sex, in two specific ways.

First, although bathroom limitations and light-bottomed dress codes do not specifically single out menstruating students for worse treatment, they impose a heightened burden—what antidiscrimination law would call a "disparate impact"—on them. In multiple contexts, antidiscrimination law responds to situations where a facially neutral policy has a disparate impact as to a statutorily protected characteristic. The response usually is to require the policies to be changed or for exceptions to be granted. Here, these bathroom and dress-code policies burden not only the students who are actually menstruating on a particular day but also the other students who worry that their periods may start at school, such that both categories of students may choose to stay home or miss class instead. By burdening the entire group of students who think it is possible that they might start menstruating at school, the policies are essentially having a disparate impact on *all* students who menstruate. To be sure, not every student who menstruates identifies as female, but the correlation is strong enough to support an argument that frames the issue as one of disparate impact on the basis of sex.

Title IX regulations have already embraced the disparate-impact concept in areas such as admissions testing and preferential recruiting, so there is some precedent for the Department of Education to also promulgate regulations and guidance against policies that have a disparate impact on menstruating students. Such regulations would not need to prohibit bathroom limitations or dress codes altogether; rather, the regulations would need to be crafted in ways that avoid disparate impacts on the basis of sex. At a minimum, exceptions should be afforded to menstruating students. Even better would be policies that prohibit singling out menstruating students, such as by allowing *all* students to wear dark pants rather than light-colored ones, and by establishing ways for all students to be allowed to access the bathroom as needed, without having to disclose that they are menstruating.

Second, policies that burden menstruation at schools can also be analyzed through the lens of accommodation. Title IX's regulations already require schools to make certain accommodations for pregnant students. Specifically, schools must treat "pregnancy, childbirth, false pregnancy, termination of pregnancy and recovery therefrom as a justification for a leave of absence for so long a period of time as is deemed medically necessary by the student's physician, at the conclusion of which the student shall be reinstated to the status which she held when the leave began."[83] This is true regardless of whether the schools provide similar accommodations to other students. In this way, Title IX goes further than Title VII's Pregnancy Discrimination Act, which, as discussed in chapter 2, only requires such accommodations for pregnant employees if they are also being given to similarly situated nonpregnant employees.

Moreover, in the Title IX guidance documents regarding pregnancy, the Department of Education's Office of Civil Rights (OCR) has gone even further. In the accompanying pamphlet to a "Dear Colleague" letter, OCR states that "[t]o ensure a pregnant student's access to its educational program, when necessary, a school must make adjustments to the regular program that are reasonable and responsive to the student's temporary pregnancy status. For example, a school might be required to provide a larger desk, *allow frequent trips to the bathroom*, or permit temporary access to elevators."[84] It is true that OCR only says that a school "*might* be required" to do this. It is worth noting, though, that OCR then goes on to list "examples of possible strategies . . . [that] are *not* legally mandated by Title IX or its regulations,"[85] such as "allowing excused absences for parenting students (both male and female) who need to take their children to doctors' appointments" or "[d]esignat[ing] a private room for young mothers to breastfeed, pump milk, or address other needs related to breastfeeding during the school day."[86] Given that the OCR states that these additional accommodations are *not* required, a reasonable inference is that the earlier accommodations *are* mandatory.[87] In the same way, Title IX regulations around menstruation could be crafted to ensure that the needs of menstruating students are accommodated when bathroom-access and dress-code policies are developed and enforced. The best policies would do so in ways that do not single out menstruating students or put the onus on them to disclose that they are menstruating.

Combating Teasing and Harassment

Underlying all aspects of menstruation at school is the fear—and sometimes the reality—of menstruation-based teasing and harassment. In the surveys of menstruating students, a strikingly common finding is the sense of urgency that most respondents feel about concealing one's period. While students have multiple reasons for wanting to keep their periods private, one of them may be concern about being teased or even harassed. In sociologist Laura Fingerson's 2006 book *Girls in Power: Gender, Body, and Menstruation in Adolescence*, she describes how teenage boys "talked about PMS and other menstrual symptoms in exaggerated terms, stressing how 'bitchy' girls get and blaming menstruation for any moodiness or unfeminine behavior displayed by girls." She notes, too, that "[m]any boys think menstruation is 'gross' and some boys engage in gross joking." Moreover, Fingerson explains that because "menstruation is defined as secretive and shameful in cross-gender interactions," girls are a "ripe target for teasing and embarrassment"—and that schools, in particular, are places where that behavior occurs. Interestingly, although some girls told Fingerson about being "teased and embarrassed by the boys, the boys [did] not admit to this in her interviews" with them.[88]

These findings are echoed in a 2011 article reporting the results of a study of college-aged men who reflected on their earlier experiences in middle and high school.[89] One participant commented, "The first time I can remember hearing about menstruation was probably around sixth grade. I remember my peers joking about periods and blood often. It always seemed like something that guys could make jokes about to make girls embarrassed or to seem superior to them." Indeed, the study's authors observe that "girls who had the misfortune of being marked with blood or other evidence indicating their status as currently menstruating, were put at an extreme disadvantage, and boys would use fear of the situation to empower themselves in social interactions." The authors conclude that "[m]enstruation-related sexual harassment in schools is common," noting that "[t]he young men in this study recalled some severe incidents of girls being teased, although no boy actually admitted to teasing a girl in this manner."[90]

This phenomenon is not limited to the United States. In October 2020, a team of researchers published the results of their study of "period teasing" in secondary schools in Northern Tanzania. They studied nearly one thousand boys and girls in the region, and found widespread fear of period teasing. Although 13% of girls reported having experienced period teasing themselves, 87% feared being teased because of menstrual odor and 80% feared being teased because of leaking. Male peers were the "most commonly feared perpetrator of period teasing," with 46% of girls identifying them as potential antagonists; 34% stated that they feared being teased by female peers as well. These fears about teasing were not unfounded: 18% of boys reported that they had personally teased a girl about her period, and 29% stated that they had observed their close friends teasing girls about their periods. Boys stated that they teased girls about their periods because "periods are embarrassing" (43%), because other boys were doing it (21%), and because "periods are unnatural" (20%). The fear and reality of menstrual teasing also took a direct toll on girls' education: 31% said that they did not participate in class as much as normal, and 33% concentrated less in school. Students attributed these feelings and behaviors to the combination of fear and shame with cramps and pain. (Additionally, 47% of respondents described leaving school early, but only 4% said that it was because of teasing as opposed to physical discomfort.)[91]

Again, law has a role to play in addressing these issues. In the United States, Title IX again is the starting point. Since its 1999 decision in *Davis v. Monroe County School Board of Education*, the Supreme Court has recognized that student-on-student sexual harassment can be a form of sex discrimination that violates Title IX.[92] Menstruation-based harassment almost certainly fits into that category. Importantly, *Davis* provides that schools can be held liable for monetary damages when peer sexual harassment is "so severe, pervasive, and objectively offensive that it effectively bars the victim's access to an educational opportunity or benefit," when the school exercised "substantial control over both the harasser and the context in which the known harassment occur[ed]," when the school had "actual notice" of the harassment, and when the school's response was deliberately indifferent to it.[93] This is a very high bar. While some cases of menstrual harassment may satisfy all four of these requirements, often they will not. Under the case law, "severe and pervasive" has been interpreted stringently; most instances of teasing will probably not qualify. Additionally, if the harassment does not occur in front of a teacher or administrator (or other school staff member) who sees it, the school will not have actual notice unless a student reports it. And, as discussed above, students may be self-conscious about discussing their periods with school personnel. Furthermore, the standard also gives school officials wide latitude in how to respond to harassment; only if their response was "clearly unreasonable" can they be held liable.

For many years, OCR set its threshold for administrative enforcement of Title IX lower than the standard set by the *Davis* Court. Notwithstanding the *Davis* limitations on damages liability for peer sexual harassment, OCR stated in its guidance that it would still hold schools responsible for sexual harassment that was serious enough to limit a student's ability to participate in school. Furthermore, OCR's policy was to hold schools responsible not only for the harassment that they had actual notice of but also for the harassment that they reasonably *should have known* about.[94] But in the waning days of the Trump administration, the Department of Education weakened the administrative enforcement standard by aligning it with the *Davis* test. Yet unlike its changes regarding restroom status, the Trump administration codified the changed limitations on damages in new regulations.[95] It is possible that the Biden administration (or another future administration) will revert to the lower standard for actionable harassment, but it will take time to change those regulations. And even if the OCR were to revert to the lower standard, that guidance probably would still not sweep in all instances of menstruation harassment, such as lighter teasing or harassment that occurs off the school's radar altogether.

In the interim, federal and state lawmakers, as well as individual school districts, should consider additional ways to protect menstruating students from teasing or harassment that impairs the ability to function and thrive at school. Beyond legal mandates to address the more severe types of menstrual harassment, comprehensive and accurate education is another important step in eliminating harassment and helping menstruating students.

Menstrual Education

Complicating the conversation about menstruation and schools is the fact that the state of menstrual education in the United States is profoundly uneven. Not all states require any sex education at all, let alone specific instruction about menstruation. That means that students who do not receive menstrual education at home or elsewhere may be unprepared for their periods to begin. Studies have shown that low-income girls, in particular, often do not receive sufficient education about menstruation. A comprehensive review of the 2000–2014 literature on low-income girls' menstrual education found that "[a]cross studies, girls reported feeling a lack of information and readiness to cope with the onset of menstruation" and that "[g]irls who felt unknowledgeable or unprepared for menstruation were more likely to report having worse experiences of menarche, negative attitudes about menarche, and more menstrual distress."[96] In particular, researchers found strong support for the ideas that "[g]irls were uncertain what to do after they first got their period" and that girls "viewed their experience of menarche in a negative light, describing their experiences as horrifying, traumatic, scary, and confusing ... often initially misinterpret[ing] blood from menstruation as a serious medical problem." The researchers also found moderate support for the idea that "[g]irls viewed school education about menstruation as inaccurate, negative, and late." Specifically, students felt embarrassed to ask questions in school and were dissatisfied with the amount of time devoted to discussion.[97]

In addition to failing to prepare menstruating students for their first periods, inadequate menstrual education also contributes to the larger culture of menstrual stigma, shame, and silence. In the literature review described above, the researchers found that "[g]irls also reported receiving implicit and explicit messages that puberty—specifically menstruation—is something to keep hidden, especially from males."[98] These messages may have come both from the way menstrual education is (or is not) provided to girls and from the lack of any menstrual education for boys. In the 2011 study of college-age men who were asked about their earlier experiences, the researchers specifically linked boys' lack of understanding about menstruation to their sense of discomfort about it, and their resultant teasing behavior. "Boys know that they can never fully understand menstruation and may feel this puts them at a disadvantage when the topic comes up," the authors wrote. "Perhaps in response to this discomfort, a prevalent theme in the narratives was that menstruation is gross and should be hidden—and that *believing* that menstruation is gross and should be kept hidden is a normal and acceptable male response."[99] They concluded,

> Families and schools have important roles in future efforts to influence boys earlier in development to better understand menstruation as a valuable biological process and to better explore and confront the social context surrounding it. In addition to the facts of "28 days," schools need to address the cultural ideology of menstruation and deconstruct negative messages about women's bodies.[100]

The 2020 study of menstrual teasing in Northern Tanzania echoes this recommendation, and adds an important nuance. One of the study's researchers later noted that, to their surprise, they found that "secondary-school boys in the schools we surveyed in Tanzania are actually quite well informed about the biological side of menstruation. . . . This goes against a sort of common assumption that adolescent boys know very little about periods and that that is the main issue that needs to be addressed."[101] Remarkably, however, the researchers found "knowledgeable boys were equally likely to engage in period teasing as their less knowledgeable peers." They concluded that scientific education about menstruation for all students was necessary but not sufficient; menstrual education must also include "social programming that aims to change social norms and period stigma."[102]

Providing widespread menstrual education is valuable, further, because it ensures that all students who may begin menstruating in the future—not only cis girls—get the information that they need. There are thus multiple benefits to developing a menstrual-education curriculum that includes all students and covers the biological, social-emotional, and cultural aspects of menstruation.

This, too, is an area where law has some role to play. Currently, Title IX's regulations specify that "[c]lasses or portions of classes in elementary and secondary schools that deal primarily with human sexuality may be conducted in separate sessions for boys and girls."[103] To the extent that schools are taking that as an invitation to discuss menstruation with girls only, more guidance might be appropriate here. More broadly, it is a worthwhile endeavor to advocate for laws that require sex education, including menstrual education. Ultimately, though, much depends on *how* schools provide the education—and as to that, legal mandates are relatively ineffective. Historically speaking and continuing to the present day, the law has been a very blunt tool for improving disparities in educational quality across the United States.

What is encouraging, though, is that the specific tangible problems that law *is* well suited to address—like the lack of access to free products in school restrooms—also are closely connected to larger intangible problems like menstrual silence and stigma. Law thus may be an effective tool in the larger push for menstrual equity. As politicians, advocates, educational leaders, and students of different ages have all observed, putting free products in bathrooms does more than address the problem of access. It also signals to menstruating students that they are valued, that they are seen, and that their needs matter, as Justice Kagan recognized when she was the dean of Harvard Law School. In both tangible and intangible ways—from fewer absences and missed classes to less menstrual stigma and shame—increasing access to menstrual products in schools will likely have positive and continuing reverberations in years to come.

4

Periods in Public

On June 21, 2016, New York City made history when it became the first city in the nation to require free menstrual products in public schools, prisons, and homeless shelters. The legislation—which the New York City Council passed unanimously—consisted of three distinct bills: one for schools, one for prisons, and one for shelters. The bills were closely intertwined both philosophically and logistically. Philosophically, they shared two core principles: first, that menstrual products are necessities; and second, that the government should make them accessible to vulnerable populations who may have trouble obtaining menstrual products on their own. Logistically, all of the bills resulted from months of research about how to address menstrual equity within New York City, and they were introduced together as a package.[1] Jennifer Weiss-Wolf, whose 2015 meeting with New York City councilmember and Finance Committee chair Julissa Ferreras-Copeland first catalyzed this work, later reflected on the bill's passage: "New York is not just acknowledging that menstruation is part of people's experience. . . . It's zeroing in on the people—public school students, homeless or incarcerated women—for whom it's most difficult to manage."[2]

New York City's 2016 passage of this legislation was a key moment in the menstrual-equity movement, illustrating law's potential to create and ensure access to menstrual products. During the year prior to the enactment of the New York City legislation, greater awareness of "period poverty"—particularly among the homeless—had already started galvanizing philanthropy and activism by private actors throughout the United States. In the summer of 2015, a Maryland business owner named Dana Marlowe started a nonprofit organization called "I Support the Girls" to collect bras and menstrual products for homeless shelters. At around the same time, in South Carolina, sisters-in-law Stephanie Arnold and Sharron Champion founded the Homeless Period Project, which donates "period packs" to people living in shelters and on the streets. And in Michigan, Lysne Taite and Amy Stephenson founded a nonprofit called "Helping Women Period," which likewise focuses on providing menstrual products to homeless and low-income people.

In all three cases, the founders explained that they began their menstruation-focused work after reading articles or social media posts that resonated strongly. Arnold and Champion, for example, learned about period poverty by way of an article about the plight of homeless women in the United Kingdom. "Never once had I thought about what homeless women do while on their periods," Champion reflected. After reading the article, the women called several South Carolina shelters to confirm that the problem existed there as well, and it did. "Everyone said very rarely do they see donations of menstrual products, and if they do, they're the first things gone," Champion said.[3] After starting as small, home-grown efforts publicized through word of mouth and social media, all three programs—I Support the Girls, the Homeless Period Project, and Helping Women Period—and many others like them have evolved into larger organizations with broader missions. Just as Weiss-Wolf has explained that she became involved in menstrual advocacy after seeing an acquaintance's Facebook post seeking donations of menstrual products, organizers like Marlowe, Arnold, Champion, Taite, Stephenson, and many others have been inspired by stories of those in need.

Social media facilitates the speed at which these stories can be shared and the number of people they can reach. Social and traditional media also play a role in publicizing the charitable work that responds to the menstruation-related needs of vulnerable populations. As word spreads about efforts to combat period poverty, talking about menstruation and menstrual products becomes normalized in public discourse. That, in turn, helps to reduce stigma and shame related to menstruation.

Greater awareness of period poverty among the homeless has not been limited to grassroots nonprofit organizations. It has also prompted national legal change as well. Even before New York City's June 2016 passage of its groundbreaking law, United States representative Grace Meng of New York had persuaded the Federal Emergency Management Agency (FEMA) to add menstrual products to the list of essential items that homeless assistance providers (including shelters, nonprofit organizations, and local government agencies) can purchase with federal grant funds from FEMA's Emergency Food and Shelter National Board Program. Representative Meng initially became aware of this issue after receiving a letter from a high school girl who lived in Meng's Queens congressional district. The girl expressed concern that homeless people in shelters did not have access to menstrual products.[4] "When I first started studying up on this issue I sort of just assumed, OK, this affects people in underdeveloped countries," Meng said. "Then the more I learned about it, I realized that it's happening to people right here in our country."[5] In January 2016, Representative Meng wrote a letter to then-secretary of Homeland Security Jeh Johnson, urging him to add menstrual products to FEMA's list of eligible items, which already included things like soap, toothpaste, and toilet paper. In her letter, Meng explained,

> In the last year, we have seen a significant increase in public awareness and conversation surrounding menstruation and a lack of access to feminine hygiene products for low-income and homeless women. I am heartened to see that this awareness has led to a corresponding increase in donations of feminine hygiene products to homeless shelters. There are now drives, projects, and even non-profits created for the purpose of providing feminine hygiene products to homeless and low-income women. Unfortunately, this increase in donations does not come close to meeting the hygiene needs of homeless women. Including feminine hygiene products in the list of eligible costs for the Emergency Food and Shelter National Board Program is a small but necessary step towards filling a necessary healthcare need for homeless women and girls.[6]

On February 1, 2016—within one month of receiving a copy of the letter—FEMA administrator W. Craig Fugate wrote Representative Meng to inform her that FEMA had added menstrual products to the list. He reported, in fact, that the Emergency Food and Shelter National Board had voted to do so the day after receiving her letter.[7] At the state level, the following year, Maryland passed a law to ensure that homeless shelters would be provided with sufficient menstrual products to meet their residents' needs.[8] Few states have followed suit, however.

Representative Meng has made menstrual equity a signature issue of her work in Congress. In 2020, she introduced a new bill to support philanthropic efforts to combat period poverty: the Good Samaritan

Menstrual Products Act.[9] This legislation proposed to limit civil and criminal liability for manufacturers, distributors, nonprofit organizations, and other persons for "apparently usable menstrual products . . . donate[d] in good faith," by holding them liable only if their action "constitute[s] gross negligence or intentional misconduct that results in injury to or death of a user or recipient of the menstrual product."[10] Because tampons are considered Class II medical devices, fear of liability can be a potential deterrent to donations, which this legislation—modeled after an analogous federal law called the Bill Emerson Good Samaritan Food Donations Act[11]—was designed to address. Numerous nonprofit leaders such as Dana Marlowe spoke out in favor of the Good Samaritan Menstrual Products Act. Marlowe called it "essential," noting that "[i]ndividual menstrual product donations are the lifeblood of our organization."[12]

As leaders like Representative Meng have recognized, law has a crucial role to play in achieving menstrual equity. Philanthropic efforts are important and beneficial, and certain legal changes—such as the proposed (but not passed) Good Samaritan Act—can help to facilitate them. But it is clear that charitable efforts on their own will not be sufficient to meet the needs of all vulnerable people. Charitable efforts are dependent on fundraising and individual initiatives, and cannot create enforceable legal rights. Moreover, private citizens and charitable organizations largely cannot reach one of the public spaces raising important menstrual-equity concerns: prisons.

Menstrual Products in Prisons

Periods do not stop when someone gets arrested and goes to jail, and detainees and prisoners are uniquely dependent on the government to provide them with menstrual products. But current law does not uniformly ensure detainees' and prisoners' access to such products. Although important progress has been made on this issue since New York City passed its comprehensive law in 2016, there are still significant gaps in access to menstrual products in federal, state, and local incarceration and detention facilities.

For the roughly 12% of all incarcerated individuals who are held in federal prisons,[13] there is now a directly applicable law: the First Step

Act, a sweeping prison reform bill passed by Congress with bipartisan support in 2018.[14] Among many other provisions, the First Step Act includes a mandate that federal prisons provide to prisoners "for free, in a quantity that is appropriate to the healthcare needs of each prisoner . . . tampons and sanitary napkins" that "conform with applicable industry standards."[15] This provision had been part of a proposed bill, entitled the "Dignity for Incarcerated Women Act of 2017," introduced by Democratic senators Cory Booker, Richard Durbin, Kamala Harris, and Elizabeth Warren the prior year.[16] Meanwhile, in the House of Representatives, Meng had proposed the Menstrual Equity for All Act of 2017, which (among other things) sought to require all state prisons that receive federal funding to provide menstrual products at no cost to their inmates and detainees.[17] Even before she had proposed the Menstrual Equity for All Act, Representative Meng had written to the United States attorney general to urge federal prisons to make menstrual products available to federal inmates and detainees at no charge, as opposed to its then-current practice of charging federal prisoners for them.[18]

Although neither the House nor the Senate bills from 2017 ever advanced, the Federal Bureau of Prisons did change its approach in August 2017, by releasing an operations memorandum requiring the cost-free provision of tampons, pads, and panty liners to inmates.[19] Even after the policy change, though, compliance was uneven. Surveys conducted by prisoner advocacy groups found that in some federal prisons, free tampons did not arrive until several months after the policy was announced.[20] Worse, other federal prisons continued their earlier practice of charging prisoners for menstrual products.[21] The prices—$5.55 for two tampons and $1.35 for two panty liners[22]—were out of reach for many federal prisoners, who earn only between twelve and forty cents per hour. Indeed, the cost sometimes meant "choosing between purchasing feminine hygiene products or a phone call home."[23] Therefore, some federal prisoners remained vulnerable to bleeding through their clothes, sometimes choosing to roll menstrual pads into makeshift tampons, with serious and even potentially fatal health consequences.[24] The codification of the new Federal Bureau of Prisons policy into explicit federal law, as effectuated by the First Step Act of 2018, thus was crucial.

Additionally, in 2019, Representative Meng successfully inserted into an appropriations bill a measure that requires the Federal Bureau of

Prisons director to provide guidance on the distribution of menstrual products to federal inmates, and to put in place reporting requirements that ensure oversight.[25] The measure also specifies that prisoners must be allowed to determine for themselves what is a sufficient quantity of products. Representative Meng's press release explained that this measure had been inserted "in response to reports of pervasive and demeaning methods of product distribution."[26]

The vast majority of incarcerated individuals are in state and local facilities, not federal ones, and thus the First Step Act does not help them. Representative Meng's proposed Menstrual Equity for All Act of 2017 would have reached state prisoners by making those facilities' receipt of federal funds contingent on their provision of free menstrual products to inmates, but that provision did not become law. Encouragingly, numerous states also took action after the passage of the First Step Act. For example, Alabama (2019), California (2021), Colorado (2019), Connecticut (2018), Florida (2019), Kentucky (2018), Louisiana (2018), Maryland (2018), New York (2019), Tennessee (2019), Texas (2019), and Virginia (2018) all passed laws requiring their state correctional facilities to provide free menstrual products to prisoners.[27] This reflected a sweeping change: prior to 2018, no laws existed to protect prisoners' access to menstrual products in state facilities. The wave of state reform that followed passage of the First Step Act is encouraging, but makes plain the work that remains in additional states.

Moreover, passing legislation is only the first step; ensuring compliance is critical. In 2019, the *Washington Post* ran an article exposing the fact that months after passage of the Maryland legislation, some inmates still had to buy boxes of tampons, at much higher prices than retail.[28] The article noted similar problems with compliance in Virginia prisons.[29] Encouragingly, Maryland's Public Safety and Correctional Services secretary Robert Green, who had recently stepped into his role, immediately took action: he visited the prison described in the article, confirmed that the new law was not being followed consistently throughout the state system, and promised, "I'm taking immediate steps to make sure we are meeting the law. It will be done. This is going to be fixed."[30]

Meanwhile, in the majority of states, there remains no statutory guarantee of any kind for prisoners' access to menstrual products. In Arizona, for instance, Representative Athena Salman introduced a bill in 2018 to require free menstrual products in prisons. At that time, Arizona's policy was to give incarcerated women in state prisons twelve free pads each month and require inmates to ask an officer if they needed more pads. Tampons were only available at a cost. "We need to make this commitment to our female prisoners in our prison system who deserve just basic dignity and respect," Salman said in support of her proposed bill.[31] Unfortunately—but not surprisingly—Salman's bill ran directly into expectations of silence and issues of stigma that often characterize discussions about menstruation. When Salman presented the bill to the all-male Committee on Military, Veterans, and Regulatory Affairs, one of the representatives interrupted her as she was explaining that "[i]n our prison system . . . a 16-count of Always ultra-thin, long pads cost $3.20." He interjected, "Rep. Salman, [c]an you keep your conversation to the bill itself? Please?" Because "the bill itself" addressed that exact issue, Salman kept speaking. The same representative, Jay Lawrence, later commented, "I'm almost sorry I heard the bill. . . . I didn't expect to hear [about] pads and tampons and the problems of periods."[32]

Indeed, the members of the Arizona committee had to hear about these issues repeatedly, as several former prisoners testified about how damaging the current policy was. One former Arizona prisoner described having had to ask guards for additional toilet paper to fashion into makeshift menstrual products. "Being there and going through this is untenable and unconscionable," she told them. "And it affects you for the long term." Another witness testified that, as a nurse, she had treated incarcerated women who made tampons out of maxi-pads. "That can increase bacteria and cause toxic shock syndrome, and I think that they shouldn't have to do that," she stated. Despite Representative Lawrence's discomfort with the discussion, the bill narrowly passed out of committee by a vote of five to four.[33] However, it did not ultimately progress, largely because the Arizona Department of Corrections agreed to adopt a new, more generous policy on its own.[34] Although such policies are obviously better than nothing at all, the lack of an actual legal mandate in many states remains problematic.

Disparities also exist in how prisons at the state, county, and local levels handle access to products, even in the states that have passed laws. For example, before being put up for a vote, Tennessee's law regarding free menstrual products in prisons was specifically amended to make clear that it only applies to state correctional facilities. Similarly, even after California passed its law guaranteeing free products at state prisons, the products were still not uniformly being provided at the county jails, as lawyer Paula Canny learned when she visited a client in San Mateo County jail. Canny's client told her that she was menstruating but did not have money to buy a tampon at the jail's commissary; indeed, Canny looked down and saw blood streaming down her client's legs. Canny contacted the San Mateo County sheriff, who was receptive to Canny's concerns and agreed to change the policy. But Canny was so disturbed that she began looking into practices at other county jails and found that the lack of menstrual products was pervasive. "I was so ashamed of myself that I didn't know" that this was happening, Canny later said. "I wanted it to change."[35]

Canny ultimately filed a class-action lawsuit against the California Board of State and Community Corrections, as well as the sheriff of Sacramento County, who had initially resisted Canny's demands. But the sheriff ultimately agreed to stop charging for products once Canny made clear that she would drop her lawsuit and not seek legal expenses if he did so. "I just want him to give inmates tampons when they want one. . . . [b]ecause that's a completely reasonable request in the 21st century," Canny stated.[36] The ultimately successful result, echoing New York's and Florida's repeals of the tampon tax after being sued, is yet another example of how actual or threatened lawsuits can help achieve menstrual equity.

Carceral Use of Menstruation to Shame and Control

The failure to provide free menstrual products to all prisoners does more than create a risk of significant physical harms, such as bacterial infections and toxic shock syndrome. It also imposes serious psychological injury. As described above, it can force prisoners to forego phone calls with loved ones, due to the need to use their money for products instead. And it creates tremendous potential for abuses of power. Chandra Bozelko, who served time in a Connecticut prison (before Connecticut passed its 2018 law mandating free menstrual products in prisons), recalled,

The reasons for keeping supplies for women in prison limited are not purely financial. Even though keeping inmates clean would seem to be in the prison's self-interest, prisons control their wards by keeping sanitation just out of reach. Stains on clothes seep into self-esteem and serve as an indelible reminder of one's powerlessness in prison. Asking for something you need crystallizes the power differential between inmates and guards; the officer can either meet your need or he can refuse you, and there's little you can do to influence his choice.[37]

Limiting access to menstrual products, then, is a way that the prison system seeks to exercise power over both the bodies and the minds of incarcerated individuals.

Too often, prison officials use menstruation as a vector for the humiliation and control of prisoners. The withholding of necessary menstrual products is one such method for doing so, as Bozelko explained. Betty-Ann Whaley, a former prisoner at Rikers Island in New York, described a particularly extreme version of this "when a correction officer threw a bag of tampons into the air and watched as inmates dived to the ground to retrieve them, because they didn't know when they would next be able to get tampons."[38] Forcing women to scramble for tampons like candy from a piñata makes a degrading spectacle out of the distribution of a basic necessity. Whaley added that, on other occasions, tampons were distributed unevenly, saying that guards "only dispensed to certain individuals—you had to be sort of chummy-chummy in order to receive them."[39] The scarcity of menstrual products creates particularly ripe conditions for abuses of power. Menstrual products should be a right, not a reward.

Invading the physical privacy of menstruating prisoners is a type of abuse related to the denial of products. At the Bedford Hills Correctional Facility, one prisoner was menstruating when she was strip searched after a scheduled visit with her father. Christine, the prisoner, later recounted to a *New York Times* reporter that she had not been given any menstrual products by the prison, and so blood was dripping down her legs. According to Christine, the female guard conducting the search told her "how disgusting I was, [saying] 'It's disgusting' . . . I was so embarrassed."[40] In 2019, Los Angeles agreed to a $53 million settlement of a class-action lawsuit alleging that female detainees in the Los Angeles

County Jail had been subjected to brutal, degrading group strip searches. Tomi-Ann Roberts, an expert who worked on the case, later wrote that

> [d]uring the procedure, to determine which inmates would need clean menstrual products, deputies asked them to raise their hand in front of the entire group if they were menstruating, forcing women to "out" themselves to strangers as being on the bleeding days of their menstrual cycle. At this point, those having their periods were required to remove tampons or pads or other menstrual products in the presence of the group, and then wait some period of time—until completion of the visual body cavity inspection portion of the search—before replacing them. According to both inmates and deputies, some of the women were heavily bleeding.[41]

Roberts further stated that in their depositions, the inmates described the psychological trauma of these experiences, saying things like, "I felt less than human," and "I felt like an animal."[42]

These accounts mirror anecdotes about law enforcement officials' use of menstruation as a shaming device in contexts outside prison. In 2016, the police approached Natalie Simms, who was sitting on a curb in San Antonio, Texas, and asked to search her car nearby. After searching the car and finding nothing, the police officers would not permit her to leave until she herself was searched by a female officer. Referring to Simms's pants, the officer asked, "Do you have anything down here before I reach down here?" Simms said she had nothing in her pants but informed the officer that she was menstruating. The officer, in full public view and in the presence of five male officers, told Simms, "I'm not gonna reach. I'm just gonna look," but then proceeded to reach into Simms's pants and underwear without Simms's consent. According to Simms's complaint, the female officer "decided at one point to run her fingers along Natalie's vaginal lips. She even commented on the amount of pubic hair on Natalie's body."[43] The officer then pulled the string attached to the tampon that Simms was wearing and pulled the tampon out of Simms's body.[44] The officer then "held the tampon up in the air for approximately 23 seconds, asking rhetorical questions and making statements about the tampon."[45] Ultimately, after finding no illegal items, the officers permitted Simms to leave the scene. Simms later filed a lawsuit; her complaint stated that "[e]ven though Natalie was allowed to leave the scene, a part of her dignity and self-worth was left behind."[46] The case was settled out of court in 2019;[47] according to press reports, the City of San Antonio paid Simms $205,000.[48]

Prison Visitors

Prisons' restrictive policies about menstrual products can even extend beyond prisoners, applying to their visitors as well. In 2018, the Virginia Department of Corrections issued a policy that banned visitors from wearing tampons or menstrual cups during inmate visits.[49] Prison officials defended this policy by citing "many instances" of attempted drug smuggling by visitors concealing illegal substances in body cavities, including the vagina.[50] Because body scanners supposedly could not distinguish between contraband and certain menstrual products, the policy banned visitors from wearing tampons or menstrual cups.[51] Kaye Kory, a member of the Virginia House of Delegates, called the policy "harassment, discrimination and a violation of privacy."[52] The American Civil Liberties Union of Virginia expressed concerns about the policy's "very negative effect" and the possibility it would "discourag[e] people from visiting those who are incarcerated."[53] The ACLU called upon the Department of Corrections "to reverse any policy or practice that limits the visitation rights of visitors who are menstruating without regard to which hygiene product they choose to use."[54] Five days after the announcement of the policy, the Virginia secretary of public safety announced the suspension, but not rescission, of the policy, meaning that it could be revived at any time.[55] While negative publicity can be an effective way of getting some facilities to change their policies, without actual laws in place, prison visitors remain vulnerable to changing institutional policies that limit their use of menstrual products.

In January 2019, the Virginia House Committee on Militia, Police, and Public Safety finally passed a bill requiring the Department of Corrections to revise its policy, which largely left unchanged the ban on visitors wearing tampons and menstrual cups, but giving those who did not wish to remove their products the option of a no-contact visit.[56] The version of the bill passed by the legislature and signed by the governor also requires the DOC to revise its policies "to permit . . . visitors to wear tampons or menstrual cups," without specifying whether visitors wearing those products will be limited to no-contact visits.[57] The DOC's website provides no information. By leaving the DOC to make its own policies, Virginia lawmakers thus failed to secure rights of prison visitors to address their own menstruation in the manner of their choosing.

Virginia is not the only place with these sorts of visitor policies. In 2014, three different Tennessee residents, identified in court documents by the pseudonyms Jane Doe #1, Jane Doe #2, and Jane Does #3, each went to a state prison to visit an inmate at separate times. All three visitors were menstruating on the day of their visits. After Jane Doe #1 underwent security screenings with a menstrual pad in her pocket, corrections officials took Doe #1 to a restroom, where she was forced to permit a female corrections officer to visually inspect her genitalia for evidence of menstruation. Jane Doe #2 also underwent security screenings and passed a sealed menstrual pad through the metal detector. Correctional officers told Doe #2 that she was not permitted to take the pad into the visiting area; she was made to change her pad in front of a female correctional officer and then show her bloody pad. Jane Doe #3 had held two wrapped tampons in her hand when passing through security and then was told that she could not bring tampons into the facility. A corrections officer accompanied Doe #3 to a restroom and told Doe #3 to remove the tampon she was wearing, show the corrections officer the bloody tampon, and replace her tampon with a pad, which Doe #3 did. A month later, when Doe #3 returned to the prison for another visit, she was menstruating again. A corrections officer accompanied to the restroom Doe #3 and Doe #3's three minor children. This time, the corrections officer required Doe #3 to change her menstrual pad, show the bloody pad to the officer, and submit to a visual genital inspection in the full view of her children.

The three Does later sued the prison and various officials for violating their constitutional rights; they also asserted claims of negligence, infliction of emotional distress, assault, invasion of privacy, and false imprisonment.[58] Shortly before trial, the case was settled and the terms of the settlement are unknown.[59] Because the prison is run by a private corporation, not the state itself, the corporate defendant is exempt from public records requests.[60]

Notably, when Representative Meng proposed the Menstrual Equity for All Act of 2019 (an updated and expanded version of her proposed 2017 act), one of the new provisions she added was a prohibition against the sorts of restrictive prison-visitor policies used in Virginia and Tennessee. In addition to requiring all state facilities receiving federal funding to provide menstrual products to their inmates and detainees at no cost (as the 2017 proposed bill had), the 2019 bill also proposed that states must certify that "no visitor is prohibited from visiting an incarcerated individual due to the visitor's use of menstrual hygiene products."[61] Unfortunately, although one piece of the Menstrual Equity for All Act of 2019 later became law—the provision allowing individuals to purchase menstrual products from their health flexible spending accounts, which was incorporated into the Coronavirus Aid, Relief, and Economic Security (CARES) Act of 2020, as discussed in chapter 1—the bill did not move forward. However, Representative Meng did succeed in inserting into an appropriations bill a measure to prohibit these sorts of visitor policies in federal prisons.[62] Whether the measure will succeed on the ground has yet to be tested.

Turning to Litigation

As several of the above-described incidents show, litigation has been a key strategy for challenging the harsh treatment of menstruation by prisons and law enforcement officials. In many of the cases described above, the parties ultimately settled, a common outcome in cases alleging particularly disturbing practices or policies related to menstruation. For example, in 2016, a New York City woman, Jennifer Flores, was arrested on charges of obstruction of justice when she attempted to advise teens being questioned in a public park by police. When she was taken into custody, she informed the booking officer that she needed to change her tampon, but was told that the precinct did not have any menstrual products. She was told to use toilet paper, which she stuffed into her underwear. Her underwear soon became bloody, staining her clothes. Flores said, "I tried to put as much toilet paper as I could but my underwear was ruined and bloody. I could actually smell it. No one should have to smell the blood soaking through their underwear because they didn't have a tampon available."⁶³ Although her attorney was able to bring her a tampon after about six hours, Flores was kept in police custody for a total of thirteen hours. She was arraigned the next day in her bloody clothes.

The obstruction-of-justice charges against Flores were ultimately dismissed, and Flores sued the city for a violation of her constitutional rights because of lack of access to menstrual products. After several defendants moved to dismiss the lawsuit, the United States District Court, Eastern District of New York ruled that the plaintiff's claim could proceed with multiple constitutional claims, including, most notably, her claim of sex discrimination under the Equal Protection Clause of the Fourteenth Amendment; the case settled shortly thereafter.⁶⁴

A similar case had arisen in Indiana in 2014, where Melissa Houglin was detained in an Indiana jail for thirty-six hours, ultimately receiving three pads and one tampon during her time there. Houglin initially did not receive a tampon from the jail staff for over twenty-four hours. During this time, Houglin bled through her jean shorts. She was left to sit and sleep in her own blood until another prisoner provided her with a towel. Houglin was finally issued a prison jumpsuit but no clean underwear; she subsequently bled through the jumpsuit. She was not issued a new one and was not permitted to shower. Houglin was forced to attend her court appearance in the soiled jumpsuit.⁶⁵ Houglin sued various members of the county sheriff's department for violating her constitutional rights, given their refusal to provide her with menstrual products and adequate clothing. Three other women who were formerly detained or incarcerated in the same facility as Houglin later joined her suit, asserting rights on behalf of similarly situated women likewise denied access to menstrual products and other basic rights.⁶⁶ The case was settled out of court in 2017 for an undisclosed amount of money.⁶⁷

Constitutional Rights of Prisoners to Menstrual Products

It is worth considering how these cases would have been decided, if they had not settled. Beyond the First Step Act and the new state laws relating to menstrual products, what underlying constitutional protections do prisoners have against menstruation-related abuse? There are several constitutional rights implicated, including the Eighth Amendment's protection against cruel and unusual punishment, as well as the Equal Protection and Due Process Clauses.

In cases involving extreme mistreatment and abuse—in which menstruation-specific abuse was present—courts have been willing to recognize constitutional claims related to access to menstrual products in jail or prison. For example, in *Darnell v. Piniero*, a group of pretrial detainees from the Brooklyn Central Booking facility (a temporary holding facility for recently arrested pretrial detainees awaiting arraignment) sued to challenge the conditions of confinement there. The plaintiffs, both men and women, alleged a variety of abuses, including overcrowding, unusable toilets, cells infested with vermin and insects, lack of toiletries and other hygienic items (including menstrual products), inadequate food and water, extreme temperatures, poor ventilation, and sleep deprivation. As to menstrual products, one plaintiff who had been menstruating during her detention specifically testified that she was "bleeding all over [her]self,"[68] that the officers were dismissive of her requests for products, and that another detainee was reprimanded and even threatened with delayed arraignment for requesting them. The Second Circuit held in 2017 that the detainees' constitutional challenge—which arose under the Due Process Clause of the Fourteenth Amendment rather than the Cruel and Unusual Punishment Clause of the Eighth Amendment, since they had not yet been convicted—could go forward.[69] The case settled out of court in 2018.[70]

The *Darnell* court's suggestion that the detention facility's refusal to provide menstrual products was unconstitutional echoed previous rulings by the Third and Eighth Circuits. In 2015, the Third Circuit had noted that former New Jersey Department of Corrections inmate Alexandra Chavarriaga "clearly" alleged cruel and unusual punishment by stating in her complaint that "officers denied her sanitary napkins and medications while she was menstruating."[71] Chavarriaga allegedly also had been denied medication for migraine headaches and menstrual cramps during her period, deprived of potable water and clothing, and subjected to a painful and unjustified manual body cavity search of her rectum and vagina.[72] On remand, the district court dismissed the complaint with prejudice after the plaintiff failed to prosecute the case (for reasons that are not clear).[73] In 2006, the Eighth Circuit held that Patti

Johnson, an inmate at Missouri's Jasper County Detention Center, had brought a cognizable Eighth Amendment claim in alleging that she had been deprived of menstrual products while menstruating. She allegedly also had been thrown to the floor, choked, and maced by a corrections officer.[74] There is no record of what happened in the case on remand. While it is encouraging that all three of these menstruation-specific abuse claims—in *Darnell*, *Chavarriaga*, and *Johnson*—were allowed to go forward, the denial of menstrual products occurred in the context of such broad and wide-ranging mistreatment that it is difficult to extract a precise rule.

Indeed, when the abuse has not been quite as egregious, courts have sometimes been more deferential to prisons. In Michigan, female prisoners brought a class action challenging the conditions of their confinement at the Muskegon County Jail. The prisoners, represented by the ACLU, alleged that opposite-sex guards were viewing them while naked (including "while attending to their menstrual periods") and that they were not being provided with adequate menstrual products. "Plaintiffs and other female inmates who menstruate and are denied pads bleed into their clothing and are often not provided with clean clothing until the next laundry day, which only occurs once a week," their complaint alleged. The plaintiffs described pleading for menstrual products and being forced to share an insufficient supply.[75] However, the district court ruled that these deprivations did not rise to the level of cruel and unusual punishment, since the plaintiffs only described delays in receiving menstrual products in terms of "hours," or, in one plaintiff's case, "approximately two days." The court suggested that this deprivation was merely *de minimis*. That ruling was later appealed, and the parties ultimately settled. The prison agreed to a new policy of providing menstrual products at the same time as medication. Notably, the court nevertheless did find that the allegations regarding the guards' viewing of the prisoners while they were naked and attending to their menstrual periods amounted to a cognizable Eighth Amendment claim.[76]

Courts should go much further in recognizing the constitutional rights of state, county, and local prisoners (and all pretrial detainees) to menstrual products. Making such products only available for sale at often-unattainable prices, or subjecting menstruating prisoners to routine delays in accessing the products they need, not only amounts to cruel and unusual punishment. These practices also raise equal protection concerns. As with the tampon tax, one way to view the denial of menstrual products to prisoners is as a facial sex-based classification. As discussed in chapter 2, menstrual products are so closely tied to female biology that they can be considered a proxy for female sex. Indeed, the withholding of menstrual products (including functionally withholding them by selling them at inflated prices) amounts to a special form of punishment that can be inflicted only upon prisoners who menstruate—i.e., predominantly women. One may also examine these policies through the disparate-impact lens, given their sex-based effect. The misogynistic comments and abuse that sometimes accompany such policies, such as telling menstruating prisoners that their bloody condition is disgusting or forcing them to beg for menstrual products, provides further evidence of the animus against menstruating prisoners or detainees. Again, as with the tampon tax, both the facial-classification and disparate-impact lenses make the sex discrimination clear.

Indeed, one court has already identified the equal protection implications of prisons' withholding of menstrual products. In 2017, Cynthia Turano filed a class-action lawsuit relating to her treatment at the Santa Rita Jail in California, where her requests for menstrual products were denied for hours, to the point where she bled all over her clothes and onto the floor. Even after a prison guard finally gave Turano two pads, Turano was given no soap or paper towels to clean her bloody hands. The court was receptive to Turano's claim that the jail had violated the Equal Protection Clause through its "failure to provide feminine hygiene products and the means to maintain personal cleanliness. . . . [T]he complained of actions apply only to women, and no further discriminatory intent need be established," the court wrote. "[T]his claim may proceed."[77] In fact, in a footnote, the court even cited United Nations research about menstrual-hygiene management, quoting a UN statement that "the widespread stigma associated with menstruation ha[s] a negative impact on gender equality and the human rights of women and girls."[78] While this opinion is not binding in other jurisdictions, the reasoning of the court suggests that judges may be increasingly receptive to claims alleging sex discrimination on account of denial of access to menstrual products to detained or incarcerated individuals.

Immigration Detainees

The scarcity of menstrual products is a problem for immigration detainees, too. In 2019, nineteen states and the District of Columbia sued various officials in the Trump administration in federal court in California, alleging that detained children were being held in cramped conditions without access to basic necessities (including menstrual products), in violation of a longstanding settlement agreement requiring immigration agencies to hold minors in facilities that are safe and sanitary.[79] These allegations were supported by an affidavit by one of the investigators for the Washington State Attorney General's Office; representatives of that office interviewed twenty-two children who had been detained in facilities maintained by US Customs and Border Patrol at the Mexico-US border. The affidavit of the principal investigator stated that one girl, who was detained for ten days, was "never offered a shower, even though she was on her period and was given only one sanitary pad a day." It added that "[a]fter a number of days, she summoned her courage and asked for a shower, and was given one."[80] This girl recalled that there was another girl in the facility who was also menstruating; each of them was given just one pad per day. The affidavit went on to state that "[a]lthough the guards knew [the girls] had their periods, they were not offered showers or a change of clothes, even when the other girl visibly bled through her pants. This girl had no choice but to continue to wear her soiled underwear and pants."[81] As in the prison context, lack of access to menstrual products is used to control and humiliate detainees.[82]

Right after the filing of the multistate lawsuit, Representative Meng sent a letter—signed by thirty-eight other members of the House of Representatives—to express "outrage over the appalling treatment of children who are in Customs and Border (CBP) custody at the southern border." The letter specifically highlighted the issue of inadequate access to menstrual products, linking it to sex discrimination and stating that "[o]n top of all the other inhumane violations against children's well-being, this type of sex-based discrimination is repugnant." The letter questioned why access to menstrual products had been limited and asked what protocols were in place "to ensure that migrants' access to sanitary products, particularly menstrual products, are [sic] met."[83]

The 2019 version of Representative Meng's Menstrual Equity for All Act had sought to address issues faced by immigrant detainees by including a requirement that the secretary of Homeland Security "take such actions as may be necessary to ensure that menstrual hygiene products are distributed and made accessible to each alien detained by the Secretary of Homeland Security, including any alien in a facility administered by a private detention entity, at no expense to the alien."[84] This differed from the previous version, which had only applied to state prisons. As noted above, however, the bill did not progress into becoming law.

The problem of inadequate menstrual products for detainees did not begin with the Trump administration. In 2014, a *Mother Jones* article entitled "No Water, No Toilet Paper, No Tampons" described the terrible detention conditions of Alba Quinones Flores, who started menstruating while in the custody of the US Customs and Border Protection near the Texas/Mexico border. She was forced to wear a single pad for her entire period, and when it became saturated, she bled through toilet paper, her underwear, and clothing.[85] Quinones later filed a federal lawsuit related to the conditions of her confinement; the case ultimately settled for eighty thousand dollars.[86]

Menstrual Products in Other Public Buildings

Beyond confined government settings like schools, homeless shelters, prisons, jails, and detention facilities, the concept of providing free menstrual products in public buildings has also started getting more attention in recent years. The need certainly exists: a 2013 Harris Interactive poll found that 86% of female respondents reported getting their periods at a time when they were in public and did not have the necessary menstrual supplies at hand. Their actions in response to an unexpected period in public ranged from improvising a pad out of toilet paper or other material (79%), going to a store to purchase supplies (62%), and asking another woman for supplies (53%) to going home (34%).[87] Until recently, though, the notion of making menstrual products freely available in public spaces has not been a topic of public discussion, let alone legislation.

In 2018, United States representative Sean Patrick Maloney brought national attention to the issue of lack of access to menstrual products in public buildings when he used his congressional office budget funds to purchase tampons for employees and visitors to his office. He then sought reimbursement from the Committee on House Administration, as all members of Congress are permitted to do for basic supplies like paper towels, hand sanitizer, and letter openers. The committee denied his reimbursement, saying that tampons were a "personal care item" and thus could not be reimbursed.[88] Maloney criticized the action, saying, "It goes to the heart of who they think matters and whose needs matter.... It portrays a mindset that doesn't see women's needs as equal to men's."[89] Jennifer Weiss-Wolf similarly described the denial as an example of "yet another way that women's bodies are devalued as a matter of policy."[90] Although Maloney subsequently received permission to use his office budget for these purchases, the official policy was not changed until several months later, in response to a clarification request from Maloney and two other congressional representatives.[91]

Some localities have taken steps to provide free menstrual products in their municipal buildings. In May 2019, Brookline, Massachusetts, became the first municipality to offer free menstrual products in all of its town-owned restrooms, including the restrooms in the town hall, libraries, and recreation center.[92] The catalyst for this change was a column in the Brookline High School newspaper by high school senior Sarah Groustra. "[M]ost people would balk at the idea of having to pay for toilet paper in a public restroom," Groustra observed, in an opinion piece that explored the stigma and shame around menstruation, as well as the tangible costs of menstrual products.[93] One member of Brookline's local government, Rebecca Stone, read the article and decided to take action. "In the United States, girls learn very early that this is their problem," Stone later reflected. "You are expected to keep it from other people, to be discreet. And so we tuck the tampons, and if we're in trouble we try to find friends, and we talk about it quietly, and we use euphemisms, and we do not impose this on others."[94] Seeking to change these expectations of menstrual silence and concealment, Stone worked with Groustra and other Brookline students to draft a local law on this issue, which passed unanimously. The law gave Brookline a specific deadline for installing dispensers and stocking them with menstrual products, in both male and female bathrooms, at an estimated cost of forty thousand dollars in the first year and then seventy-five hundred dollars a year thereafter.[95]

In 2019, the city council of Salt Lake City, Utah, passed a budget direction encouraging, but not mandating, the provision of menstrual products at some municipal facilities. One of the proposal's cosponsors, council member Erin Medenhall, said, "We don't charge people for toilet paper, and women's access to feminine hygiene products shouldn't be charged either."[96] Another cosponsor, council member Ana Valdemoros, said, "Pads or tampons are a necessity, not a luxury. . . . I hope we draw attention from those in charge at schools and other public institutions in Utah to start thinking of similar policies."[97] The city council designated funds in its budget for a pilot program, and indicated that it would "encourage" city-owned libraries to follow suit.[98] The products were initially available at City Hall. The communications director of the Salt Lake City International Airport said that it hoped to make products available by September 2020, but there has been no update since.[99]

Also in 2019, the city of Columbus, Ohio, made free menstrual products available in all bathrooms in city-owned recreation centers, after a successful pilot program in 2017.[100] Council member Elizabeth Brown explained the policy as a matter of common sense. There is no "restroom outside your own home where you are expected to bring your own roll of toilet paper. . . . Yet there is a nearly ubiquitous expectation for women to supply their own tampons and pads," she said. Brown also cited two other factors in the city's decision: the cost of the products and the frequency of being out in public and having a period start unexpectedly. She reflected,

> On an errand, in a meeting, or in school, being caught without an accessible tampon or pad derails thousands of women every day. . . . For an adolescent, the experience can lead to insecurity, embarrassment, and sometimes shame. For the most vulnerable populations, like homeless women, the cost of obtaining reliable menstrual products can even compete with the costs of supporting a family.[101]

The Columbus program is the product of a partnership with the menstrual-product company LOLA, although it is not clear precisely how the costs are shared or for how long they will be shared.[102] The Columbus airport also began making tampons available for free in women's restrooms, at a cost of approximately two thousand dollars per year.[103]

The momentum for free menstrual products in public buildings continued into 2020, when the Los Angeles City Council passed a measure authored by member Bob Blumenfield to direct the Los Angeles Department of Recreation and Parks and the Department of General Services to prepare a feasibility study and cost estimate for what it would take to provide free menstrual products in all restrooms in city-owned facilities.[104] Blumenfield described his motivation for sponsoring the measure by saying, "Providing feminine hygiene products at no cost in City-owned facilities should be just as normal as providing toilet paper or soap." He cited not only the high cost of menstrual products but also the need to end stigma around menstruation.[105] Despite initial enthusiasm for the project, however, free menstrual products are not yet available in Los Angeles public facilities.

In 2021, the city council in Melbourne, Australia, approved a one-year pilot program to make menstrual products for free in six public buildings in the city at a cost of approximately $10,000 AUS (approximately $7,760 US), but in a city with a population greater than five million, it is not clear how widely that program will reach without additional funding or support. Notably, the resolution introduced by Councillor Jamal Hakim passed unanimously. Other than Hakim, the only other speaker on the motion was the former lord mayor, Nicholas Reece, who added, "Let's face it, if blokes had periods, we would have done this decades ago."[106]

At the federal level, Representative Meng has also taken up the issue of providing menstrual products in public buildings. In 2019, the updated version of Meng's proposed Menstrual Equity for All Act included a new provision requiring that all public federal buildings, including buildings on the Capitol campus, provide free menstrual-hygiene products in the restrooms.[107] Although that bill did not become law, Representative Meng subsequently succeeded in inserting a measure into an appropriations bill to direct the Veterans Health Administration to ensure that free menstrual products are available in public female, unisex, and family restrooms in all VA facilities.[108]

The growing momentum on this issue suggests that free menstrual products may become more widely available in public facilities in the years to come. The long-held idea that menstrual products should not be discussed or seen in public—let alone provided for free—has begun to crumble through a combination of increased publicity (especially on social media) about menstruation-related issues, grassroots organizing, threatened and actual litigation, and local, state, and federal legislative initiatives. Relatedly, there is growing recognition of the cis male norms underlying the assumption that the "typical" bathroom user requires nothing more than toilet paper in the stall. With efforts proceeding simultaneously on all of these fronts, there is reason for hope that free menstrual products in public buildings might become the norm in the future.

5

Periods at Work

Joyce Flores, a dental hygienist, was at work one day in July 2019 when she went to the restroom and realized that she needed to change her tampon. Unfortunately, she had none at hand. Like countless others who have been caught in this situation, she discarded her used tampon and "made do" by placing some toilet paper in her underwear until she could get back to her office to retrieve a new tampon. Unfortunately, that commonsense solution quickly went awry. Flores's employer was the Virginia Department of Corrections (VDOC)—the same entity that had recently attracted negative national publicity for its policies prohibiting prison visitors from wearing tampons, as discussed in chapter 4. The VDOC's poor understanding of menstruation-related needs ended up ensnaring Flores as well.

When she reported to work that morning, Flores—who was experiencing heavy perimenopausal bleeding and wearing a tampon—had passed through the prison's body scanner without incident. But on the trip from the restroom back to her office, she had to pass through the scanner again. Because she was no longer wearing a tampon, the second scan image differed from the one taken upon her arrival at work. Corrections officers took Flores to a private room for questioning about the fact that the "suspicious item in her vagina" from the first body scan was no longer there. Flores did everything possible to prove that the "suspicious item" had only been a tampon—including going into the restroom with two female officers, showing them the bloody toilet paper that was in her underwear, inserting a new tampon, going through the body scanner again, agreeing to a full search of her car, and later pleading with the warden to speak to the manufacturer of the body scan equipment, because of known difficulties the scanners had in distinguishing menstrual products from contraband items that might be placed in the vagina. But Flores's protests were to no avail. Flores was suspended and ultimately terminated due to "suspicion of contraband," although none had ever been found. The VDOC thus distorted an ordinary moment of personal forgetfulness—failing to bring to the bathroom a needed tampon—into "suspicion of contraband," when the only thing Flores was guilty of was menstruating while at work.[1]

Flores sued the VDOC, alleging that her termination amounted to sex discrimination in violation of Title VII of the Civil Rights Act. And, in February 2021, the United States District Court for the Western District of Virginia ruled that her case could go forward. The court clearly and persuasively explained, as further discussed below, that menstruation-based mistreatment is indeed a form of sex discrimination. The *Flores* decision is important for all other menstrual discrimination claims—including, but not limited to, those involving menstruation in the workplace.

So far, issues involving menstruation at work have not been a primary focus of the menstrual-equity movement. This is not surprising. As compared to the tampon tax, or the special needs of vulnerable populations like students, prisoners, and the homeless, problems involving menstruation in the workplace may be less widespread and less visible. But for some employees, menstruation *does* function as a barrier to full participation at work. Thus, employment is another area where the law can and should become more responsive to human needs. At a minimum, laws should be clarified and expanded to embrace two key principles. First, adverse action against an employee or prospective employee because of that person's menstruation is indeed a form of impermissible sex discrimination. Second, all employees should have the ability to address their menstruation-related needs in a timely, private, and safe manner.

Firing an Employee for Menstruating Is Sex Discrimination

The most extreme examples of how menstruation can limit employees are cases like Flores's, where menstruation directly leads to termination. Even in these types of cases, though, not all courts have recognized the inherent sex discrimination. Consider, for example, the case of Alisha Coleman, who was a call taker for a nonprofit agency called the Bobby Dodd Institute. After Coleman began working there, she entered perimenopause and began experiencing uncontrollable and unpredictable heavy bleeding. She told her supervisors about the situation and always kept menstrual products with her at work to try to prevent accidents. But in August 2015, Coleman suddenly experienced heavy bleeding that stained her chair. She told her supervisor, who gave her permission to leave the premises to change her clothing. Coleman was then given a disciplinary write-up and warned that she would be fired if this ever happened again.

Coleman tried to take extra precautions to prevent a reoccurrence. About seven months later, though, she got up to walk to the bathroom and some of her menstrual blood leaked onto the carpet. She immediately cleaned the spot with bleach and disinfectant. Nonetheless, Coleman was told to leave work and then terminated for failing to "practice high standards of personal hygiene and maintain a clean, neat appearance while on duty."[2] Coleman later wrote about the experience, recalling, "They told me I lacked high standards of cleanliness. I never heard anyone get fired for anything like that before. When I walked out the door, I felt so numb. I was shocked and ashamed."[3]

There was never any evidence of any wrongdoing or failure on Coleman's part. A person cannot "hold in" menstrual blood the way one can control one's bladder, and as anyone who has ever had a period knows, menstrual bleeding does not stop and start according to a fixed schedule. Essentially, Coleman was punished for violating the cultural imperative that menstruation should be hidden. As Professor Margaret Johnson has observed about Coleman's treatment, "low-wage workers without job security are particularly vulnerable to the whims and biases of their supervisors that menstruators should be banished."[4] Had Coleman been an executive with a private office, she might have been able to clean up the chair or carpet before anyone else knew what had happened. But because her menstrual blood was briefly visible to others, Coleman was fired.

Coleman sued her employer for violating Title VII by terminating her, just as Flores later did. Under Title VII, it is unlawful for an employer to "discharge any individual, or otherwise to discriminate against any individual with respect to his compensation, terms, conditions, or privileges of employment, because of such individual's . . . sex."[5] Akin to claims under the Equal Protection Clause of the Fourteenth Amendment, sex-discrimination claims brought under Title VII generally fall into two categories: (1) "disparate treatment" claims, which challenge employment practices that are facially discriminatory, and (2) "disparate impact" claims, which challenge employment practices that, while facially neutral, are discriminatory in effect.

In 1978, Congress passed the Pregnancy Discrimination Act (PDA), which amended Title VII by adding two important clauses. The PDA's first clause provides that "[t]he terms 'because of sex' or 'on the basis of sex' include, but are not limited to, because of or on the basis of pregnancy, childbirth, or related medical conditions."[6] The PDA's first clause thus elaborates on the meaning of Title VII's general prohibition on discrimination in employment "because of sex." The PDA's second clause adds that "women affected by pregnancy, childbirth, or related medical conditions shall be treated the same for all employment-related purposes . . . as other persons not so affected but similar in their ability or inability to work."[7] This second clause addresses situations where, for example, an employer accommodates other employees' requests for light-duty work but does not accommodate such requests by pregnant employees—as in *UPS v. Young*, discussed in chapter 2. (A bill that would provide even stronger protection for pregnant workers—the Pregnant Workers Fairness Act—is discussed later in this chapter, as well as in chapter 2.)

Coleman alleged that her termination violated Title VII in two related ways. First, she argued that the termination violated Title VII's general prohibition against sex discrimination. Second, she argued that the termination specifically violated the first clause of the Pregnancy Discrimination Act. There, her argument was that menstruation and menopause counted as "related medical conditions" to pregnancy and childbirth.

The district court, however, dismissed her complaint. The court essentially combined her two arguments and rejected them in one fell swoop. The court acknowledged that there was some precedent that "could be construed to extend [the PDA's] protection to uniquely feminine conditions beyond pregnancy, such as pre-menopausal menstruation."[8] But the court declined to take that path, emphasizing that Coleman's "excessive menstruation was related to pre-menopause, not pregnancy or childbirth." Additionally, the court suggested that even if the PDA *did* cover menstruation, that would still not be enough for Coleman to win. "Coleman was not terminated simply because she was pre-menopausal or menstruating," the court stated. "Coleman was terminated for being unable to control the heavy menstruation and soiling herself and company property."[9] The court added that the only way Coleman might have been able to prevail was by showing that "her excessive menstruation was treated less favorably than similar conditions affecting both sexes." Since Coleman could not point to a nonmenstruating comparator who had been treated more favorably—such as a colleague suffering from incontinence, as the court suggested—her case could not proceed.[10] The court did not discuss the more general sex-discrimination argument. Coleman appealed the dismissal, and the parties later settled.[11]

The *Coleman* court's reasoning was incorrect. There is no legal basis for requiring a comparator in cases involving employees who are punished for menstruating. This is true whether such menstruation cases are viewed through the general sex-discrimination lens or the more specific PDA lens. To be sure, the PDA uses a comparative frame in its *second* clause, which states that pregnant employees (including employees with related conditions) cannot be treated worse than "other persons not so affected but similar in their ability or inability to work."[12] But this clause applies in the context of pregnant employees' requests for benefits or accommodations. It is not relevant to cases like Coleman's (or Flores's), where no accommodations were sought. By the same token, it is true that comparators are sometimes used in sex-discrimination cases when there is no direct evidence of discrimination. In those cases, the differential treatment of a comparator serves as the key circumstantial evidence. But this, too, is irrelevant in cases where an employee is *overtly* fired for menstruating. In such cases, there is no factual dispute about what happened and why, so there is no need for a comparator.

In contrast to the *Coleman* opinion, the *Flores* opinion grasped these points and their relevance to menstruation-based discrimination. The *Flores* court explained that it did not need to address whether menstruation was covered by the PDA (although it thought there was a "strong argument" that it did). Rather, what happened to Flores simply was sex discrimination: "*but for* Flores's menstruation and the use of a tampon—conditions inextricable from her sex and her child-bearing capacity—she would not have been discharged."[13] This recognition that menstruation-based discrimination *is* sex discrimination is profoundly important.

The court added that there was no need for Flores to identify a nonmenstruating comparator. It approvingly cited the argument of Flores's attorney: "[T]he fact that menstruation is inapplicable to men demonstrates that Flores was . . . treated differently because of an inherently female characteristic."[14] Moreover, the *Flores* court pointed out that a comparator requirement here would impose an illogical, nearly insurmountable hurdle. As the court explained,

> [C]omparing menstruating females to men and non-menstruating females in this [body scanner] context is an awkward fit; reality and common sense demonstrate that most males and non-menstruating females typically do not have any *legitimate* reason to have any objects in their body cavities prior to entering a prison facility. The best comparison that courts have discussed is fecal incontinence, as it can affect men and women alike, and individuals can insert anal plugs into their rectums. But fecal incontinence is a medical condition that is treatable and hopefully short-lived for those that suffer from it. Menstruation, on the other hand, is a normal physiological cycle that women, in their reproductive years, experience approximately one quarter of the time.[15]

Indeed, the notion that menstruating employees have no recourse unless they happen to have an incontinent colleague—and then happen to learn that this person has had a urinary or bowel accident, or is using an anal plug—is absurd.

Nor is it reasonable to suggest that employees like Coleman and Flores were terminated for the mere *effects* of their menstruation, instead of the fact that they were menstruating. An employer's defense that "I didn't fire her because she was pregnant; I just fired her because I knew that at some point she would go into labor and that might happen at work," would never be an adequate defense to a claim of pregnancy discrimination; firing someone because she might go into labor is tantamount to firing someone for being pregnant. An argument that "I didn't fire her because she was menstruating; I just fired her because the body scanner revealed an object in her vagina, and there is nothing she can do to convince me it was a tampon" should be equally unavailing, as should "I didn't fire her because she was menstruating; I just fired her because some menstrual blood leaked onto the carpet and that means she is unclean." Such defenses are circular, reflecting an underlying attitude that is discriminatory. Treating menstruating employees as untrustworthy or impure perpetuates old stereotypes that have no place in the modern workforce.

The employers' actions in *Coleman* and *Flores* are even more outrageous in light of the fact that the employers suffered no harm from the employees' menstruation. Coleman immediately cleaned up the "mess" herself. And the prison security guards merely needed to take a short time to confirm that Flores was indeed menstruating and that there was no contraband in her office or even her car. The employers' perceptions of the harms allegedly caused by these employees' menstruation were thus irrational. And their conclusions that any sort of sanction, let alone *termination*, was warranted for an involuntary bodily process were even worse.

In some sense, the law does not need to be amended to deal with these sorts of extreme situations. Title VII, properly understood, already addresses them—as the *Flores* court, at least, recognized. To prevent decisions like *Coleman*, however, the law should be clarified either through regulatory guidance or by amending the statute.

Clarification via Regulatory Guidance or Statutory Amendment

One way to prevent employment discrimination based on menstruation would be for the EEOC to issue regulations, or at least guidance, stating that menstruation-based discrimination is a form of sex discrimination. The EEOC could do this in two different ways. The first option is simply to make clear that menstruation-based discrimination counts as a type of sex discrimination. As Professor Deborah Widiss has written, the benefit of the EEOC's taking this approach with respect to Title VII is important: if menstruation discrimination is broadly recognized as "discrimination on the basis of 'sex' itself," that reasoning would likely be persuasive in other contexts.[16] For example, it would be relevant to cases involving deprivations of menstrual products in prisons.

The second option would be for Congress to amend the Pregnancy Discrimination Act to explicitly cover menstruation. To be sure, there is a good argument that menstruation is already covered by the PDA, given the close relationship between menstruation and pregnancy. During the first part of the menstrual cycle, the uterine lining builds up in anticipation of pregnancy. If a fertilized egg implants in the uterus, pregnancy occurs; if not, the uterine lining is released through menstruation. But at least for purposes of Title VII, it is not a settled doctrinal matter that pregnancy and menstruation are related enough to fall within the same legally protected status.[17] A simple amendment would remove any possible ambiguity about the PDA's reach. The first clause of 42 U.S.C. § 2000e(k) could be revised to state, "The terms 'because of sex' or 'on the basis of sex' include, but are not limited to, because or on the basis of pregnancy, childbirth, *menstruation*, or related medical conditions."

Such an amendment would presumably carry over to the PDA's second clause as well. In other words, the PDA would then require that employees affected by menstruation "shall be treated the same for all employment-related purposes" as other employees "not so affected but similar in their ability or inability to work." This would mean, for instance, that if an employer let employees with other medical conditions take extra bathroom breaks or rest time, the employer would have to do so for menstruating employees who requested them, too. The next section explores in more detail the current—and possible future—legal options for pursuing menstrual accommodations at work. These issues raise thorny, sometimes polarizing questions about how the law should account for sameness and difference in achieving gender equity.

Menstruation-Related Accommodations at Work

Not all menstruating employees need accommodations at work. For employees with regular, predictable menstrual cycles, and periods that are not particularly heavy or painful, menstruation may pose no obstacle at all to workplace success. This is particularly true when the job does not involve limited access to restrooms, restrictions on bathroom breaks, or heavy physical labor. But for other employees, especially those with jobs that involve one or more of those challenges, menstruation can be an obstacle to workplace performance or advancement. There are clear class dimensions to this issue: the movements of low-wage, low-income workers are far more likely to be restricted and monitored than those of highly compensated employees. Recall that Alisha Coleman, the call-center operator, had to request permission to leave her workplace in order to change her stained clothes after the first bleeding incident. Had a high-ranking corporate officer of the call center started to menstruate at work, the officer probably would not have needed anyone's permission to leave the office.

The lack of bathroom breaks may be especially acute in factories and similar settings. In 2016, for example, Oxfam America issued a report called "No Relief: Denial of Bathroom Breaks in the Poultry Industry."[18] The report stated that out of all of the workplace challenges for poultry workers, "the thing that offends their dignity most is simple: lack of adequate bathroom breaks, and the suffering that entails, especially for women."[19] Based on a several-year study of numerous poultry companies, the report found that workers were routinely denied breaks to use the bathroom, required to wait on extremely long lines when breaks were available, and otherwise threatened with discipline if the trip took too long. Some workers resorted to wearing adult diapers to avoid any penalty at work.

The Oxfam report specifically noted the toll that these restrictive bathroom policies take on menstruating employees, quoting one worker from a Pilgrim's plant in Alabama as having "witnessed many women crying about not getting to go to the bathroom, even if they were menstruating." It also quoted employees who described their degrading interactions when they had to tell their supervisors that they were menstruating and ask to use the bathroom. One of them, Rebecca, stated, "When we have our [menstrual] cycle, we need to go more often to the bathroom, but they don't let us, they don't like it." Another worker, Laura, echoed that "[a]s women, we take a little longer to assess our needs and feel clean. Instead of letting us use the bathroom, they threaten us, humiliate us to the point of filing claims with human resources to discharge us."[20]

To be clear, unreasonable limitations on employees' bathroom access are already illegal. The Occupational Safety and Health Administration (OSHA) has a sanitation standard requiring employers to provide their employees with toilet facilities. In a memo, OSHA stated that "this standard requires employers to make toilet facilities available so that employees can use them when they need to do so" and that "all employees must have prompt access to toilet facilities."[21] Indeed, unreasonable bathroom policies harm *all* employees, not only those who are menstruating. As the Oxfam report noted, though, OSHA does not have anywhere near the resources to inspect all workplaces for compliance with this standard. This is an area where the law "on the books" may not provide any practical protection for many employees, especially those who are fearful of losing their jobs and have little choice but to tolerate the employer's practices.

Separately from the OSHA standard, restrictive bathroom break policies can also be challenged as a form of sex discrimination, under a disparate-impact theory. Under Title VII, a facially neutral policy that has a disparate impact on the basis of a protected characteristic like sex can be struck down even without a showing of discriminatory intent. In this way, disparate-impact challenges under Title VII are easier to win than those brought under the Equal Protection Clause (where an intent to discriminate must be shown). For a Title VII disparate-impact claim, the plaintiff employee simply must show that the policy is having a statistically significant disparate impact as to sex. If so, the employer's only valid defense is to show that the policy is "job-related and consistent with business necessity." And even there, the plaintiff employee can still win by showing that an alternative policy would work instead.[22] A Title VII disparate-impact claim is thus a viable strategy for challenging restrictive work policies that are particularly harmful to menstruating employees, given the link between menstruation and so-called female biology. Indeed, when a 2014 story revealed that one company had installed equipment to monitor its employees' bathroom use and tried to limit them to six minutes of bathroom use per day, an EEOC spokeswoman said that the rule might constitute sex discrimination because of its effect on menstruating women.[23]

In fact, Joyce Flores's initial sex-discrimination claim against the VDOC included a disparate-impact allegation as well. She had argued that the VDOC had a "policy and practice of using body scans to screen employees, and then terminating employees based on the body scans." That claim failed, but only because Flores could not show that the VDOC actually had such an employment policy and had used it against other menstruating employees.[24] Flores's only evidence was her own experience. But had she offered evidence of a broader policy and statistical proof of the impact it was having on female employees, which would seem easy to show, her disparate-impact claim likely would have proceeded alongside her disparate-treatment claim.

More complicated legal questions arise when a menstruating employee needs an exception from or alteration to an otherwise reasonable policy that is *not* having a statistically significant disparate impact. For example, the employee might need accommodations, such as days off or break time, for significant menstrual pain. Or the employee might need some sort of heightened bathroom access while menstruating, due to the particular nature of her periods. If the employee is "disabled," as defined under the Americans with Disabilities Act, then an accommodation might well be required under the law. The ADA requires employers to make "reasonable accommodations" for disabled employees, unless those accommodations impose an undue hardship (defined as an "action requiring significant difficulty or expense").[25] But there is a high threshold for what counts as disabled. The ADA defines a "disability" as "a physical or mental impairment that substantially limits one or more major life activities . . . a record of such an impairment; or . . . [individuals] being regarded as having such an impairment."[26] A menstruation-related disorder, such as endometriosis or dysmenorrhea, might qualify as a disability under the ADA, depending on the circumstances.[27] But for less severe menstrual issues that do not rise to the level of creating a disabling condition, the ADA—at least in its current form—has less of a role to play.

Another potential legal basis for a menstrual accommodation is, as noted above, the Pregnancy Discrimination Act, which requires employers to treat "women affected by pregnancy, childbirth, or related medical conditions . . . the same for all employment-related purposes" as "other persons not so affected but similar in their ability or inability to work."[28] If menstruation counts as a "related medical condition" to pregnancy, then the PDA requires menstruating employees to receive the same accommodations as other analogous employees. This circles back to the *Coleman* court's idea that the plaintiff would have had a better case if she had shown that "her excessive menstruation was treated less favorably than similar conditions affecting both sexes." Again, that requirement did not fit with Coleman's particular claim since she was not seeking an accommodation. It does, however, explain where the court got that idea.

But the PDA is a limited source of protection here, too. First, as discussed earlier in this chapter, it is not entirely settled yet whether menstruation counts as a "related medical condition" to pregnancy. Second, even if menstruation is covered, the PDA only requires that menstruation not be treated *worse* than other conditions. Thus, if an employer is generally parsimonious with accommodations, then the menstruating employee has little to go on. Indeed, in the Supreme Court's leading pregnancy-accommodation case—*Young v. UPS*, discussed in chapter 2—the Court leaned into the comparison-based approach of the PDA. It suggested that if an employer is "accommodat[ing] a large percentage of nonpregnant workers while failing to accommodate a large percentage of pregnant workers," then a pregnant employee will have a strong case.[29] But if the employer is *not* doing so—say, the employer is only accommodating the employees who have ADA-qualifying conditions that must be accommodated by law—then the case becomes weaker.

Indeed, the PDA's narrow reach has repeatedly prompted members of Congress to propose a new law: the Pregnant Workers Fairness Act (PWFA).[30] The narrowness of the PDA has had tragic consequences. Stories abound regarding pregnant workers who have been denied breaks or light-duty reassignments, sometimes suffering miscarriages as a result.[31] The PWFA addresses this problem by creating an *independent*, rather than contingent, entitlement to accommodations for pregnant workers. The PWFA essentially copies the ADA's accommodation protections, requiring employers to make "reasonable accommodations to the known limitations related to the pregnancy, childbirth or related medical conditions of a qualified employee,"[32] unless the employer can show an undue hardship. This legislation has been introduced in every Congress from 2012 on. For years, it did not have much success, but it passed the House of Representatives in September 2020 and again in May of 2021. If the PWFA does become law—and if menstruation is treated as a "related medical condition" under the PWFA—then menstruating employees will be on their strongest footing yet in seeking accommodations that prevent menstruation from being a hurdle at work.

Menstrual Leaves?

An intriguing possible source of protection for menstruating employees is a menstrual-leave system. This idea has never taken hold in the United States. But several countries—including Japan, South Korea, Indonesia,

Zambia, and certain provinces in China—follow this approach, at least on the books. Japan, for instance, passed a law in 1947 allowing any woman with painful periods to take time off, although the leave was not necessarily paid. Passed in World War II's aftermath, the law aimed to improve labor conditions. But today, that policy is rarely used. Indeed, the number of employees taking menstrual leave in Japan has steadily dropped, from approximately 26% (in 1965) to 16.6% (in 1976) to 13.4% (in 1981) to less than 1% (in 2017).[33] A study on Japanese menstrual leave in the mid-1980s attributed the decline to several factors, including an improvement in working conditions (with fewer physical demands) as well as the idea that "nowadays young women are ambitious, want to achieve in their jobs, and do not see themselves as incapacitated by menstruation."[34]

More recent articles about menstrual leave in Japan have emphasized cultural reasons for the decline, including the norms around menstrual concealment as well as the fear of sex discrimination. One 2019 piece quoted Sachimi Mochizuki, an event management employee who had worked in Japan for two decades, as stating that she had never taken a day off for her period because she was not comfortable telling her managers that she was menstruating.[35] "It's very private and, especially in Japan, that's still kind of a taboo.... We don't want to talk about it with any men," she said. Yumiko Murakami, head of the Organization for Economic Co-Operation and Development's Tokyo Center, commented that "[i]f you tell people you're taking leave because of your period, that will be seen as you're not as good as men."[36] Another female employee, Kyoko (last name withheld), expressed similar views: "If you take menstrual leave, you're basically broadcasting to the entire office which days of the month you have your period.... It's not the sort of thing you want to share with male colleagues, and it could lead to sexual harassment."[37]

With such a small number of employees now taking menstrual leave in Japan, Murakami believes that some employees do not even know the option exists, especially given her anecdotal sense that most employers do not mention it. Indeed, another employee of a Japanese firm said that no one at her company encouraged employees to take time off due to menstrual pain. "[I]f you're trying to prove yourself in a man's world, you're not going to take menstrual leave in case it's interpreted as a sign of weakness," she added.[38]

When the Anhui province in China adopted legislation in 2016 allowing women to take one or two days off from work each month for severe menstrual cramps, Yang Lan wrote an editorial expressing similar pessimism. "Take a look at Shanghai, where a similar policy was introduced nearly 30 years ago," she wrote. "[F]ew if any women dare take leave from their jobs when suffering from period pain, with a great majority not even being aware of their rights to." She listed several reasons why employees do not take leave: they will simply have to make up the work when they come back; they fear getting on their bosses' bad side; and they are concerned that it will harm their chances for raises or promotions. "[T]he 'bloody' fact is that accepting paid leave whenever a woman has cramps will ultimately do more harm than good for our cause, as it weakens us at the workplace," she concluded.[39]

In 2017, Italy considered adopting a menstrual-leave policy, prompting a similar discussion over whether that would be positive or negative for female employees. The proposed bill would have given Italian women up to three paid days of leave per month, if they could present a doctor's diagnosis of dysmenorrhea. A *Washington Post* headline captured the debate: "Giving Italian Woman 'Menstrual Leave' May Backfire on Their Job Prospects."[40] The article noted that women's magazines in Italy were split on the issue, with the Italian version of *Marie Claire* arguing that the proposed menstrual-leave law would function as "a standard-bearer of progress and social sustainability," while a piece in *Donna Moderna*, another Italian magazine, expressed concern that "employers could become even more oriented to hire men rather than women."[41] Ultimately, the legislation did not move forward in Italy.

The debate over menstrual leave raises familiar issues. It implicates what feminist legal theorist Martha Chamallas has called "double binds and dilemmas of difference," meaning that "women constantly face dilemmas in which they are forced to predict which less-than-ideal course of action will prove to be the least hazardous."[42] Italy's menstrual-leave policy, for instance, would have protected employees who genuinely need time off for dysmenorrhea—but raised the concern that if many employees began taking such leaves, then all employees who might menstruate could become less desirable to employers.

Meanwhile, in the United States, menstrual-leave legislation has not been proposed anywhere. Gender-specific protective labor laws in this country have a long and complex history. During the late nineteenth and early twentieth centuries, numerous states passed laws limiting the numbers of hours women could work. In *Muller v. Oregon*, decided in 1908, the Supreme Court upheld the right of states to do so.[43] Such legislation, according to the Court, was a proper exercise of the state's police power, because of women's physical weakness ("[H]er physical structure and a proper discharge of her maternal functions—having in view not merely her own health, but the well-being of the race—justify legislation to protect her from the greed as well as the passion of man.") and the fact that "woman has always been dependent upon man."[44] In the Progressive Era, reformers sought to improve conditions for all workers, and legislation that protected women became part of what legal scholar Arianne Barzilay has called "an entering wedge strategy"—the idea that once labor laws changed favorably for women, they would be easier to change for men, too.[45]

Today, of course, any such limitations on women's ability to work would be rightly regarded as discriminatory—indeed, they would be blatantly unconstitutional under the Equal Protection Clause. Reflecting on the *Muller* decision one hundred years later, Justice Ruth Bader Ginsburg observed, "Having grown up in years when women, by law or custom, were protected from a range of occupations, including lawyering, and from serving on juries, I am instinctively suspicious of women-only protective legislation. Family-friendly legislation, I believe, is the sounder strategy."[46]

Ginsburg's skepticism about workplace laws that single out women for "protection" resembles some of the concerns about menstrual-leave laws. Of course, menstrual-leave laws do not limit women's ability to work in the way that the maximum-hours laws did; employees would not be *prohibited* from working while menstruating. Moreover, a law that required employers to grant menstrual leave in cases of significant physical discomfort would be constitutional. The Supreme Court explained in *California Federal Savings and Loan Association v. Guerra* that policies or mandates requiring accommodations for employees' actual physical impairments caused by pregnancy, childbirth, and related conditions do not amount to impermissible sex discrimination, because such rules are designed to promote equal employment opportunities and remove barriers to workplace participation.[47] Far more problematic, on the other hand, are standards that are untethered to physical impairments and otherwise reflect "archaic or stereotypical notions about pregnancy and the abilities of pregnant workers."[48] Accordingly, a law that required employers to give menstrual leaves to *all* menstruating employees (regardless of need) would likely be struck down, while a law requiring employers to give such leaves to menstruating employees with an actual need for them would likely be upheld. But even though narrow menstrual-leave legislation would be constitutional, there does not appear to be much popular support for it in the United States, as evidenced most clearly by a comprehensive study published in 2019.

In that study, researchers Jessica Barnack-Tavlaris, Kristina Hansen, Rachel Levitt, and Michelle Reno surveyed six hundred adults living in the United States about their attitudes toward menstrual-leave policies and what effects they thought such policies might have in the United States. The participants ranged in age from eighteen to sixty-five and included both men (52.5%) and women (47.2%). Slightly under half (45%) of the participants claimed that they would support menstrual leave if it were implemented in the United States, with an additional 16.3% saying that they would support it with certain conditions, such as the leave being unpaid and/or the leave being limited to employees whose menstruation-related discomfort was significant enough to require medical intervention. But when asked what types of effects a menstrual-leave policy might have in the United States, people expressed negative views. Out of all participants, 23% thought there would be positive effects, 49.3% thought there would be negative effects, and 13.3% thought there would be both positive and negative effects. (The remaining people were uncertain or thought there would be no effects.) For the most part, the results were not cross-tabulated by gender, so it is not clear whether views differed widely based on whether the respondent was male or female.

The researchers identified five main themes that emerged from the survey participants' comments. The first theme was positive: 10% of the study participants thought that a menstrual-leave policy would support women in several ways, including giving menstruating employees time to rest and recover, promoting greater understanding of menstruation, and reducing menstrual stigma and related concealment imperatives. But the other four themes to emerge all were negative. Approximately

20% of the participants felt that a menstrual-leave policy would be unfair to men because it would give women extra time off, leading to a backlash against women. Relatedly, about 34% of the participants thought that a menstrual-leave policy would harm the workplace because employees would use it to unnecessarily skip work, reducing business productivity and putting an added burden on the employees working that day. Another view, expressed by 11% of the participants, was that menstrual-leave policies were unnecessary because menstruation was not onerous. The last theme, expressed by slightly more than 16% of the participants, was that a menstrual-leave policy would make women "look bad." These participants noted the stigma surrounding menstruation and also said that they believed such a policy might deter employers from hiring women.[49]

These negative themes point to a dynamic lurking under the surface of the movement for menstrual equity. The previous chapters have described a wave of recent successes: the elimination of the tampon tax in numerous states, the First Step Act's inclusion of a provision requiring free menstrual products for federal prisoners, the CARES Act's inclusion of a provision allowing menstrual products to be purchased with funds from flexible spending accounts; legislation in a growing number of states to provide free menstrual products in schools and prisons; and more. These changes share some common aspects. They are monetary and mostly impose no direct real burden on nonmenstruating people (other than, perhaps, a tax increase that is so small as to be *de minimis*). These other changes do not have the effect of making some people feel as though they are missing out on "special treatment." There is no evidence, for example, that nonmenstruating students are envious of the free tampons and pads in the school restrooms. Nor are there accounts of nonmenstruating prisoners objecting to the provision of menstrual products to inmates who have their periods.

Menstrual leave, however, is different. The idea of regular days off from work is broadly appealing to virtually *all* employees. A menstrual-leave policy, therefore, raises the specter of winners (menstruating employees) and losers (nonmenstruating employees). And, indeed, 20% of participants in the study raised concerns about fairness, making comments like, "It discriminates against men who have to work all the time" or "I think men would probably come up with a 'condition' in which they would request off, such as men menstruation." Compounding the survey participants' discomfort was the idea that the nonmenstruating employees could be doubly penalized. Not only would they miss out on "extra" days off, but they might have to do extra work to pick up the absent employees' slack. Indeed, participants expressed worry about the "burden" that such a policy would impose on other employees, and even suspected that women would abuse the policy by lying about when they had their periods or by exaggerating their symptoms.[50] These sorts of suspicions, too, are much less prevalent with the tampon tax or in the school or prison contexts. It is generally accepted that menstruation exists and requires products to absorb the flow. Most people do not doubt that others are buying or using menstrual products out of necessity. But because the physical effects of menstruation vary widely from person to person, there is much greater skepticism about the level of need for menstrual leave.

The results of this study of attitudes toward menstrual leave gesture towards the types of menstrual-equity initiatives that are likely to gain widespread support, and why. In short, policies that seem like a "zero-sum game"—with clear winners and losers—will have the least support. Of all possible ways to address menstrual equity in the workplace, therefore, a menstrual-leave policy is probably the least viable. But, as Barnack-Tavlaris and Levitt note in a later piece, there are also workplace policies that could address the needs of menstruating employees while being more broadly applicable, such as "workplace flexibility more generally (for example, more time off, the ability to work from home, customized work schedules)" and/or "equipping workplaces with rest/break rooms for anyone who is feeling under the weather—physically, mentally, or emotionally."[51] Widely available, gender-neutral policies are much less likely to trigger resistance or resentment; they are precisely the type of "family-friendly" policies that Justice Ginsburg said she favored over the protective legislation in *Muller v. Oregon*. They are also safer legally, since they do not raise the specter of sex discrimination.

That said, some global employers have voluntarily adopted menstrual-leave policies, and it is possible that employers focused primarily on domestic US markets will follow suit. Nike, for instance, referenced menstrual leave in a prior version of its Code of Conduct for contractors, stating that the contractor hereby "certifies that it complies with all provisions for legally mandated benefits, including but not limited to . . . sick leave; emergency leave; pregnancy and menstrual leave; vacation, religious, [and] bereavement and holiday leave."[52] The wording of this policy, though, suggested that contractors only must offer menstrual leave if doing so was legally mandated. Nike's current Code of Conduct does not mention menstrual leave; its Leadership Standards provide that "[n]o physical exams may be conducted to verify eligibility for menstrual leave if it is a benefit mandated by local law."[53] Other companies have gone further in support of menstrual-leave policies. A British social enterprise company called Coexist made headlines back in 2016 when it became the first UK company to introduce a menstrual-leave policy. Under Coexist's policy, a "flexitime" approach is used, whereby menstruating employees can shift their work schedules so that they do not work during their periods but then make up the time at other points. In a TED Talk, the company's director, Bex Baxter, explained the genesis of the policy as follows:

> I saw a member of staff bent double, white as a sheet, clearly in a lot of pain, over reception and still serving customers. I did what any compassionate human would do, and as her line manager, I obviously told her to go home. But it wasn't as simple as that. She started to shoo me away with those four very familiar words: "it's just my period." I knew those words in my own mind, and in hundreds of thousands of women across the UK. . . . In that moment, I got this bizarre sort of excitement because I knew I could do something. This was a basic human rights issue. And as an innovative company, maybe we could trial something—we could test drive something new—and end the suffering and the taboo around menstruation in the workplace.[54]

More recently, Zomato—an Indian food delivery startup—announced in August 2020 that "all women (including transgender people)" could take up to ten days of paid "period leave" per year. The company's founder and CEO, Deepinder Goyal, wrote in the company's blog,

> Zomato understands that men and women are born with different biological realities. It is our job to make sure that we make room for our biological needs, while not lowering the bar for the quality of our work and

the impact we create. There shouldn't be any shame or stigma attached to applying for a period leave. You should feel free to tell people on internal groups, or emails that you are on your period leave for the day.

Goya added that "these leaves should only be availed if you are *really* unable to attend to work. . . . Do not abuse these leaves or use them as a crutch to take time out for other pending tasks."[55]

Given the long history of suspicion and mistrust surrounding menstruation, menstrual-leave policies like Zomato's may well give rise to allegations that some employees are taking unfair advantage. At the same time, as the studies of menstrual-leave policies in Japan and China reveal, many eligible employees may be reluctant to avail themselves of this benefit in the first place, because of a desire to maintain privacy, fears of projecting weakness in the workplace, and/or concerns about losing ground vis-à-vis other employees. These tensions are likely to vary depending on particular workplace cultures, but any employer implementing a menstrual-leave policy should be sensitive to them.

Menstrual Products at Work

As compared to menstrual leaves, a less controversial idea for promoting menstrual equity at work is providing free menstrual products in workplace restrooms. Both the 2017 and the 2019 versions of Representative Grace Meng's proposed Menstrual Equity for All Act included a provision requiring employers with one hundred or more employees to provide free menstrual products for employees. Specifically, the bill proposed amending OSHA to direct the secretary of labor to promulgate a requirement along these lines. The bill did not advance, but may have better prospects in the future.

Meanwhile, employers are of course free to take this step on their own. Some employers have already been leaders in this respect. Nancy Kramer, the founder of a nonprofit organization called Free the Tampons, recalls having a "eureka" moment back in January 1982, "when I walked into the women's restroom in Apple's corporate headquarters in Cupertino, California, and there on the counter was a collection of tampons and pads for everyone to freely access." She remembered, "I thought, wow, that makes so much sense. A public restroom that has everything that I, as a woman, need to tend to my normal bodily functions." Kramer noted that after her trip to Apple, "I immediately stocked our restrooms at our business with women's supplies."[56] She added that over the years, she had also convinced a number of other employers to do so.

Indeed, with the rise of free menstrual products in the restrooms of secondary schools, universities, and certain public spaces, it seems likely that some employees will begin to request or even expect free menstrual products in workplace restrooms, too. The more workplaces that do so, the more other workplaces are likely to follow. The presence of free menstrual products in workplace restrooms may, in turn, help usher in a broader reduction of menstrual stigma and concealment throughout the workplace and beyond.

6

Menstruating While Male

On June 6, 2020, J. K. Rowling—author of the well-known *Harry Potter* series—posted a tweet that quickly went viral. Commenting on an op-ed bearing the title "Creating a More Equal Post-COVID-19 World for People Who Menstruate,"[1] Rowling sarcastically wrote, "'People who menstruate.' I'm sure there used to be a word for those people. Someone help me out. Wumben? Wimpund? Woomud?"[2] She was, in essence, objecting to the framing of menstruation in gender-neutral terms.

Rowling was not the first to raise this issue. Greater awareness and visibility of trans people in recent years had already prompted discussion and debate about what language to use for discussing menstruation, pregnancy, and related issues. But Rowling's tweet became a flashpoint: it received over eighty-five thousand likes, and many critical comments as well, with some calling Rowling a "TERF" (the acronym for "transexclusionary radical feminist"). Daniel Radcliffe, who portrayed Harry Potter in the movies based on Rowling's series, soon entered the discussion by writing a blog post for the Trevor Project, an LGBTQ youth suicide-prevention group. Radcliffe wrote, "Transgender women are women. Any statement to the contrary erases the identity and dignity of transgender people and goes against all advice given by professional health care associations who have far more expertise on this subject matter than either Jo [Rowling] or I."[3] Emma Watson, who portrayed Hermione Granger in the movies, also spoke out: "Trans people are who they say they are and deserve to live their lives without being constantly questioned or told they aren't who they say they are."[4] Legions of Harry Potter fans expressed feelings of hurt, disappointment, and anger over Rowling's tweet.[5]

Undeterred by criticism, Rowling expanded upon her first tweet in a blog post. "[T]he inclusive language that calls female people 'menstruators' and 'people with vulvas' strikes many women as dehumanizing and demeaning," she wrote. "I understand why trans activists consider this language to be appropriate and kind, but for those of us who've had degrading slurs spat at us by violent men, it's not neutral, it's hostile and alienating." Rowling linked her comments to a broader objection, asserting that "the arguments about femaleness not residing in the sexed body, and the assertions that biological women don't have common experiences" are "deeply misogynistic and regressive."[6] Rowling's blog post, in turn, sparked further controversy, one that has shown no sign of abating.

A similar but less well-publicized reaction had earlier met Megan Murphy, a feminist blogger at the site *Feminist Current*, when Murphy objected in 2016 to a tweet by Planned Parenthood that referred to "menstruators" and celebrated the end of the tampon tax in New York. Murphy wrote, "Every single person who menstruates has a female body. Does this make you feel uncomfortable? Apparently it makes Planned Parenthood uncomfortable, which is odd, as they, of all people, should understand these basic facts about women's bodies, as experts and educators on the very topic of women's bodies."[7] Some commenters called Murphy a TERF, endorsing the term "menstruator" as more accurate.[8] Other commenters agreed with her, saying that "[b]eing called a 'menstruator' ... [is] like calling someone an incubator."[9] Another said, "Why can't we be women and menstruators? If transmen don't want to be included in the category woman, fine but as a female I won't be reduced to my body parts I am a whole person, female is a whole real person not just pieces without a face to appease a cult."[10]

The reactions to Rowling and Murphy provide a window into some of the complexity in talking about menstruation in the current moment. Just as greater awareness of period poverty crossed over into popular consciousness in roughly 2015, so too did greater trans awareness. As markers of this growing cultural and legal awareness, consider the 2014 series premiere of the television show *Transparent*; the June 2015 cover story on Caitlyn Jenner in *Vanity Fair*; the July 2015 series premiere of the reality TV series *I Am Jazz*, a reality show about the life of a trans girl, Jazz Jennings; and the December 2015 issuance of guidance by the New York City Commission of Human Rights that announced "strong protections for [the] City's transgender and gender non-conforming communities in housing, employment and public spaces."[11]

Indeed, recent years have yielded more public discussion than ever before about *both* menstruation and gender identity—and the two topics intersect in complex ways. This chapter aims to unpack and explore that intersection. We begin with the premise that the dialogue about how law and society can and should address matters of menstruation is both complicated and enriched by the facts that not all girls and women menstruate and that not all who menstruate are girls and women. Indeed, although this chapter is entitled "Menstruating While Male" to gesture at the linguistic complexity of describing the universe of people who menstruate, that phrasing is also incomplete. In addition to cisgender (or "cis") girls and women, some of the people who menstruate are trans men and boys. Furthermore, others who menstruate are gender nonbinary, meaning that their gender identity (internal sense of self) and/or gender expression (presentation to the world through appearance, names, pronouns, and the like) do not conform to either side of the male/female binary. Still others who menstruate are genderqueer, meaning outside those categories altogether.[12] For any individual, the medical markers of sex (such as external genitalia, hormone levels, or genes) may or may not match an individual's gender identity or expression. The term "trans" can apply without regard to biology, and regardless of the medical steps a person does or does not take to align the physical body with the internal sense of self. And, of course, not all cis girls and women menstruate, for reasons ranging from age to various health and medical conditions.

Given the complexities in talking about sex and gender, menstrual-equity advocates face two challenges worthy of equal attention and effort. The first is to use language that does not pathologize or "other" trans, gender-nonbinary, and genderqueer people by leaving them out of the discussion. The second is to craft arguments that will be convincing to courts, legislatures, and administrative agencies—as well as to public opinion, which plays an important role in influencing those entities. Particularly when legal arguments are framed so as to dismantle widespread menstruation-based disadvantages or barriers, such as the tampon tax, those goals can sometimes appear to be in tension. After all, the most straightforward legal strategy is to characterize unfavorable treatment of menstruation as a form of discrimination against women. Deemphasizing the link between women and menstruation, therefore, runs the risk of undermining that approach. There are effective ways to navigate this challenge, and it must be addressed both clearly and carefully.

This chapter begins by sketching the larger landscape and context giving rise to linguistic controversies like the firestorm over Rowling's tweet. It also attempts to provide a fuller account of menstruation as experienced by people beyond those who are cis girls and women. We then turn to a consideration of inclusive and effective legal strategies for the menstrual-advocacy movement.

Increasing Awareness of Issues Relevant to Trans and Gender-Nonbinary Populations

Trans, nonbinary, and genderqueer people have gained more visibility in the twenty-first century, but the overwhelming majority of Americans have limited awareness of the complex issues they face. In recent years, there have been different attempts to estimate how many people in the United States identify as transgender. Researchers affiliated with the Williams Institute at the University of California–Los Angeles used data from the 2014 Behavioral Risk Factor Surveillance System to make state-level estimates of self-identified transgender adults. They estimated that 0.6% of all adult individuals in the United States, or approximately 1.4 million people, self-identify as transgender.[13] The estimated trans population by state ranges from a low of .30% in North Dakota to a high of 2.8% in the District of Columbia.[14] A 2018 study of Minnesota high school students estimated that 3% of all students identified in a way that is different from the sex they were assigned at birth.[15] According to a 2017 GLAAD-Harris poll of 2,037 individuals, somewhere between 88% and 97% of the population self-identifies as "cisgender." Other respondents to the same survey identified as "agender" (zero to 3%), "gender fluid" (zero to 3%), "transgender" (zero to 2%), "unsure/questioning" (2% to 3%), "bigender" (zero to 1%), and "gender queer" (zero to 1%).[16] The age group with the lowest percentage of self-identified cisgender people was the eighteen- to thirty-four-year-old cohort (88%), followed by thirty-five- to fifty-one-year-olds (94%). Because the GLAAD-Harris poll does not report publicly how many respondents were in each age category, however, it is not possible to estimate the numeric size of the various population segments.

One of the many problems with surveys that rely on self-reporting, particularly by individuals who may be vulnerable to discrimination, is that they likely undercount. In other words, there probably are more people who identify in categories other than cisgender than people who self-identify that way on a survey. Another challenge with survey data is that large population studies are, by definition, comprehensive and time-consuming, and so a report like the Williams Institute's necessarily makes use of data that is already a few years old. Given the relatively rapid increase in the (still limited) visibility of transgender individuals in the media and the (slowly improving) social attitudes about trans issues, there may be a higher percentage of people identifying as trans as the years go on. Also, because more young people currently tend to identify as transgender than older people do, any survey that is limited to "adults" in any particular year may not accurately forecast the future size of the trans population.[17] For all of these reasons, it is difficult to know the precise size of the trans population in the United States. The message of the Harris-GLAAD poll is nonetheless clear. An increasing number of young people identify as not cisgender.

Gender-Neutral "Menstruators" and the Challenges of Language

For hundreds of years, conventional descriptions of gender difference have relied on words like "men" and "women." But in the twenty-first century, we have become increasingly aware that these terms do not capture the full range of human experience. Indeed, trans, nonbinary, and genderqueer people have always existed; what is new is that their voices are increasingly being heard by others. Nudging the culture in the direction of more inclusive language was likely the goal of the journalists who wrote the headline about "people who menstruate" that caught J. K. Rowling's attention and prompted the famous author's subsequent tweet.[18] Indeed, the headline echoed a November 19, 2019, tweet by the ACLU: "There's no one way to be a man. Men who get their periods are men. Men who get pregnant and give birth are men. Trans and nonbinary men belong."[19] Language of inclusion and belonging is a response to the strong feelings that can be provoked by bright lines that some people wish to draw around categories relating to sex and gender.

There are some feminists, such as Rowling and Murphy, for example, who understand menstruation as a function deeply tied to female biology and identity. They resist or object to gender-neutral language like "menstruators" because they feel such language is reductionist (to body parts) or because the language fails to acknowledge the gendered nature of menstruation, insofar as most people who menstruate, numerically speaking, are cis girls and cis women. Yet others, including the critics of Rowling and Murphy, understand menstruation as a bodily process separate from an understanding or existence of the self as female or as a woman. They explain that gender-neutral language like "menstruators" more accurately and completely describes the universe of people who menstruate, while simultaneously avoiding any suggestion that trans women are not "real" women because they do not.[20] Each side in these exchanges feels deeply pained, angered, and marginalized by the language of the other. These controversies, like others that have plagued feminist organizing in the past, reflect deep resentments and feelings of exclusion that divide groups of people who otherwise share goals of equality and freedom for all, without regard to sex or gender.

In the current cultural climate, when conversations about sex and gender touch on trans issues, they risk quick descent into line drawing, misunderstandings, and even name calling, which stifle—rather than enhance—an exchange of views. For fear of being labeled TERFs, many feminists even attempt to side-step trans issues entirely. How, then, to talk about menstruation in a way that is inclusive of all people who menstruate without reducing them to their bodily functions? The analysis running throughout this book is generally consistent with a liberal feminist interest in enabling all people to participate fully in society, on their own terms. Autonomy to designate what one is called and how one moves through the world is consistent with basic American values like privacy and respect for human dignity. This means that there may always be some diversity in the language surrounding menstruation and those who menstruate, but the first step is greater understanding. Indeed, it is helpful to hear more about what trans, gender-nonbinary, and genderqueer individuals themselves say about their own experiences with menstruation, and so we now turn there.

The Fraughtness of Menstruation for Some Trans People

Given the pervasiveness of negative cultural attitudes about menstruation discussed in chapter 1, it is not surprising that many cis girls and cis women have negative feelings about their periods. For some trans men, trans boys, gender-nonbinary individuals, and genderqueer people who menstruate, these larger cultural messages, combined with their own discomfort, can lead them to avoid acknowledging menstruation at all. As trans writer Wiley Reading explains, "Most trans guys have to deal with their periods at some point or another. It's not something we talk about—a lot of us are ashamed, which is understandable." Reading adds, however, that in his experience, "talking about our bodies is sometimes the best way to fight dysphoria and learn new things about how to improve our lives."[21]

In his essay, Reading uses the term "dysphoria," referring to the medical diagnosis of gender dysphoria that replaced "gender identity disorder" in the fifth edition of the American Psychiatric Association's *Diagnostic and Statistical Manual of Mental Disorders* (the "DSM-5"), issued in 2013. But this language, too, is controversial and not adopted by all. Some believe the diagnosis of dysphoria is necessary in order to allow trans people to advocate for the healthcare coverage they need. Others argue that it pathologizes people for failing to meet heteronormative expectations for bodies and lives.

Reading's discussion of menstruation makes two points in particular. He argues that, in his experience, talking about menstruation has particular associations with shame for trans boys and men: it is a reminder that they have at least one ovary and a uterus, which for them may be subjectively at odds with their male identities. Second, Reading uses an inverse quasi-Descartian reasoning ("I think, therefore I am") to challenge the understanding of particular anatomies as "female." His argument is that menstruation does not make him less than the trans man he is. "[T]here's no reason bleeding makes me feminine," he writes. "I'm not going to get ejected from the realm of masculinity because my set of gonads produces blood from time to time. . . . [M]en can have periods. My body is not female. My menstruation is not female. It just *is*. My body just is."[22]

Sociologist Sarah Frank's study of trans and nonbinary experiences of menstruation yields similar reflections. On the basis of surveys with nineteen trans or gender-nonbinary individuals, Frank draws attention to the ways that trans and nonbinary individuals navigate menstruation. Given the study's small sample size, one should not rush to overgeneralize about trans experiences with menstruation, but Frank's groundbreaking study centers trans voices, bringing attention to an understudied area. It also provides a blueprint for possible future work. Frank's interviews with participants yielded four important observations: (1) menstruation is an experience that "contributes to a contested self" for many of the study participants;[23] (2) many trans and nonbinary people are uncomfortable with the "aggressive gendering" of menstrual products as feminine;[24] (3) navigating men's bathrooms while menstruating can be a fraught experience for some trans individuals; and (4) many trans people have negative experiences with healthcare providers around menstruation and other issues.[25]

The individuals who participated in Frank's study suggest that there is no single way to talk about trans and gender-nonbinary experiences with menstruation. On the subject of contested identity, some of the trans men and gender-nonbinary individuals in Frank's study describe menstruation as disruptive to their sense of selves. Like Reading, one participant explains, "[O]n the one hand menstruation is seen as very, you know, something that happens to cis women so I guess kind of an invalidation of what my identity, what I strive to be, but on the other hand if we try to raise more awareness that this isn't something that happens only to cis women, kind of breaking down the assumption and more 'Hey this can happen to anyone,' sort of deal."[26] These types of comments illustrate what Martha Chamallas has called the "double binds and dilemmas of difference" problem in feminist legal theory. As chapter 5 describes, this double bind refers to facing two either/or choices that are equally suboptimal.[27] On the one hand, for some trans and gender-nonbinary people, discussions about experiences of menstruation may disrupt their masculine or gender-fluid identity. At the same time, silence about their experiences of menstruation obscures the fact that some trans men, gender-nonbinary individuals, and genderqueer people menstruate, too, reducing the likelihood that the law will evolve in ways that take this into account.

Although the experiences of trans, gender-nonbinary, or genderqueer people with menstruation are not well documented, it is an emerging area of inquiry. For example, Klara Rydström, the project manager at MENSEN, a Swedish nonprofit organization that focuses on spreading awareness around menstruation and fighting menstrual taboos, has interviewed nine Swedish trans people about their experiences with menstruation. As in Frank's study, Rydström found that trans people described feeling "othered" in the context of menstruation, particularly in connection with public bathrooms, menstrual products, and experiences with the healthcare sector.[28] The marketing and terminology surrounding menstrual products has recently become a focal point for criticism by trans consumers and their allies, with some notable developments.

Hyper-Gendered Marketing of Menstrual Products

The hyper-gendered nature of menstrual products and their marketing makes some trans and nonbinary people uncomfortable. Reading, for example, described the mental tricks he goes through when having to buy "any sort of quote-unquote 'feminine product,'" including making jokes in his head and avoiding repeat interactions with the same cashier. One of Frank's interviewees observed, "[W]hat I'd like to see is, you know like I said, the aggressive gendering of products, including the wrappers of the pads. Like I'd like to see more gender neutral. . . . Like so just having more neutrality and making it easier for trans people to look at this and say this is a product that does not make me feel less trans."[29] One blogger for *Period Media* similarly remarked,

> Menstrual health aisles more often than not look as flowery and feminine as a field of fresh daisies. Adverts promoting sanitary products more or less always depict cis women (naturally-born women whose psychological gender identity is also female). This is of course understandable in marketing terms due to the core demographic of their buyers. However, the diversity of those who use sanitary products isn't yet being fully represented.[30]

Frank says that for her participants, the packaging of menstrual products contributes to "negative conceptions of the self."[31] Rydström similarly observes that "[t]he Othering of trans menstruators in relation to menstrual products is present on various levels," from the term "feminine hygiene products" to the "packaging of menstrual products—feminine-coded colors and patterns."[32]

Concerns about the gendered marketing of menstrual products prompted at least one company to change the packaging of its products.

In March 2019, one Twitter user reacted to the woman symbol on Always brand menstrual products: "Hey @Always since today is #TransVisibilityDay it's probably important to point out the fact that this new packaging isn't trans* friendly. Just a reminder that Menstruation does not equal Female. Maybe rethink this new look."[33] In October 2019, Procter & Gamble, the company behind the Always brand of menstrual products, announced that beginning in 2020, it would eliminate the woman sign—also called a Venus symbol—from some of its packaging. Some news outlets reported that this was the company's capitulation to a "transgender lobby" and to "transgender activists," but it seems that the company made the change in response to a few tweets on social media and a direct complaint from an eighteen-year-old transgender man.[34] The company wrote to him directly with the news that in the near future, its product wrapper would not contain the "feminine symbol," and added, "We are absolutely grateful for having people like you voicing their opinions."[35]

The decision by Procter & Gamble attracted controversy. In language similar to Rowling's concerns about referring to "people who menstruate" rather than "women who menstruate," one UK woman objected,

> Removing the female symbol from sanitary towel packaging is basically denying the existence of women. We're now moving towards the total elimination of women's biology. The women's symbol has been used by feminists for decades. This is pure cowardice and virtue signalling from these big corporate brands who are capitulating to the trans agenda.[36]

This comment reveals that some consumers view menstruation as so intertwined with female sex and gender identity that the shift to more gender-neutral packaging and the elimination of "feminine" or "female" colors or symbols strikes them as an erasure or denial of cis women's existence and experience. That leaves even well-intended (but still profit-seeking) companies with a conundrum: gender-neutral packaging might attract trans, gender-nonbinary, genderqueer, and some cis gender customers, but alienate some other cis gender customers. To make matters more complicated, some trans, nonbinary, or genderqueer people may not object to stereotypically female-gendered packaging, while some cis women may be turned off by it. Thus menstrual-product companies may actually find a ready market if they diversify their packaging and advertisements.

The terminology surrounding menstrual products themselves is another aspect of this issue. As Rydström noted, the "feminine hygiene products" phrase presupposes that the users of these products are solely women. Reading also described his discomfort with the term "feminine products," which conflicts with his own efforts to reframe his period as "less like I'm a lady flower experiencing lady uterus ladyship" and "more like myself experiencing a medical condition."[37] Concerns such as these resonate in the June 2020 announcement by the New Zealand supermarket chain Countdown that it would stop using words like "sanitary products," "personal hygiene," and "feminine hygiene" in advertising certain products, instead just referring to "period care." The two words removed by Countdown—"feminine" and "hygiene"—are both worth emphasizing. First, as one commentator noted about the change, "by using the word 'feminine,' supermarket chains are not respecting every single one of their customers and may harm some of their identities. Simply utilizing the word 'period' is far more respectful and encourages more inclusivity for some of those in the LGBTQIA+ community."[38] Second, the removal of the term "hygiene" communicates that there is nothing dirty or problematic about menstrual periods. As a spokesman for Countdown put it,

> Words like "personal hygiene" and "sanitary products" give the impression that periods—which are an entirely natural part of life—are somehow something to hide to yourself, or that they're unhygienic. They absolutely aren't, and we can play an important role in helping change that. We want to help normalise the language around periods and continence as well as making products like pads, tampons and menstrual cups much easier to find when our customers are shopping online.[39]

This view connects with Reading's focus on removing the emotional valence from buying menstrual products. (Interestingly, Countdown also shifted toward using the term "continence care" and "continence products," as opposed to the phrase "incontinence," on the similar rationale of "de-stigmatis[ing] what is again a natural part of life" and avoiding "euphemisms.")[40] Sarah Mikkelsen, a cofounder of the New

Zealand nonprofit The Period Place, heralded Countdown's decision: "[T]o see a big brand jump on a train that they haven't really even been asked to jump onto is very cool, very inspiring."[41]

Pink Packages and Pink Taxes

Issues surrounding the marketing and terminology for menstrual products also present a unique twist on what cultural critics and scholars call the "pink tax." Generally speaking, the phrase refers to a variety of different problems related to gender differences in economic life. The tampon tax, as discussed in chapter 2, is one such example. The term "pink tax" also refers to the gender pay gap and to gender-based pricing differentials in products intended to be used by "female" and "male" consumers. A 2015 study by the New York City Department of Consumer Affairs, for instance, found that across five different industries and thirty-five categories, "women's" products cost 7% more than the equivalent "men's" product.[42] Researchers found differences in supportive braces ($94.99 for the women's product and $84.99 for the men's product), razors ($8.99 for the 5-blade razor for women and $8.49 for the 5-blade razor for men, made by the same company), and clothing ($39.94 for a woman's sweater; $34.94 for the same style and pattern of sweater for men), to provide just a few examples.[43] Gender-based pricing discrimination in the provision of services has been prohibited in California since 1995,[44] although a bill to prohibit similar discrimination in the provision of goods was withdrawn in 2016 in response to lobbying pressure.[45]

In New York, a new "pink tax" ban went into effect on September 30, 2020, in connection with Governor Andrew Cuomo's execution of the fiscal year 2021 budget. The new law prohibits any individual or entity from charging different prices for substantially similar goods or services due to the gender for whom the goods or services are marketed. The state government's press release about the change explained that "the same children's swimming pool product brand and dimensions offered in pink at $89.99 and blue at $69.99 would constitute a violation of the law," as would "dry cleaning a woman's suit jacket for $12 and a man's suit jacket for $8."[46]

To be sure, issues surrounding the marketing and terminology for menstrual products do not technically fall under the "pink tax" umbrella, since they are about presentation, not cost. But New York's law does suggest a growing attentiveness to the negative aspects of gendered marketing, in ways that may cross into the menstrual-product space as well—especially given the growing awareness that not all who menstruate are cis women and girls.

Inclusive and Effective Advocacy

Just as some stores and companies selling menstrual products have begun adapting their language to be more inclusive, so has the menstrual advocacy movement. In her 2017 book *Periods Gone Public: Taking a Stand for Menstrual Equity*, Jennifer Weiss-Wolf reflected,

> [I]n framing this book, my focus has been on a historical exploration of menstruation and the more recent policy agenda—the vast majority of which pertains to cisgender women and girls. As an advocate and writer, I've struggled with how to reconcile a fuller array of perspectives, doing my best to employ gender neutral language—using "menstrual products" instead of "feminine hygiene," for example; in my advocacy, I urge policy makers and other influencers to do the same.[47]

For that reason, numerous authors and advocates have begun using the word "menstruators" in their work—similar to the gender-neutral language that attracted J. K. Rowling's attention.

How can and should the increasingly inclusive language of menstrual advocacy get incorporated into legal arguments? Here, it is helpful to begin by distinguishing between two categories of legal advocacy involving menstruation. The first category involves broad, large-scale reform, such as eliminating the tampon tax, requiring schools to provide free menstrual products, and so on. These efforts can take the form of impact litigation as well as legislative and public relations campaigns. The second category involves challenges to specific cases of menstrual mistreatment, such as the employment terminations described in chapter 5 of Alisha Coleman and Joyce Flores for menstruating at work. Efforts in this second category will typically take the form of individual lawsuits, though the issues can also implicate larger questions about the need for legal reform.

For the first category, a helpful organizing theme—one that is both inclusive and effective—is that legal reforms are necessary because negative treatment of menstruation reflects a form of sex discrimination that then harms all who menstruate. This argument has two aspects: the "sex discrimination" piece and the "harms all who menstruate" piece. Each is crucial.

The first aspect of the argument, which emphasizes the sex-discriminatory aspect of what is occurring, helps situate menstrual advocacy within the existing constitutional and statutory frameworks for challenging discrimination. To be clear, stating that menstrual deprivations and mistreatment constitute a form of sex discrimination does not mean that only cis women and girls menstruate, any more than it means that all cis women and girls menstruate. Rather, this piece of the argument draws on (1) the cultural and biological associations between menstruation and female sex, (2) the sexist—at times, even misogynistic—roots of menstrual mistreatment and deprivations, and (3) the disparate impact of the burdens that result. As Jennifer Weiss-Wolf and former ACLU attorney Gabriel Arkles (now with the Transgender Legal Defense and Education Fund) put it in a 2019 column,

> Not all Jewish people wear yarmulkes, and some people who aren't Jewish do wear yarmulkes (for example, if attending a Jewish religious service). Still, if a legislature decided to tax people for wearing yarmulkes, or to impose sales tax on yarmulkes but not similar items, that would be anti-Semitism, and it would violate the constitution. Similarly, imposing a sales tax on menstrual products but not similar items is sexist, and violates the constitution....
>
> We don't need to erase trans or non-binary people to show that barriers to menstrual equity, such as the tax on menstrual products, are unconstitutional sex discrimination. This tax targets a bodily function associated with women for less favorable treatment. It relies on sexist ideas that women's needs are frivolous and unnecessary.[48]

Weiss-Wolf and Arkles thus helpfully show how the sex-discrimination argument can fully coexist with recognition that people other than cis women and girls menstruate, too.

The second piece of our proposed framing—emphasizing the harms to all who menstruate—highlights the ultimate goal of menstrual advocacy: helping ensure that menstruation does not limit people's full participation in public life. Indeed, our language here emphasizes that the legal reforms must reach all who menstruate. In some situations, like elimination of the tampon tax, this occurs naturally: once the tax is repealed, no one buying menstrual products has to pay it. But in other situations, this will not be automatic. Schools need to take affirmative steps to make menstrual products available to all menstruating students, rather than solely placing them in the girls' restrooms. Similarly, prisons must be sure to provide products to all menstruating prisoners; and employers must ensure that any policies that accommodate menstrual needs are equally available to all menstruating employees.

That brings us to the other category of legal advocacy involving menstruation: individual cases, particularly those that reach the point of being filed in court, as opposed to wider reform efforts. Here, the argumentation in any one case must be specifically tailored to the facts and circumstances of the particular plaintiff, and so the legal rhetoric will necessarily be less sweeping. But the underlying theme—that menstruation-based discrimination is a form of sex discrimination that then harms all who menstruate—is relevant here as well. In *Flores*, for instance, the plaintiff was a cis female employee who was terminated because the toilet paper that she had temporarily put in her underwear to absorb her menstrual flow tripped the security body scanner of the prison where she worked, since she had earlier been wearing a tampon. In her complaint, she alleged that she "was terminated because she was a menstruating female utilizing a feminine hygiene product when she arrived to work."[49]

The *Flores* court's analysis of why she had adequately alleged sex discrimination perfectly captured the underlying themes of this chapter. First, the court stated that "Flores has sufficiently alleged that she was discriminated against on the basis of her sex," explaining that "but for Flores's menstruation and use of a tampon—conditions inextricable from her sex and her child-bearing capacity—she would not have been discharged." But the court also went further, by noting that "[t]he court understands that transgender men (individuals who were assigned female at birth and transitioned to living as men) and nonbinary individuals may also menstruate."⁵⁰ The court thus showed not only that it was aware of the diverse population of people who menstruate but also that this awareness could coexist with viewing menstruation-based discrimination as a form of sex discrimination.

Moreover, the logic of the *Flores* court's analysis makes clear that, were a menstruating employee other than a cis woman terminated under similar circumstances, that employee would also have a cognizable claim. If employers cannot punish female employees for menstruating, they also cannot punish trans male and/or gender-nonbinary employees for menstruating. Doing so would clearly violate the Supreme Court's decision in *Bostock v. Clayton County*, which held that Title VII's prohibition of sex discrimination necessarily prohibits gender-identity discrimination as well.⁵¹ After all, the only difference between the menstruating cis female employee and the menstruating trans male employee would be gender identity. It is worth noting that with the Department of Justice's March 2021 conclusion that *Bostock* applies to Title IX as well, this reasoning is equally helpful for menstruating students.⁵²

The framing of menstruation-based discrimination as an actionable form of sex discrimination thus ultimately redounds to the benefit of all who menstruate. Not only does it provide an organizing principle for large-scale reform, but it also provides a road map for individual lawsuits. The precise framing of effective and inclusive menstrual advocacy will continue to evolve. Its broad outlines, though, are now discernible.

7

Menstruation, Health, and the Environment

Imagine a shopper at the grocery store. If she wants to know whether a bottle of salad dressing contains any dairy products that might aggravate her food allergies, she can consult the label. That is because federal labeling laws, enforced by the Food and Drug Administration, require nutrition labels on most food products. Next envision a shopper considering a sweater. If he wants to know whether it contains wool that itches his sensitive skin, he can consult the garment tag. Once again, federal laws require disclosure, at least about the garment's fiber content.[1] Now consider a purchaser of menstrual products who wants to know more about various tampons, pads, menstrual cups, or period underwear, in order to compare their safety. That customer is left almost entirely to guess. No laws require menstrual product manufacturers to reveal all chemicals in their products or to affirmatively demonstrate product safety.

This chapter takes up a discussion of the sustainability of menstrual products. We use "sustainability" in the broadest context, to mean safety, health, and affordability for current and future generations, as well as preservation of the environment and the planet's natural resources and systems.[2] After exploring historic and ongoing health and safety concerns surrounding menstrual products, as well as the risks they pose to the environment, we evaluate existing and possible future legal efforts to enhance menstrual-product sustainability. We address consumer disclosure laws, federally financed scientific research, public awareness, public law interventions around safety and manufacturing, and private governance initiatives that might respond effectively to a changed legal landscape in which menstrual products are commonly available in schools, jails, prisons, detention centers, public buildings, and places of employment. Robust procurement rules, in combination with other strategies, could have a powerful impact on the behavior of consumers and manufacturers. It is possible to imagine a future with menstrual products that are sustainable, in the broadest sense of the word.

Categories and Use of Menstrual Products

To frame the discussion of the health, safety, and environmental impacts of menstrual products, we start with an overview of the products themselves. Tampons and menstrual cups are worn inside the body; pads and period underwear are worn externally. Tampons may come with or without a cardboard or plastic applicator. Applicators are usually a compressible component part of the tampon's cardboard or plastic casing, allowing the user to insert the tampon into the vaginal canal without inserting one's own finger. Tampons usually can be worn for between four and six hours, depending on flow; they are removed by pulling on the string that attaches to one end of the tampon. Disposable tampons typically are made with cotton or rayon surrounded by a thin synthetic layer of polyethylene or polypropylene. Tampons marketed in the United States as being made of "organic" cotton must meet additional federal requirements applicable to all companies that describe their cotton as organic.[3]

Disposable menstrual pads are worn externally, attached to regular underwear via one or more adhesive strips. Users change their pads every four to six hours, as needed. Conventional pads typically have a polyethylene bottom layer, a permeable top layer made out of polyethylene or polypropylene, a layer of cellulose, and some sort of inner core made of undisclosed ingredients.[4] Pads marketed as "organic" usually are comprised of cellulose and cotton; as with tampon manufacturers, such pads must meet additional federal requirements.[5] There are also reusable pads made from fabric or natural fibers; they are designed to be washed after each use, which can last between four and six hours.

Menstrual cups, designed for internal use, are manually inserted into the vaginal canal. The user places the cup's open side against the cervix; the reservoir "stem" extends downwards. Menstrual cups may be worn for up to twelve hours at a time. They typically are made from rubber or silicone and may last up to ten years. Menstrual cups must be sanitized after each monthly use; users also should wash their hands before and after each handling.

Finally, period underwear is essentially like "regular" underwear, but has an additional layer designed to absorb menstrual flow. This layer may contain tiny silver particles designed to act as antibacterial agents and control odor.

According to studies from the early 2000s, in the United States, the most frequently used menstrual products are tampons and pads, with 50% to 86% of women using tampons; 62% to 73% using pads; and 75% using panty liners (smaller, thinner pads designed for days when one's flow is particularly light or to keep underwear free from vaginal discharge between periods).[6] Rates of utilization of menstrual products may differ by race or ethnic group. A study of white, Black, and Mexican American females, for example, found that product choice indeed varies: 22% of Mexican American females, 31% of Black females, and 55% of white females reported that they used tampons in the last month. Sixty-three percent of Mexican American females, 69% of Black females, and 59% of white females reported that they used pads in the same time period. (The study did not include any information about the practices of Asian Americans, Native Americans, members of other Latinx groups, or other consumers.) Survey participants were not asked about use of reusable menstrual cups or period underwear.[7]

From the perspective of market size, in 2018, US consumers spent a total of $1.04 billion on tampons, $1.76 billion on pads, and $630 million on reusable menstrual cups.[8] Consumers in the United States buy approximately 5.8 million tampons each year; the average menstruating individual will need between five thousand and fifteen thousand pads or tampons over the course of a lifetime, unless using a menstrual cup or alternative products.[9] Menstruation is big business.

Limited Federal Regulation of Menstrual Products

In the United States, responsibility for regulation of the manufacture and marketing of menstrual products rests with the Food and Drug Administration (FDA), an agency within the federal Department of Health and Human Services. Tampons were initially legally classified as "cosmetics," but they became medical devices when President Gerald Ford signed the Medical Device Amendments in 1976.[10] The FDA places all medical devices into one of three classes, depending on their use and the level of risk they pose; each successive class is subject to increasing levels of agency control.

Manufacturers of Class I medical devices (such as bed pans, examination gloves, and elastic bandages) are subject to general controls for "good manufacturing" processes; they must register themselves and their devices with the FDA, and are required to report any serious death or illness caused by a device.[11] Manufacturers of Class II devices—menstrual products, blood pressure cuffs, contact lenses, hearing aids, syringes, absorbable sutures, x-ray machines, and pregnancy test kits, for example—are subject to the same requirements as manufacturers of Class I devices. They also must meet any further "special controls" the FDA deems necessary. Those special controls may include performance standards, assurances about the device's safety, or compliance with any other guidelines or recommendations the FDA deems appropriate.[12] For manufacturers of tampons and pads, the FDA recommends, but does not require, that companies provide general information about the contents of their products. Compliance is entirely voluntary.[13] The FDA has not chosen to require manufacturers to guarantee the safety of menstrual products.

The final category, Class III medical devices, includes items like breast implants, pacemakers, and defibrillators. A Class III device is one for which the "general controls" applicable to Class I devices are insufficient "to provide reasonable assurance of the safety and effectiveness of the device," and the "special controls" applicable to Class II devices fail to "provide reasonable assurance of its safety and effectiveness."[14] Because Class III medical devices are considered higher-risk items, they generally are subject to premarket approvals.[15]

In the years immediately following the enactment of the Medical Device Act in 1976, the safety of menstrual products remained mostly off the radar of both the government and the general public. Soon after, though, menstrual-product safety took on a sense of urgency, when the deaths of several women were linked to tampon use.

Superabsorbent Tampons and Toxic Shock Syndrome

In 1975, the Procter & Gamble company began testing new, superabsorbent tampons under the brand name Rely in markets in Rochester, New York, and Fort Wayne, Indiana. After the company flooded those local markets with advertising and free samples, a writer for a local Rochester newspaper, the *Patriot*, surmised that Procter & Gamble was using area women as "guinea pigs" for a product that contained carboxymethylcellulose, a material derived from wood pulp, as well as polyurethane, a type of plastic linked to cancer. The paper ran a picture of a dissected Rely tampon, revealing chunks of carboxymethylcellulose and compressed polyurethane foam chips.[16] Carboxymethylcellulose is a hydrophilic (and thus highly absorbent) material used in products ranging from laundry detergent to ice cream.[17] In 1975, Procter & Gamble declined to answer a Rochester reporter's questions about the possibility of polyurethane from Rely tampons leaking into the human body and what consequences any leakage might have.[18]

Initially, Rely tampons were very popular with consumers. By 1980, an estimated 25% of all tampon users were using the Rely brand. Procter & Gamble competitors began to develop their own versions of tampons made of highly absorbent materials, all containing synthetic elements.[19] Superabsorbent tampons soon became national news, but not for the reasons that the companies hoped they would.

Researchers had first reported a condition they called "toxic shock syndrome" in 1978. A group of seven children ages eight to seventeen all presented with high fever, headaches, vomiting, skin rashes, and peeling of the skin on hands and feet.[20] Five of those patients were found to carry a particular strain of *Staphylococcus aureus* bacteria. In July 1980, the Centers for Disease Control and Prevention (CDC) issued a report linking a potentially fatal form of toxic shock syndrome (TSS) with tampon use, even though the mechanisms of infection were not well understood at the time.[21] Procter & Gamble took Rely tampons off the market in September 1980.[22]

In 1980, the CDC received reports of over eight hundred cases of menstruation-related TSS;[23] these represented approximately 91% of all TSS cases in the country[24] and an infection rate of approximately 8.9 per one hundred thousand menstruating-age women.[25] That year, thirty-eight women died from menstruation-related TSS.[26] By March 1982, the company was facing over four hundred lawsuits related to illnesses or deaths of users of Rely tampons.[27] Although menstruation-related TSS rates declined after the withdrawal of Rely tampons from the market, there were still 2,021 menstruation-related TSS cases and ninety-five fatalities during the period 1981 to 1986.[28] As of 2013, researchers reported that the overall number of TSS cases in the United States had been relatively stable for approximately ten years, occurring at a rate of

0.3 to 0.5 cases per 100,000 people (not just those in a certain age range who regularly menstruate).[29] Menstruation-related cases represented approximately half of those.[30]

Ineffective Federal Tampon-Safety and Disclosure Rules

Despite the CDC's report in 1980 and the evidence that otherwise healthy women were dying from tampon use, the FDA took no action with respect to tampons until two years later. When the agency finally did act, its response was anemic. In 1982, the agency implemented rules requiring manufacturers to affix to their products a caution that consumers should select the lowest-absorbency tampons needed. To be sure, the warning labels were effective, at least in part; scientists attribute a decline in menstruation-related toxic shock syndrome to these new labeling requirements, among other factors such as increased consumer awareness of the risk of TSS.[31] In 1988, the FDA issued proposed rules to make absorbency terms consistent industry-wide, so that words like "regular" or "super" would have the same meaning across brands.[32] After receiving hundreds of comments, the FDA issued different proposed rules in 1989,[33] hastened in no small part by a lawsuit from the Public Citizen Health Research Group. This consumer-advocacy organization, cofounded by Ralph Nader in the 1970s, had been pressing the FDA for more accurate labeling since as early as 1982.[34] In 1990, the labeling laws finally took effect; again, researchers credit these labeling rules with leading to "a substantial reduction in the risk" for toxic shock syndrome.[35] However, at no time during the TSS crisis or afterwards did the FDA take any steps to require menstrual-product manufacturers to disclose the contents of their products or make assurances about their safety.

In 1997, United States representative Carolyn Maloney (D-NY) first introduced into Congress the Tampon Safety and Research Act. The act sought to provide funding for independent research into the health risks associated with the presence of certain chemicals, including dioxins, in menstrual products, and to require manufacturers to submit their own research to the FDA.[36] Although Representative Maloney has introduced some form of the proposed legislation in several successive Congresses—most recently in 2019—none of the bills has ever advanced. In 2017, Representative Grace Meng (D-NY) first introduced into the Congress the Menstrual Products Right to Know Act, a bill that would require all manufacturers of menstrual products to list the names of each ingredient or component on product packaging.[37] This bill, too, has been repeatedly introduced without advancing.

The Mystery of Menstrual Products' Contents

Given the lack of federal regulations or laws requiring disclosure of the contents of menstrual products or assurances of their safety, scientific researchers—along with nonprofit and advocacy groups—have repeatedly raised questions about actual or potential toxicants in menstrual products. But there has been limited federal research, most of it decades old, about the contents of menstrual products. More contemporary research from nongovernment sources suggests that many of the common menstrual products that millions of people use regularly for several days every month for multiple years may, in fact, contain chemicals with harmful or unknown long-term effects on human health.

In 1992, the United States House of Representatives Committee on Government Operations issued a staff report asserting that the FDA had failed to investigate the presence in tampons of dioxins, which are chemical by-products from the chlorine bleaching of paper products, as well as menstrual products.[38] In 1994, the Environmental Protection Agency (EPA) called dioxins a "probable carcinogen." Although there is conflicting scientific information about whether dioxins are linked to an increased risk of endometriosis,[39] the EPA did warn that dioxin exposure was linked to other negative health effects, such as a suppressed immune system, decreased fertility, increased risk of pelvic inflammatory disease, and possible problems with fetal development.[40] There is further research that suggests that "average background levels [of dioxins] may lead to non-cancer health effects, including developmental delays, birth defects, hormone disruption and immune cell suppression. With repeat exposure, such as the use of tampons, the toxin accumulates and is stored in humans, especially in women's body fat and in breast milk."[41] To this day, there is no public evidence that the FDA has ever investigated the danger of dioxins in menstrual products, although the FDA website states (without supporting research) that today's tampons are manufactured without using elemental chlorine in the bleaching process, which "prevents products from having dangerous levels of dioxin."[42]

Bleaching methods have changed since 1992, at least in part because of consumer activism.[43] Nevertheless, there are studies that suggest that several brands of tampons and pads currently on the market contain other toxic chemicals in their cotton or rayon component parts.[44] Nanosilver is one chemical of possible concern that may be present in some disposable pads[45] as well as some period underwear.[46] Nanosilver is commonly used as an odor reducer in athletic clothing; it has been shown in animal studies to be toxic to epithelial cells in the vagina and to enter the bloodstream after exposure to vaginal tissue.[47] Another concern is the fragrance added to some menstrual products. As early as 1979, a study conducted in the United States linked perineal rashes to a chemical used in scented menstrual pads.[48] In 1996, a study published in the *Canadian Medical Association Journal* linked significant vulvar irritations to the use of Always brand pads in particular.[49] A 2007 study from Australia identified methyldibromo glutaronitrile, a substance used in the adhesive material of menstrual pads, as the cause of dermatitis in some users.[50]

In 2017, researchers at the University of Illinois at Urbana-Champaign undertook broad-based testing of multiple brands of menstrual pads and diapers obtained from six different countries.[51] The tests revealed that a majority of the samples contained both volatile organic compounds—known to cause burning of the skin, disruption of endocrine levels, and defects in fetal development—as well as phthalate concentrations, associated with endocrine disruption and reduced fertility.[52] A 2018 study conducted in Hungary confirmed multiple earlier studies' findings of the presence in menstrual products of phtalic acid esters—potentially the cause of reproductive harm and neurological damage—as well as the presence of tributyl phosphate, a known neutrotoxicant and skin irritant. The researchers noted that these detected compounds "could be hazardous or irritating being in direct contact with skin and the mucous membrane for over a period of time."[53]

In addition to the FDA's previously mentioned nonbinding recommendations that manufacturers disclose the contents of menstrual products, the agency also recommends (but does not require) "that tampons be free of 2,3,7,8-tetrachlorodibenzo-p-dioxin (TCDD)/2,3,7,8-tetrachlorofuran dioxin (TCDF) and any pesticide and herbicide residues."[54] But research by the consumer advocacy group Women's Voices for the Earth suggests that manufacturers do not necessarily follow those recommendations. A 2013 study found that one brand of tampons contained low levels of the pesticides malaoxon and malathion, dichlofluanid, mecarbam, procymidone, methidathion, fesulfothion, pyrethrum, and piperonyl butoxide—substances known to be carcinogens, neurotoxicants, or otherwise harmful to human reproduction.[55] The detected levels were below those permissible for food, but certainly do not comport with the FDA's recommendation for pesticide-free tampons.[56] In the same study, Procter & Gamble's Always pads were found to contain detectable levels of chloroform, chlorethane, and styrene. Styrene is classified by the World Health Organization as a carcinogen.[57] The presence of all of these chemicals is cause for concern at any level, because membranes in the vagina and vulva can absorb chemicals more quickly than other parts of the body. Thus it is difficult to compare the rates of exposure from ingested food or drink to exposure through products that are used in the vagina or genital area.[58]

In addition to concerns about the health and safety of tampons and pads, so-called alternative products are not without risks either, as indicated above in the case of period underwear containing nanosilver. In the case of menstrual cups, because these typically can be left in place much longer than tampons, they may foster the growth of dangerous bacteria. In 2015, researchers reported a confirmed case of toxic shock syndrome in a woman who had been using a menstrual cup.[59] Furthermore, there is evidence to suggest that menstrual cups are not necessarily safer than tampons in terms of growth of the *Staphylococcus aureus* bacteria and production of the associated toxic shock syndrome toxin 1 (sometimes referred to as TSST-1), but further research is necessary.[60] Consumers, activists, and scientists thus have begun sounding the alarm again about the connection between menstrual products and toxic shock syndrome.

Similarly, many consumers have heralded menstrual underwear as a welcome alternative to pads and tampons, but in early 2020, researchers found that the period underwear Thinx contained high levels of PFAS—a diverse group of perfluoroalkyl and polyfluoroalkyl substances used in most nonstick and stain-resistant products. Some PFAS compounds are no longer produced in the United States or Europe because of deleterious health effects.[61] PFAS compounds have been linked to cancer, liver damage, disruptions to the immune system, thyroid disease, dyslipidemia, pregnancy-induced hypertension, and reduced fertility.[62] In 2020, the Environmental Protection Agency issued rules under the Toxic Substance Control Act that require prior EPA review and approval for the use of certain "long-chain" PFAS.[63] A 2021 study of human breast milk samples from women in the United States found PFAS at levels ranging from fifty parts per trillion to greater than 1,850 parts per trillion; the US Department of Health and Human Services recommends that drinking water have no more than fourteen parts per trillion.[64] Thinx disputed the finding that the company's underwear contained PFAS and published on the company's website results of its own testing showing the absence of these chemicals.[65] But critics point to contradictory studies and the fact that Thinx's patent application itself acknowledges that the company's products "may be treated with . . . polyfluoroalklylacrylates," fluoropolymers that can potentially give off PFAS over time.[66] The Royal Australian and New Zealand College of Obstetricians and Gynaecologists has raised further concerns about "increasing the potential risk of infection" from use of period underwear, due to continuous contact between the genital area and blood-soaked material.[67]

Somewhat ironically, had menstrual products retained their pre-1976 classification as cosmetics, manufacturers would have been required to disclose the products' contents under the Fair Packaging and Labeling Act.[68] A quick check of an eyeshadow palette or face powder compact reveals more about the chemicals applied to one's face than the consumer can learn about chemicals placed inside one's body via a tampon. That said, some scientists assert that menstrual products still present far less of a risk of exposure to dioxins than food consumed on an everyday basis. Due to long-term effects of pollution, food may contain far more dioxins than any tampon or pad does.[69] Even so, the lack of information stands in the way of meaningful reform.

Consumer Backlash in South Korea and Kenya over Health Problems Caused by Menstrual Products

In 2017, thousands of South Korean women began reporting adverse effects from using the Lilian brand of menstrual pads manufactured by the Korean company Klean Nara; consumers reported rashes, cramps, and disruptions to their menstrual cycles.[70] South Korean women took to online "mom cafes"—internet meeting sites for women—to share their experiences using Lilian pads and to mobilize against the company. Because of the negative publicity generated in the press and organized consumer pressure, the manufacturer pulled the pads from the market.[71]

Around the same time, the Korean government launched a formal investigation into multiple menstrual products available in that country. Shortly thereafter, the South Korean Ministry of Food and Drug Safety announced that in over six hundred menstrual products tested, the detected levels of volatile organic compounds were sufficiently low as to pose no health risks to consumers.[72] A women's health advocacy group countered that the government's inspections were incomplete because the government had not tested for other potentially harmful chemicals. Echoing the need for more testing, South Korean actress Joo-young Lee revealed in the press that she had been "taken to the hospital emergency twice this year alone due to severe cramps after having used the Lilian sanitary pad for more than a year." She added, "I cannot trust the government's ostrich belief."[73]

On behalf of tens of thousands of women who claimed they had been harmed by the Lilian pads, attorneys filed a class-action suit against Klean Nara, requesting damages of $7.97 million (USD).[74] The plaintiffs lost at trial after the court found that there was insufficient evidence that Klean Nara could foresee any harm to human health by the chemicals used in their Lilian pads.[75] Regardless of the findings of any governmental agency or court, though, ample scientific studies discussed earlier in this chapter provide evidence to support what South Korean consumers already knew first-hand: not all menstrual products are necessarily safe to use.

A similar consumer backlash occurred in Kenya in 2019. Procter & Gamble, the company that was behind the Rely tampons of the 1970s and 1980s, also manufactures the Always brand pads. This is the same brand of pads that previous research had linked to vulvar irritations in 1996.[76] Kenyan users of these pads seized upon the company's #MyAlwaysExperience social media campaign to report widespread itches, rashes, and burning from using the products. Always is a market-dominant brand in Kenya, accounting for approximately 65% of the commercial products used there. As of mid-2019, the top layer of the pads that were sold in Kenya appeared to be different from the same layer of pads sold to customers in the United States or Europe. Activists and consumers in Kenya raised concerns that the polyethelene film used as a "top sheet" on the menstrual pads sold in Kenya might be responsible for the complaints about itching and burning.

Procter & Gamble denied that the company's products could cause irritations, dermatitis, or rashes in their Kenyan customers. But after the social media outcry, the company agreed to begin marketing higher-quality products in Kenya in the future.[77] As with South Korea, the Kenya example shows that once health concerns associated with menstrual products become visible (i.e., rashes and other negative side effects), consumers can and do mobilize to demand change. Indeed, both South Korean and Kenyan women did so especially effectively using the power of the internet and social media.

What explains the lack of attention to the safety of menstrual products, even as progress on menstrual equity is being achieved in other areas? Lack of salience likely plays a large role. In other menstruation-related contexts, injustices are plainly visible. When menstruating students or prisoners bleed through their clothes, the stains vividly demonstrate the need for menstrual products. Similarly, the tampon tax appears right on store receipts for people to see. And those issues have clear, straightforward solutions, such as providing free menstrual products to vulnerable populations and eliminating the tampon tax. But questions about the contents and safety of menstrual products—like those products themselves—tend to fall into the "out of sight, out of mind" category for most consumers, advocacy groups, and lawmakers, at least until consumers start reporting visible health problems. Legal scholar Claudia Polsky has also explained that, broadly speaking, governmental regulation of the chemicals in consumer items tends to focus less on "articles," meaning tangible objects people use (such as couches, guitars, or tampons, for example) than on "formulations," meaning consumer products that get dissipated with use (like bug spray or floor cleaner).[78] Even so, the silence, lack of interest, and even apathy about the potential risks associated with use of menstrual products should also be understood as connected to the longstanding cultural attitudes, explored in detail in chapter 1, that treat menstruation as not a topic for public conversation, let alone scientific inquiry.

The Planetary Cost of Menstrual Waste

Related to concerns about the human health consequences and safety of menstrual products is the "cost" of these products from an environmental perspective. Here, the discussion of the cost of menstrual products moves beyond the literal. Sales of tampons and pads in the United States are close to $3 billion each year,[79] but a complete discussion of the "cost" of menstrual products must also take into account their associated waste and contributions to the degradation of the environment.

Shortly after the introduction of commercially available disposable menstrual pads in 1921 and the filing of the first patent for a tampon with an applicator in 1933, US consumers became hooked on disposable menstrual products.[80] Bulky pads and tampons ultimately evolved into individually wrapped products with sleek, low-profile designs. These easily transportable and disposable products are appealing to both consumers and manufacturers alike: consumers like the convenience,[81] and manufacturers like the profit margins.[82]

Unfortunately, most conventional tampons and pads tend to rely heavily on plastic—in wrappers, applicators, strings, polypropelene base layers, polyester fibers, adhesive "wings," and packaging. Most of that nondegradable plastic ends up in landfills or waterways. Conventional pads may take between five hundred and eight hundred years to biodegrade.[83] In the case of conventional tampons, even if the cotton itself might break down in approximately six months, the interior plastic used in the tampon body may never break down.[84] (The fact that many conventional tampons can contain interior plastic is not well known, even among consumers who otherwise demonstrate a high level of awareness of the environmental impact of menstrual products.)[85] In part because microorganisms cannot recognize polyethylene as food, a large portion of menstrual products, their plastic wrappers, and plastic applicators cannot biodegrade.[86] While organic cotton tampons with cardboard applicators may seem like the more ecologically friendly choice, cardboard with menstrual blood cannot be recycled, either.[87]

A 2020 study of OECD countries estimates that menstrual products represent between 0.3% and 0.8% of municipal waste by weight in Europe and North America, and 1% or more by weight in Bolivia, Cuba, El Salvador, Guatemala, Guyana, Haiti, Honduras, and Suriname.[88] The problem of menstrual products in landfills is not limited to one country; it is a global concern.

In addition to contributing to landfill waste, plastic tampon applicators are a persistent and visible source of waste in rivers and oceans. In 2017, UK beach clean-up participants found plastic applicators from tampons at a rate of nine per kilometer.[89] In the United States, the Ocean Conservancy, a nonprofit environmental advocacy group, has been sponsoring an International Coastal Cleanup since 1986. Participants in one of the group's recent projects collected twenty thousand tampon applicators from beaches.[90] These applicators threaten wildlife because animals like seabirds, sea turtles, and seals can ingest plastic, causing starvation and death.[91]

Disposal of menstrual products also may create problems for residential plumbing and for municipal wastewater facilities. In the United States, the majority of tampons are flushed down the toilet or thrown into the trash; even sophisticated consumers may not know that tampons should not be flushed.[92] Flushed tampons can cause pipe blockages in homes or sewers, and even larger problems for wastewater treatment systems, as discussed in greater detail in chapter 9. In major metropolitan areas all over the world, municipalities spend millions of dollars each year to remove nonbiodegradable material, including wet wipes and menstrual products. Sydney, Australia, recently spent an estimated $8 million on removing flushed debris from its water system. In the United States, the National Association of Clean Water Agencies launched a "Toilets Are Not Trashcans" campaign designed to raise consumer awareness of which material cannot be flushed.[93] In the UK, consumers flush an estimated two billion menstrual products in toilets each year.[94] When menstrual products and other items damage wastewater treatment infrastructures, untreated sewage and solid materials get released into streams, rivers, lakes, and sources of drinking water.

To shift consumer behavior toward menstrual products that are less environmentally harmful, better education and information are key. Researchers at Anglia Ruskin University asked focus-group participants what single step might reduce the negative environmental effects of menstrual products. Study participants favored school-based education about available menstrual products (23.4%) and clearer information about product disposal (21.4%). Providing more detailed labeling information about products' content was another popular choice (19.4%), as well as some sort of government stamp (17.2%) or universal environmental rating for products (16.4%). Presumably any intercompany ratings would be controversial and subject to political and other pressures.[95] But the study does suggest the possibility of changing the behavior of consumers.

There is at least an embryonic movement toward more reusable or natural products. One UK company called Dame makes a reusable tampon applicator that, if widely adopted, could mitigate the problems associated with both plastic applicators and the inability to compost cardboard ones that have any menstrual blood.[96] There are also tampons and pads made entirely of organic cotton, tampons without plastic applicators, reusable pads, and reusable menstrual cups. For some users, the level of laundering or cleaning required by reusable products, their higher initial cost, and/or their perceived inconvenience may make these options less desirable or practical. Absent a significant change in consumer behavior, though, vast amounts of environmental waste from menstrual products will persist.

The Planetary Costs of Menstrual-Product Production

In the manufacture of menstrual products, one significant environmental concern is the chemical processing of the "filling" material used in tampons and pads. Cotton, rayon, or a combination of the two are the main components of these products. The cotton goes through a chemical-intensive process involving sodium hydroxide, either bleach or hydrogen peroxide, and lubricants. Rayon is a synthetic fiber that is less expensive than cotton. To make rayon, wood pulp or residue cotton fibers are steeped in caustic soda, dried, and churned with liquid carbon disulfide to create sodium cellulose xanthate, which is again bathed in caustic soda and then stored. That viscose solution is made into fiber strings and then spun into yarn.[97] Dioxins are byproducts of the process of converting the raw materials into rayon; as described above, dioxins have been identified by the Environmental Protection Agency as probable carcinogens.[98]

Among the significant by-products of making conventional tampons and pads, as well as many other consumer products, are fossil fuel emissions associated with plastic production. Low-density polyethylene, a thermoplastic made from ethylene, is the nonbiodegradable material that goes into tampon applicators and menstrual pad top layers, base layers, and wings. Its manufacture is energy-intensive and leads to substantial carbon emissions.[99] Tampon applicators may contain polypropylene, a type of plastic also used in candy wrappers.[100] One researcher estimates that the average disposable tampon or pad has a carbon footprint of 5.3 kg CO2 equivalents, whereas the silicone used in a reusable menstrual cup requires approximately 2.71 kg CO2 equivalents.[101] According to the Royal Institute of Technology in Stockholm, the creation of the low-density polyethylene components of tampon applicators and the base layer of a pad requires a greater amount of fossil fuel energy than does the making of the cotton or rayon components.[102]

To date, there has been no comprehensive study of the environmental impacts of disposable tampons and menstrual pads. Such a study would also need to take into account ecotoxicity, acidification, eutrophication, and depletion of mineral and fossil resources.[103] The precise environmental harms of menstrual products are not well studied or documented, but eliminating or even reducing the amount of plastic used in menstrual products would address one particular source of waste and fossil-fuel consumption. To be sure, there are many other consumer goods that produce even more waste and use the same (or a greater) amount of fossil fuels and other natural resources in production. Nevertheless, a robust vision for a future with sustainable menstrual products should account for the full range of their environmental harms.

Achieving Sustainability through Law

The discussion so far has revealed many obstacles to making menstrual products sustainable. The challenges include lack of disclosure rules about menstrual products' contents, concerns about harmful chemical in menstrual products and their deleterious effects on human health, lack of federal research about the contents or safety of menstrual products, the absence of administrative mechanisms to guarantee product safety, and environmental waste and degradation caused by both the disposal and the manufacture of menstrual products. How, then, might the law be effective in addressing these issues? Through a combination of targeted public action, disclosure and warning laws, more active administrative regulation, strategic public procurement policies, and actions by private-sector associations, the future of menstrual products could be made much more sustainable.

Targeted Public Interventions into Manufacturer and Consumer Behavior

One legal strategy for increasing the sustainability of menstrual products would be reducing the amount of plastic associated with them, given the amount of menstrual waste that ends up in landfills and waterways. This could be accomplished through bans on menstrual products with any plastic parts, or at least on plastic wrappers or plastic packaging. Bans on single-use plastics like shopping bags or straws have begun to enter popular public consciousness in recent years. In 2019, the United Nations unsuccessfully tried to adopt a legally binding agreement to phase out single-use plastics worldwide, but the effort was defeated largely due to objections from the United States.[104] Within their own borders, countries have adopted different approaches to the problem of plastics. Bangladesh and the Marshall Islands, for example, have an absolute ban on single-use plastic bags; Ecuador and Guyana regulate their disposal; France, India, Italy, and Madagascar ban or tax certain plastic bags (those thinner than 50 microns).[105]

In the United States, in the absence of federal limitations on single-use plastic products, some state and local governments have stepped into the void. California, Connecticut, Delaware, Hawaii, New York, Oregon, and Vermont ban plastic bags; the District of Columbia imposes a tax on carryout paper and plastic bags. Individual cities including Boston, Chicago, Los Angeles, and San Francisco all ban plastic bags.[106] Practically speaking, a city can adopt such a ban, unless the state has enacted a preemptive state law, as Arizona did with respect to plastic-bag bans.[107] In other places, some companies voluntarily have reduced their customers' use of single-use plastics.[108]

Recently, Mexico City took the drastic step of banning the sales of all tampons with plastic applicators until more "environmentally friendly" tampons become available, without knowing or informing consumers when that might be. The move attracted international attention because tampons without applicators are not ordinarily sold in Mexico City, so consumers' choices became more limited.[109] A spokeswoman for one menstruation-related NGO in Mexico City, Anahí Rodríguez, critiqued the government for its sudden and drastic action, while recognizing the environmental value in reducing plastic use. "It's the government's responsibility to take steps to protect the environment. But they should have made sure there were tampons available with applicators that used an alternative to plastic, at an accessible price, before they withdrew them," she said.[110]

In linking the plastic in tampons and other products to environmental issues, Rodríguez made a connection that may not be obvious to many people. There are no commercials or advertisements showing marine life hobbled by tampon applicators, akin to images of birds with soda six-pack plastic rings yoked around their necks, or dolphins with fins impaired by plastic bags. The absence of these types of public service ads and visual reminders, combined with likely low levels of consumer awareness of environmental waste associated with disposable menstrual products generally, contribute to the lack of momentum for a popular movement for plastic-free menstrual products. The absence of vivid public relations campaigns—or even notice in the case of the Mexico City ban on tampons with plastic applicators—is, once again, rooted in the general cultural silence about menstruation. With greater awareness, however, customers and legislators might become more open to such approaches.

Disclosure, Consumer Activism, and Partially Effective State Laws

Another key step toward a future with more sustainable menstrual products is improving disclosure about their contents. Because the FDA merely recommends, but does not require, that menstrual-product manufacturers disclose the contents of their products, some consumer-advocacy groups have engaged in traditional protest methods, along with "naming and shaming" techniques to obtain information. For example, in 2015, Women's Voices for the Earth organized a group of protestors to gather outside Procter & Gamble's Cincinnati headquarters during the annual shareholder meeting, armed with a petition signed by approximately thirty-five thousand people demanding disclosure of product content as well as the elimination of certain chemicals from menstrual products. The protestors previously had released a spoof video on the internet to pressure the company into complying with its demands.

When Procter & Gamble finally relented and posted on its website a list of ingredients in its Tampax brand tampons, it did so using vague terms such as "plant-based plastic applicator," the meaning of which is unclear.[111] The company does not report what chemicals any of the listed ingredients contain. According to FDA spokesperson Deborah Kotz, tampons are subject to some FDA checks for safety and absorbency, but manufacturers have no affirmative obligation to demonstrate the safety of their products over time. Industry representatives do claim that their products are safe, but no company has published any long-term studies in support.[112]

In the absence of federal legislation, attention has turned to state legislatures as possible sources of stronger consumer disclosure laws for menstrual products. In New York, for example, in 2016—shortly after introducing into the New York legislature the bill that eventually led to the repeal of the tampon tax[113]—Assemblymember Linda Rosenthal introduced a bill that would require all packages of tampons in the state to carry a "plain and conspicuous printed list of all ingredients with percentages of the components of the tampon and the applicator." The penalty for failing to comply with the labeling requirements was set at one thousand dollars per package or box.[114] Both that bill and a more comprehensive version introduced in the next legislative session never advanced out of committee.

By the time Assemblymember Rosenthal introduced the legislation for a third time in 2019, the bill had been watered down to require disclosure only of those ingredients "intentionally added" to menstrual products (as opposed to all ingredients). It is unclear precisely what role industry played in modifying earlier versions of the bill. This third version was signed into law by Governor Andrew Cuomo on October 11, 2019.[115] It essentially absolved manufacturers of any requirement to disclose the chemical contents of their tampons, pads, and menstrual cups, as long as the manufacturers themselves had not added chemicals to the raw materials. This change took most of the "teeth" out of the New York bill as an effective consumer disclosure law. Studies by Women's Voices for the Earth, for example, have shown that the dangerous ingredients in menstrual products are not necessarily those intentionally introduced during the fabrication process but rather those found in the materials that make up the product components.[116]

After the bill's passage, Assemblymember Rosenthal announced, "Now that my bill to require menstrual product ingredient disclosure on packaging has become law, every single New Yorker who uses tampons and pads will know exactly what's in the products they use in and on some of the most sensitive parts of their bodies for 24 hours a day, seven days a week . . . [approximately every month, every year] for as many as 40 years."[117] But this is not accurate; consumers receive some, but not complete, information. Similarly, Women's Voices for the Earth—as well as menstrual-product manufacturers like Seventh Generation, DivaCup, Nataracare, and Lola that emphasize the "eco-friendly" nature of their products—declared the passage of the New York legislation as a great victory for transparency in labeling and menstrual health generally, without mentioning the major flaws in the bill.[118]

In 2020, California passed the California Menstrual Products Right to Know Act. This law requires a "plain and conspicuous list of all ingredients" in menstrual products, but with this law, too, there are major loopholes.[119] An "ingredient" is defined as a "fragrance ingredient or other intentionally added substance or combination of substances present in the menstrual product, unless the intentionally added substance or combination of substances is confidential business information," in which case the manufacturer's disclosure obligations are limited to the ingredient's "common name."[120] The bill also provides a safe harbor for added fragrances, requiring disclosure only to the extent that added levels exceed a concentration level of ten parts per million.[121] Thus the California bill is even weaker than the New York bill: manufacturers must disclose only those ingredients that they add to the menstrual products, and even then, they can limit their disclosure by claiming the existence of "confidential business information." Furthermore, the safe harbor rules for fragrances are problematic; scented tampons that fall under safe harbor levels may alter the pH levels of the vagina and increase the risk for yeast infection and bacterial vaginosis.[122] Women's Voices for the Earth had originally supported the bill,[123] but came to publicly oppose the final version that became law, saying that "keeping ingredient secrets, especially in products that come into such intimate contact with the body, is simply not acceptable."[124]

Despite the limitations of the New York and California menstrual-product-disclosure laws, they do represent some progress in the larger effort for greater transparency. Groups like Women's Voices for the Earth, for example, typically have on staff well-informed consumer advocates with the necessary scientific expertise to translate for the general public any information that manufacturers do reveal. In this way, the laws may become useful tools in the hands of intermediary advocacy groups that have the expertise to interpret and publicize the information that is disclosed.

To a certain extent, California's existing consumer warning law known as Proposition 65 might serve as a useful model for modifications to the existing New York or California menstrual-product-disclosure laws, or even future menstrual-product-disclosure laws in other states.[125] California's Safe Drinking Water and Toxic Enforcement Act of 1986, more commonly known as "Proposition 65," is the most rigorous consumer warning law in the country. It seeks to prevent the discharge of certain harmful chemicals into the state's drinking water sources and to increase public awareness of exposure to toxic chemicals. Proposition 65 provides that businesses with ten or more employees shall not "knowingly and intentionally expose anyone to chemicals that are known to the state to cause cancer or birth defects or other reproductive harm" without first giving "a clear and reasonable warning," subject to limited exceptions.[126] The state maintains a list of more than nine hundred chemicals that trigger the obligation to give "clear and reasonable" warnings, to the extent that any listed chemical exceeds the applicable safe harbor level.[127] In other words, when exposure is at or below the "No Significant

Risk Level" for carcinogens or the "Maximum Allowable Dose Level" for chemicals linked to reproductive harms (including birth defects), no warning is required. There are safe harbor levels for approximately one-third of all of the chemicals on the state list.[128]

Significantly, Proposition 65 gives enforcement authority to both public and private actors. Compliance with Proposition 65 may be enforced by the state attorney general, any district attorney, city attorneys of cities with populations over a certain level, and city prosecutors with the consent of the district attorney. Citizens also have a private right of enforcement, meaning that individuals or groups can sue to force businesses to comply with the law.[129] By statute, successful plaintiffs may obtain attorneys' fees as well as penalties in Proposition 65 cases, and thus have financial incentives to bring litigation.[130] In the best cases, this means that citizens do not have to rely on government actors to enforce state law. Through actual litigation or threat of litigation, consumers may affect the behavior of manufacturers and other businesses in ways that benefit the larger public. On the other hand, Claudia Polsky and Megan Schwarzman point to an unintended consequence of the attorneys' fees and violations awards under Proposition 65:

> [L]itigators with little toxics expertise and unaffiliated with any environmental nonprofit group bring Prop 65 actions over comparatively health-trivial violations, [and] the pecuniary motive often appears to dominate. In the low-nuance contexts of litigation and stakeholder politics, the defense bar and the law's critics thus often use the pejorative term "bounty hunter" to stigmatize all private Prop 65 enforcers.[131]

The experiences in New York and California suggest that comprehensive menstrual-product-disclosure laws may be difficult to pass, as a political matter. Nevertheless, given the lessons from Proposition 65, any future menstrual-product-disclosure laws should be expanded to include private rights of enforcement, as well as provisions for recovery of attorneys' fees and penalties, so enforcement does not rest solely with the government. That said, fees and penalties should be available only in the discretion of the court and should be reasonably related to the quantum of public benefit achieved through litigation.[132]

State Law Disclosure Rules Meet Public Procurement Laws

Public procurement laws are another way of enhancing consumer disclosure and moving toward greater menstrual-product sustainability. In an analogous context, the New York State Green Cleaning Law provides a powerful example. Adopted in 2005, this law requires all elementary and secondary schools to use "environmentally sensitive cleaning and maintenance products," meaning those that "minimize adverse impacts on children's health and the environment," in accordance with guidelines promulgated by the State Commissioner of General Services.[133] Schools must comply with these guidelines in purchasing cleaning and maintenance products.[134] To facilitate compliance, the Environmental Services Unit of the State Office of General Services maintains on its webpage an "Approved Green Cleaning Products Listing," which, by statute, is a "sample list," arguably leaving room for schools to go outside it.[135] The items listed range from general cleaning products to hand soap, carpet cleaners, floor finishes, and floor finish strippers to vacuum cleaners.[136] By executive order, the law was suspended in 2019 to allow schools to respond to the COVID-19 pandemic with specialized cleaning and disinfectant products, but even during the suspension, schools were limited to using products registered with both the Environmental Protection Agency and the New York State Department of Environmental Conservation as effective against the coronavirus.[137]

Procurement laws can powerfully affect the targeted sector by providing strong incentives for businesses to comply with the state's guidelines, in order to capture a portion of the lucrative state business.[138] As a practical matter, procurement laws operate most efficiently when they are clear and unambiguous. In the case of the New York State Green Cleaning Law, the approved listing contains named brands, not ingredients. A menstrual-products procurement law could take a similar approach, to the extent that there are existing products that meet the desired criteria. An effective and inclusive procurement policy also would have clear benchmarks that other menstrual products would need to meet before they could be added to the "approved" list.

Note that in both New York and California, the two states that already have limited menstrual-product-disclosure laws, some or all public schools are required to make menstrual products available for free to students, as discussed in chapter 3. The same is true in numerous other states that do not yet have menstrual-product-disclosure laws. Furthermore, states and cities throughout the country have enacted or are considering laws that would make menstrual products freely available in prisons, detention facilities, and public buildings, as discussed in chapter 4. At the federal level, if the Menstrual Equity for All Act of 2019 were to become law at some point in the future, then free menstrual products would become available to employees at businesses with more than one hundred employees and in all public federal buildings.[139] Cities, states, the federal government, and even private employers are thus poised to become major purchasers of menstrual products. Many manufacturers will be eager to capture a share of that market.

Whether at the city, state, federal, or even corporate level, adopting menstrual-product-procurement rules akin to the New York State Green Cleaning Law could have a significant impact. A "Sustainable Menstrual Products Procurement Policy" should require that any products placed in schools, jails, prisons, detention centers, public buildings, or places of employment meet criteria that cluster in four distinct areas: (1) contents; (2) disclosure; (3) safety; and (4) carbon footprint. The following is a broad sketch of such a policy.

First, a Sustainable Menstrual Products Procurement Policy could limit permissible products to reusable pads, menstrual cups, or organic cotton tampons or pads without plastic parts or plastic wrappers. Second, as Laura Strausfeld, one of the cofounders of Period Equity, has envisioned, effective procurement rules should require menstrual-product manufacturers to disclose all ingredients and warn about any known toxicants. She also would require approved menstrual products to have been tested for safety.[140] Third, and relatedly, a Sustainable Menstrual Product Procurement Policy could require menstrual-product companies to use only those ingredients contained on an "approved" list of products and to actively demonstrate that their products do not contain any chemicals on the "unapproved" list. In order to verify representations made by manufacturers, the government could fund half of the cost of an independent testing program; menstrual product companies, in proportion to their market share, could fund the remainder. The testing program should be augmented by a research program, modeled after Representative Maloney's proposed Tampon Safety and Research Act;[141]

Strausfeld and others have argued persuasively for the importance of independent research in achieving menstrual-product safety.[142] Fourth, a Sustainable Menstrual Product Procurement Policy could require manufacturers to demonstrate at specified intervals that they are continuing to reduce the overall carbon footprint of their products.

Procurement policies have the power to influence not only menstrual-product companies but consumers as well. If organic pads and tampons without plastic wrappers or plastics parts are the only ones that are available in schools and other public buildings, for example, users will become accustomed to those products. Consumers also will receive the implicit message that these products are what psychologist Robert Cialdini and others have called the "descriptive norm,"[143] and then seek these same (or similar) products out when making personal purchases. The ability of procurement laws to transform the menstrual-product market should not be underestimated.[144]

Private Governance for Sustainable Menstrual Products

Apart from—or in addition to—any official Sustainable Menstrual Procurement Policy adopted by cities, states, the federal government, or private employers, menstrual-product manufacturers might be able to attract both socially minded consumers and investors by committing to a voluntary set of standards or practices for product ingredient composition and disclosure, safety testing, and environmentally sensitive manufacturing and distribution processes. These voluntary standards might include compliance with some or all of those set forth in the Sustainable Menstrual Product Procurement Policy described above. In chapter 8, we discuss the "halo effect" that certain companies seek by adopting female-empowerment-oriented advertising and in seeking B-corporation status. Voluntary compliance with industry-specific business practices aimed at creating sustainable menstrual products, if certified by an outside entity, could send similar or even stronger messages. With a push from consumer-advocacy organizations, consumers might begin to seek out the equivalent of a "seal of approval" on packages of menstrual products, indicating that the products meet certain sustainability criteria. This type of voluntary compliance also may attract investors driven by environmental, social, and governance (ESG) concerns; the ESG investment orientation is becoming increasingly significant in the marketplace, in terms of overall amounts invested.[145]

Another private-governance initiative that would help accelerate a shift to sustainable menstrual products would be a voluntary agreement by one or more large retailers, for example, to stock only those menstrual products that meet stated standards for health, safety, and the environment. While a complete analysis is beyond the scope of this project, imagine if major retailers like Walmart, Target, and CVS agreed that they would carry only those menstrual products that met the standards described in the Sustainable Menstrual Products Procurement Policy, even if there were no official law requiring them to do so. Private governance can play an important role in changing the way menstrual products are manufactured and consumed.

In combination with consumer education, both public-law interventions and private-governance initiatives hold tremendous promise as tools for achieving a world with sustainable menstrual products. Employing multiple parallel and overlapping approaches may make it possible to halt the proliferation of conventional menstrual products full of caustic chemicals and nondegradable plastic. In the push toward sustainable menstrual products, the stakes—namely, the long-term health of at least half the population and the physical planet we all inhabit—could not be higher.

8

Menstrual Capitalism

Selling tampons, pads, menstrual cups, and other period products is big business. In the United States, consumers spend more than $3 billion each year on these items.[1] Worldwide, the market for menstrual products is estimated to be $26 billion.[2] While engaged in the for-profit activity of selling products like tampons, pads, and menstrual cups, some companies that are dominant in the US market also invest heavily in advertising that emphasizes female empowerment. In addition, traditional and newer menstrual-product brands are increasingly engaging in philanthropy that draws on similar themes of female empowerment, as well as menstrual equity. By connecting their products with the increasing public awareness about period poverty and the need for menstrual equity, these companies are tapping into the cultural zeitgeist in order to increase their market share.

This chapter takes a closer look at the marketing and selling of menstrual products through feminist-oriented messaging. By employing empowerment rhetoric or themes of menstrual equity, many companies attempt to create a "halo effect" in order to generate more business for their commercial enterprises, which, at their core, seek to profit from menstruation.[3] We call this practice "menstrual capitalism"—not as a critique of capitalism itself, but to draw attention to the complex interaction of (1) profit motives, (2) the history of stigma and shame around menstruation, and (3) technological advances that simultaneously enhance management of menstruation while increasing scrutiny of the menstruating body. The chapter begins with a look at one major menstrual-product manufacturer's advertising and charitable work. It then moves to consider some newer menstrual-product companies' strategic deployment of the B-corporation form, which allows these businesses to pursue the dual motives of increasing shareholder profit and advancing social causes such as menstrual equity. We also look at the ways that some for-profit businesses outside the menstrual-products industry have undertaken private initiatives to address period poverty.

The chapter concludes by evaluating innovations like menstrual underwear, technology-driven "smart" menstrual products, and menstrual monitoring systems. Some of these products may make it easier to manage menstruation. Other products play on old fears of the menstruating body as something inscrutable, unruly, or disgusting. The use of menstrual monitoring systems, both for seemingly personal health purposes as well as for optimization of athletic performance, in particular, illustrates the dual nature of menstrual capitalism and its implications. On the one hand, the frank recognition of menstruation as an aspect of wellness and health is a welcome development. On the other hand, when menstruation becomes big business, consumers should remain vigilant about the ways that their bodies are being used as the source of profit—both materially and in the form of information collected through apps or otherwise.

Selling Female Empowerment

Procter & Gamble, the maker of the Always and Tampax brands, has a 50% share of the US market for menstrual products. It represents 25% of the global market. In other countries, Always pads are sold under the names of Whisper, Lines, Ausonia, and Naturella. Overall, sales of what the industry calls "feminine care" or "femcare" products account for approximately 6% of the company's global sales, with $3 billion of that coming from pads and $1 billion from Tampax tampons.[4] Recall that Procter & Gamble was the company behind the Rely tampons that became linked to several deaths from toxic shock syndrome, discussed in chapter 7. But through the passage of time as well as savvy advertising, the company has largely shed its association with that epidemic.

For both the Tampax and Always brands, Procter & Gamble has embraced overtly feminist advertising. For example, the company's 2020 "Time to Tampax with Amy Schumer" campaign takes on popular myths and misconceptions about menstruation through a series of humorous sketches featuring the comedian discussing tampons with others in places like restrooms and malls.[5] Schumer's comedic style embraces a frank discussion of sexuality and the human body, including menstruation. At the 2016 Emmys, when an interviewer asked her what she was wearing, Schumer cleverly replied, "Vivienne Westwood, Tom Ford shoes, and an O.B. tampon."[6] Schumer's reference in that moment to menstruation and menstrual products (whether or not she was compensated for the tampon mention) was very much "on brand" with her style of comedy and contributed to positive media coverage for her. That Schumer would later team with Procter & Gamble to promote the Tampax brand is not surprising. The relationship benefits the company—the ads *are* funny—and enhances Schumer's reputation as a feminist comic willing to take on taboo topics.[7]

Procter & Gamble has some history of working with celebrity endorsers. Actor Sofia Vergara and soccer star Lionel Messi both have appeared in ads for the company's Head & Shoulders shampoo, for example. But with menstrual products, the company uses its celebrity spokespersons to promote more than just a product. It intertwines the public figures' images with the company's product and with the larger goal of menstrual equity. In 2018, for example, actor Gina Rodriguez from the television show *Jane the Virgin* became the face of the Always brand #EndPeriodPoverty campaign. Writing in *Teen Vogue* about "What My Life Would Have Been Like If I Missed School Because of My Period," Rodriguez explained that she became involved in the company's program to donate products to "girls in need" after hearing stories from school nurses, teachers, and pantry coordinators about students missing school because of lack of access to menstrual products. The company made donations whenever consumers purchased products or posted an old school photo using the #EndPeriodPoverty hashtag. Rodriguez wrote, "Without the foundation of a FULL and UNINTERRUPTED basic education, I may not have been in a position to go to NYU. And if I hadn't had that college experience, I may not have had any of the amazing, life-changing opportunities that followed and shaped who I am today."[8] Rodriguez is active on a variety of social-justice fronts, such as advocating for disaster relief, greater Latinx representation in Hollywood, and reunification of migrant families, so her advocacy for the elimination of period poverty is no doubt genuine and heartfelt.[9] Meanwhile, having a celebrity with this type of activist profile at the helm of a social media campaign allows Procter & Gamble to reach a greater audience than it otherwise might on its own, while simultaneously "doing good." The company reported that it donated twenty million menstrual items in 2018.[10] A year later, the company teamed with actress Sophia Bush, who used her considerable social media presence to spread the same #EndPeriodPoverty message that Rodriguez had spread a year before.[11]

Since at least 2014, Procter & Gamble has also used themes of female empowerment in its advertising. Its "Like a Girl" television campaign for Always turned on its head stereotypical notions of what it means to run, throw, and otherwise behave like a girl. The ads featured adults who responded to the prompt to behave "like a girl" (complete with giggling and arms flapping) followed by young girls explaining that to run like a girl means to "run as a fast as you can," for example. A wildly successful version of the ad ran during the Superbowl in February 2015; it won multiple advertising awards.[12]

Professor Victoria Haneman critiques the "menstruation industrial complex"—companies that profit from the sale of menstrual products—for strategically deploying "woke-washing" (which she defines as "messaging designed to appeal to progressively-oriented sentimentality") in order to gain consumers. Indeed, as Haneman explains, it can be difficult to distinguish between an "authentic commitment" to female empowerment, as she describes it, and pure brand promotion.[13]

Traditionally dominant brands are not the only ones that make both empowerment and menstruation-related philanthropy important parts of their public profiles. The period underwear company Thinx has historically engaged in advertising that is blunt or playfully risqué. In 2015, the New York City subway system initially disallowed Thinx's advertisements as "inappropriate" for displaying, for example, a peeled and halved grapefruit—presumably a stand-in for a vulva—and a woman in a turtleneck sweater and underwear, each with the tagline "Underwear for Women with Periods."[14] Thinx also makes philanthropic activities part of its public-facing identity. The company has what it calls a "giveback program," telling customers that when they purchase Thinx, they are "helping give life to our programming and initiatives." The website says that the company works through partner organizations in three main areas: advocating for menstrual equity; providing a menstrual-education curriculum (including workshops and teacher training) to educators; and helping expand access to safe menstrual products.[15] But the details of these programs, or the extent to which purchases actually support them, are not made clear.

B-Corporations in the Menstrual Marketplace

One salient difference between companies like Procter & Gamble and some of the newer menstrual-product companies is the legal forms that the newer corporations select. Procter & Gamble is a traditional corporation, known as a "C" corporation, that operates to maximize profits for shareholders. By contrast, several newer menstrual-product companies are "B" corporations. Generally speaking, B-corporations commit to a rigorous external vetting system by the nonprofit B Lab, which looks to the company's "entire social and environmental performance" and evaluates how the company impacts its "workers, community, environment, and customers."[16] Examples of well-known B-corporations include King Arthur Flour, Burt's Bees, Ben & Jerry's, and Eileen Fisher.[17] B-corporations have dual purposes: (1) earning profits for shareholders; and (2) achieving larger social goals that are set forth in their charter. Unlike the traditional C-corporation that must focus on a "single bottom line," or profits, B-corporations thus have a "double bottom line,"[18] explicitly striving for profits and to advance the interests of a broader community of stakeholders.

In the menstrual-products market, two prominent B-corporations are Diva International, Inc., the maker of the Diva Cup, and Aisle (formerly known as Lunapads), the manufacturer of reusable cloth menstrual pads and underwear. Both companies engage in significant socially aware programming in addition to their main business activity of selling menstrual products.

Diva International, Inc., which has been in business since 2003, became a "certified" B-corporation in 2018, and a legal B-company prior to that. Diva International company displays its "Certified B Corporation" status prominently on its webpage and explains that its community goals are menstruation-related education, advocacy, and donation of menstrual cups. According to a recent company report, it donated over six hundred thousand dollars' worth of products to organizations like I Support the Girls.[19] Relatedly, Carinne Chambers-Saini, one of the cofounders of Diva International, was an executive producer of

Pandora's Box, a 2019 documentary that explores global period-poverty and menstrual-equity issues. Diva International promotes its menstrual products as both cost saving and environmentally friendly. The Diva Cup, which sells at Walmart for approximately twenty dollars, can be reused for a number of years, so the average consumer will spend less on the cup than on disposable tampons or pads that need to be changed every three to six hours and generate more waste.

Like Diva International, Aisle is a "Certified B Corporation" that is billed as an environmentally friendly option, because its pads and underwear are washable and reusable. The Vancouver-based company's "Dignity Projects" focus on product donations, financial donations, and "mentoring" of other organizations that center menstruation-related education and philanthropy.[20] For many years, the company employed a customer-buys-one-company-gives-one program that donated products to girls in East Africa.[21] Through its affiliation with AFRIpads in Uganda, the company's products are made by local African workers and distributed through NGOs working in the area, helping to minimize the number of women and girls who miss school or work because they do not have access to menstrual products.[22] The company emphasizes its zero-waste manufacturing process; left-over and odd-sized pieces of fabric are repurposed for furniture filling or children's clothing.[23]

By embracing both gender issues and environmental sustainability, companies like Diva International and Aisle have joined the ranks of socially conscious companies with dual missions of making profits and furthering larger social goals. According to a recent survey, a full 89% of consumers believe that businesses should support environmental causes and 74% believe that businesses should support gender-related causes.[24] Data suggest that most consumers believe that the large businesses have a greater responsibility than small businesses to embrace social causes. Yet in the menstrual-products arena, it is the small companies that have gone beyond corporate philanthropy to embrace environmental and gender issues through their corporate structures.

Interestingly, 63% of consumers say they are willing to continue purchasing from companies that remain silent about important social issues, so it is not clear whether changes by traditional manufacturers of menstrual products—to the extent that any may occur in the future—will come from consumer demands or from another source, such as activist shareholders.[25] In any event, for those consumers who are interested, Professor Haneman suggests that B-corporation certification performs an initial sorting function that allows consumers and investors to distinguish between purely profit-seeking companies and those that embrace a more sincere feminist agenda. As she explains, a company's chosen structure may "provide a metric of do-goodery and trustworthiness that has the potential to be revolutionary in the world of business," including in the business of menstrual products.[26]

Creating Need Where There Was None Before

One of the ways menstrual capitalism, and indeed any profit-driven market, operates is by creating a perceived "need" where there previously was none. Consider the examples of Bluetooth tampons, "smart" menstrual cups and pads, period subscription boxes, and period blankets. In some cases, these products may actually create new risks of their own, raising both health and privacy concerns. In other cases, the products are harmless to their users, but send mixed messages that warrant more scrutiny.

Start, for example, with a product called my.Flow. This is a menstrual-flow monitoring device that uses Bluetooth technology to alert a user when a tampon is saturated. The proprietary tampon has an extra-long string, approximately twelve inches in length, that contains a fine conductive thread. The string connects to a small clip-on monitor that can be worn on one's underwear under clothes or clipped to an external waistband. The monitor communicates with an app installed on the wearer's cell phone. The user programs the phone with information about expected menstrual flow and then receives a warning when the monitor senses that the tampon is reaching the saturation point. According to company cofounder and CEO Amanda Brief, this avoids both unnecessary waste and discomfort: "Currently, you can't check the level of your tampon as it's inside you, so many people err on the side of taking their tampon out prematurely, which is not only wasteful, but quite physically uncomfortable as well."[27] The product operates on a subscription model, with a one-time purchase of forty-nine dollars for the wearable monitor and then an additional cost for the special tampons. The user can program the app to replenish the tampon supply automatically every month.[28] While the tampon itself allegedly emits no signal of any kind, Dr. Jen Gunter, a gynecologist who also serves as a *New York Times* columnist, has warned that the product "represents a significant design change" that warrants FDA approval.[29] It is also unclear how secure the Bluetooth connection is and what the company might do with the data it gathers. Additionally, Brief's comments are not substantiated by empirical or even anecdotal evidence that "many" people take out their tampons prematurely and that doing so is "quite physically uncomfortable" for them.

The spread of Bluetooth technology to menstrual products is not limited to tampons. The LOONCUP bills itself as "the world's first SMART menstrual cup," with embedded sensors that communicate via Bluetooth technology with an app that allows users to measure and track their menstrual flow's volume and color. The Bluetooth antenna is embedded in the cup's thirteen-millimeter stem.[30] Manufactured by a Korea-based company, the product received certification from the Federal Communications Commission in June 2019.[31] The manufacturer warns that users should not wear the product while going through airport security because the antenna, embedded battery, and sensors contain materials that will set off x-ray machines.[32] Presumably the same caution applies for medical x-rays, as well. Here, too, there are questions about the security and privacy of the data collected via Bluetooth, but very little information is available about the company or the status of its product availability.

Consider next the proliferation of period subscription boxes. These can follow a simple model of delivering new menstrual products each month, but increasingly involve elaborate monthly "care packages" containing not only menstrual products but also items like snacks, candy, tea, bath oils or lotions, ibuprofen, "hygiene wipes," and even a hot water bottle at a cost of over twenty-two dollars a month.[33] There are a range of specialty subscription boxes on the market, including a "PMS Package,"[34] a "First Period Box" for young tweens and teens, a "Men's Box," and a "Gender Neutral Box" containing nongendered candies, snacks, and comfort items.[35] These products often emphasize a female empowerment theme. Kali, for instance, promotes its "teen box" with the message, "A fun start to period care. Join Kali and Girl Up [the United Nations Foundation's adolescent girl campaign] on your period journey because periods should be celebrated. Let us make that time of the month exciting for you!"[36] All of this is a welcome pushback against the historic stigma and silence surrounding menstruation. But to the extent that these products' messaging implies that periods are inevitably going to be painful or taxing, such that hot water bottles, candy, and/or ibuprofen must be on hand, there is a double-edged sword. People's experiences of menstruation vary widely. Menstruation is not necessarily burdensome for all, and suggesting otherwise perpetuates negative stereotypes about menstruation.

One relatively new (but seemingly short-lived) menstruation-related product was the "period blanket," a quilted satin blanket made by the same company behind Thinx period underwear. The blanket, which came out in 2018, cost approximately $350 and is no longer for sale on the company's website. It contained the same absorbent material as period underwear and was machine washable.[37] Thinx promoted the item by, among other things, featuring a blog post on its website entitled "Your Guide to Better Period Sex." The blog stated,

> [W]ith all that "messy perfection" it's nice to have something to save your sheets from stains—but no need to sacrifice your towels. That's why THINX came out with their Period Sex Blanket, a luxe solution that absorbs fluids while you play. Just throw it down before the action starts and let the 4-layer tech do its job—your sheets will thank you later.[38]

Some reviewers praised the blanket. According to one reviewer, it makes "period sex SO much easier."[39] Despite the blanket's small size, another reviewer was impressed by its absorbency and its ability to maintain a relatively fixed position on the bed in spite of vigorous movement on top of the blanket, ultimately concluding that the blanket might be equally practical in providing a protective layer for sleep during menstruation, to avoid leaks onto bed linens.[40] However, the *Wirecutter* columnist in the *New York Times* pointed out that "[p]utting down a towel is an effective solution to catch drips or smears of blood. . . . [S]elling a blanket at the same price as several very nice vibrators ultimately suggests that women should be spending gobs of money to make their bodily functions as pleasant as possible."[41] Once again, the messaging around the product simultaneously challenged and reinforced various menstrual stereotypes.

Are You There, Capitalism? It's Me, Period Poverty

In April 2021, the Lidl Ireland branch of the global Lidl supermarket chain launched a period-poverty initiative that attracted worldwide attention. Its program allows any customer to redeem a coupon once a month for a free box of tampons or pads at any of its 168 stores in the Republic of Ireland,[42] with plans to expand to Northern Ireland in the near future.[43] Customers can obtain the coupon by registering through the company's app; to meet the needs of those without access to smart phones or the internet, the company is making regular donations of menstrual products to a homelessness charity.[44] The company also distributes free menstrual products through clubs of the Ladies Gaelic Football Association, as an additional way of reaching people in need. The company's webpage refers to a Plan International Study that found that almost 50% of girls in Ireland "found it difficult to pay for sanitary products" and cites to Scotland's and New Zealand's efforts to combat period poverty by distributing free menstrual products in schools.[45] A Lidl Ireland spokesperson explained the reasoning behind the company's decision: "The guiding principle of this initiative is the inherent respect for the dignity of all those concerned" and the company's commitment to being a "family retailer."[46] The *New York Times* dubbed Lidl Ireland "the first major retailer to make period products available for free nationwide."[47]

In the broader context, the Lidl initiative suggests a positive aspect of menstrual capitalism—the idea that for-profit companies can play a valuable role in addressing lack of access to menstrual products. Lidl developed its program in connection with Homeless Period Ireland,[48] a charitable organization with experience addressing period poverty and getting menstrual products to those who need them.[49] Through Lidl's coupon program, a customer can present a menstrual product and coupon at the cash register, just as one would present, say, a box of cereal discounted with a particular coupon. The customer gains access to urgently needed products; in exchange, the company's app captures information about potential customers. Both for those who use the coupons and those who do not, the company's positive messaging around menstruation and alleviating poverty builds brand loyalty and enhances the company's public image.

Around the same time that Lidl Ireland announced its program, the UK grocer Morrisons posted a notice in one of its stores that customers "in need or struggling for sanitary products" could go to the customer service desk and "ask for a package that SANDY has left for you."[50] The program is available only in a few Morrisons stores; a company spokesperson says that it may expand in the future.[51] Judging from news reports, the Lidl and Morrisons campaigns differ in both the method and quantity of free menstrual-products delivery. A Morrisons customer who asks for the package from "Sandy" receives "an envelope with a sanitary product inside," as opposed to an entire *package* of menstrual products from Lidl (although presumably a customer could ask for "Sandy" more than once a day).[52] The Morrisons protocols reflect another double-edged sword. On the one hand, the code word may obviate the need to out oneself as poor and menstruating; as chapters 1 and 3 discuss, this is indeed something that many people are reluctant to do. On the other, *instructing* customers to use a code word assumes, and even reinforces, a sense of shame. A better approach would be to offer the code word as an option. Similarly, requiring such customers to go to the customer service desk, rather than giving them the option of handling the situation at the cash register, also exacerbates the sense of difference. The Morrisons method thus may unintentionally contribute to the shame around period poverty, even though the underlying program helps to reduce period poverty itself.

Despite the differences in the Lidl and Morrisons programs, both represent praiseworthy efforts by private-sector businesses to address the problem of period poverty. Uniquely among other companies that donate menstrual products, neither Lidl nor Morrisons is a manufacturer of menstrual products. They are grocery stores; yet both seem to have concluded that by addressing this need, they will receive positive public attention that is likely to increase customer loyalty and new business. The programs of Lidl and Morrisons signal to other businesses that by engaging in social welfare—with the safety, health, and vitality of one's customers as a goal—companies can grow their bottom lines.

Menstrual Data

With the rising prevalence and sophistication of smart phones, it is not surprising that one can now use an app to track and monitor one's period. Commonly used apps include Period Tracker, Clue, Eve Tracker, and Flo, to name just a few.[53] Some of the apps sync with the Apple Health app, facilitating tracking of sleep, physical activity, and water intake. Depending on the particular app, there may be places to enter one's weight, mood, and sexual activity. Indeed, some apps even predict likely ovulation dates, although medical professionals counsel against using menstrual-cycle trackers as fertility predictors. One study found that of thirty-three tracking apps, only three predicted the precise fertile window of their users. Similarly, the app may not be especially helpful for users who have irregular cycles.[54]

The proliferation of menstrual apps has an unexpected nexus with employment law. Some employers give employees a financial incentive to use health-related technologies. For example, Activision Blizzard, a videogame company, pays its employees to use the Fitbit. It also pays employees one dollar a day to use the Ovia Health planning apps, giving the company real-time data (in an anonymous, aggregated form) about employees' menstrual cycles and fertility.[55] A *Washington Post* article explained that such menstrual data then becomes available on an internal employer website accessible by human resources personnel, adding that beyond companies like Activision Blizzard, some employers "incentivize workers to input as much about their bodies as they can, saying the data can help the companies minimize health-care spending, discover medical problems and better plan for the months ahead."[56] Critics of these apps point out that even though data is aggregated and anonymized, there is still the possibility of tracing data back to the individual employee, either through security breaches, the combination of anonymous data with confidential discussions, or other means. "The real benefit of self-tracking is always to the company," Professor Karen Levy has observed. "People are being asked to do this at a time when they're incredibly vulnerable and may not have any sense where that data is being passed."[57]

Relatedly, given efforts to roll back abortion rights in some states, it is even plausible to imagine a scenario in which self-provided data about missing a period could later be used as evidence that someone was pregnant and had an illegal abortion. So, too, might data be used to identify employees who are pregnant or trying to become pregnant, raising the specter of illegal employment discrimination on the basis of pregnancy. Add these to the many general concerns about data privacy, as well as the possibility that one could lose one's phone or others could access entered personal data, and there are real reasons to be concerned about the rise in the so-called FemTech Industry, the umbrella term for these apps and other "smart" technologies.[58]

Professor Michele Gilman, a prominent legal critic of FemTech, draws attention to the ways that "[m]enstruation is being monetized and surveilled, with the voluntary participation of millions of women," with the profits flowing to a business sector estimated to grow to approximately $50 billion by 2025. The companies that sell—or more commonly, give away—technology period-tracking and fertility apps typically require users to enter their name, email address, age, and gender, along with other highly personal data.[59] That data then becomes a commodity for advertisers as well as hackers, in whose hands health-related data may be worth even more than credit-card data.[60] In January 2021 the Federal Trade Commission (FTC) settled a complaint against Flo Health, Inc., the maker of the Flo Period & Ovulation Tracker app, for the company's disclosure of millions of users' health data to companies including Facebook and Google.[61] Around the same time, the FTC also issued consumer guidance aimed at helping users of health apps protect their private information.[62]

Gilman critiques the neoliberal model of US privacy laws, which place the onus on consumers to protect their own data under a notice-and-consent framework.[63] She notes that privacy policies are difficult and time-consuming for most consumers to read (if they read them at all) and that it is almost impossible to bargain for separate terms in the event a user wishes to alter a tech company's standard privacy policies. Gilman suggests that a menstrual justice–informed approach to period trackers and fertility apps would require a shift to a nonprofit model, with consumers having input on app design and function. Gilman also advocates for greater data privacy, limits on data sharing, and meaningful consent by the end user.[64] These are salutary goals. But absent comprehensive data-privacy reform in the United States, it is unlikely that the profitable FemTech industry will change its practices any time soon.

Elite Sports and Menstrual Surveillance

In the context of elite sports, coaches of teams like the US Women's National Soccer Team have begun paying attention to menstruation, particularly as it relates to athletic performance—and that attention is increasingly taking the form of surveillance. For example, beginning in 2016, the team's fitness coach, Dawn Scott (who subsequently left the coaching staff at the end of 2019), began tracking players' menstrual cycles (along with their heart rates, hydration levels, and other metrics).[65] In the lead-up to the 2019 World Cup in France, Scott input the athletes' information into the app FitrWoman (tag line: "Track Your Period and Train Smarter")[66] and adjusted their diets, sleep, and training schedules in response to their menstrual-cycle information. Scott called period tracking one of the many strategies that "helped us win" the World Cup.[67] This initiative was backed by research showing that at certain times during the menstrual cycle, an athlete may be more prone to injuries, as well as research indicating that hormone levels can affect overall health or performance, with the body more able to adapt to high-intensity workouts during the first half of the menstrual cycle.[68]

Notably, Scott individualized the tracking for each of the team's twenty-three players. Athletes completed comprehensive surveys about their periods, in terms of when their menstrual flow started, how long their periods lasted, what types of symptoms they felt, and whether those symptoms impacted their play. "We could dial in on players with the most symptoms," Scott explained, noting that, for instance, she would "just text or say to a player, 'Hey you're in phase three and we know you get disrupted sleep, so make sure you do x, y and z.'" The fact that midfielder Rose Lavelle got her period the day after scoring a goal in the final game of the 2019 World Cup match also became part of the public narrative about Scott's coaching methods.[69] "Rose showed that, although the menstrual cycle might impact performance, you can limit those effects through diet, nutrition, recovery and sleep," Scott recounted. "World Cup medals have been won by players at disruptive phases of their menstrual cycle. For me, it is about being diligent."[70]

Even prior to the 2019 World Cup tournament, conversations and speculation about the effect of menstruation on elite athletic performance had been growing. In an interview after her 4x100 relay team narrowly missed winning a bronze medal at the 2016 Summer Olympics in Rio de Janeiro, swimmer Fu Yuanhui corrected an interviewer who attributed her pained facial expressions to a stomach ache. "It's because I just got my period yesterday, so I'm still a bit weak and really tired.... But this isn't an excuse for not swimming well," Fu told the reporter. Fu's comments were heralded as "breaking what has long been a taboo among female athletes."[71]

In contrast to Fu, who said her period was not an "excuse" for poor performance, when Jelena Jankovic, the former world number one tennis player, exited Wimbledon in 2009 in an early match against teenager Melanie Oudin, Jankovic explained her loss in part by saying she had "some woman problems," thus implying (but not explicitly stating) that she had her period.[72] Similarly, when the number one UK tennis player, Heather Watson, lost in the first round of the Australian Open in 2015, Watson said that she did not feel well, offering, "I think it's just one of these things that I have, girl things."[73] Commentator Annabel Croft, herself a former number one UK player, interpreted those comments as referring to menstruation and praised Watson's candor, saying, "Women's monthly issues seems [sic] to be one of those subjects that gets swept under the carpet and is a big secret."[74]

Here, too, there are complicated questions. On the one hand, there is anecdotal and scientific evidence of the ways that the menstrual cycle can affect athletic performance for many people, supporting the logic of Scott's period-tracking approach. And as with the "period boxes" that include hot water bottles and pain relievers, there are many positive aspects to talking more openly about menstruation's physical and psychological effects. Not only do such conversations challenge traditional expectations about menstrual silence, but they also promote greater understanding and exploration of different strategies for mitigating those effects. In these respects, these developments are consistent with this book's underlying theme of ensuring that menstruation does not prevent people from fully participating in the activities of their choosing.

On the other hand, generalizations can heighten notions of menstruation as physically and/or psychologically disabling, when in fact people's experiences vary widely. Indeed, as Coach Scott herself pointed out, the effects of menstruation vary by individual. Part of why her strategy worked so effectively was that it was specific to each player, and incorporated other aspects of their physiology, such as their heart rates and hydration levels.

Of course, the type of comprehensive body surveillance that informs the coaching of elite soccer players is not a model for how menstrual capitalism works more generally. For the most part, menstrual capitalism is a market phenomenon related to the selling of menstrual products to average consumers through female-empowerment messages. But the focus on individuals here, as opposed to the essentialization of menstruation and the commodification of menstruating bodies and their data, illustrates the many forms that menstrual capitalism can take. After all, elite athletic performance, especially at the international level, is not just about wins and losses. Not only might a top performance yield lucrative opportunities for the individual athlete, but competitions and victories are also intertwined with the economics of sports. For example, the 2019 FIFA Women's World Cup contributed approximately $318 million to the French economy.[75] In the case of the US Women's National Soccer Team, the victory on the largest international stage in turn generates interest at the youth sports level.[76] In some affluent communities, youth sports themselves can take the form of big business, too.[77]

New technologies and products related to menstruation are inevitable. Many are welcome, especially when guided by principles of individual difference, privacy, and autonomy. But depending on the messages associated with the selling of those products, it is easy to lose sight of the fact that each individual's experience of menstruation is different and that new technologies are not always necessary. Consumers should be attentive to the way that some companies are playing into old stereotypes of menstruation as messy and gross (hence the "need" for a period blanket), mysterious (hence the need for a "smart" tampon), or misery inducing (hence the need for a subscription period box with treats). And consumers absolutely must take care to protect their own data privacy, rather than thinking that companies will do so. Through greater awareness of these issues, as well as more corporate transparency about philanthropy, consumers can make more informed decisions about the ways they participate in menstrual capitalism.

9

Menstruation around the Globe

Menstruation is a unifier—an experience shared by approximately half the world's population, for several decades of their lives. This book has largely focused on menstruation in the context of United States law, society, and culture. But it is worthwhile to situate the discussion of menstruation in the global context, too. Virtually all of the topics discussed in earlier chapters—menstrual stigma and shame; period poverty; the tampon tax; menstrual products in schools and public buildings; employment accommodations; environmental and health concerns; and the business of selling menstrual products—are salient in other countries. The growth and success of menstrual advocacy, particularly since 2015, has also been worldwide. For example, in 2018, Nepal banned the traditional menstrual huts that served as a place of exile from the family home during menstruation, even offering cash payments to those who spurn the practice.[1] Legislative efforts to repeal the tampon tax coevolved in Canada (2015), India (2018), Australia (2018), Germany (2019), and the UK (2021), after Kenya led the way in 2004.[2] Colombia's Constitutional Court invalidated the country's tampon tax in 2018; it also required the city of Bogotá to provide menstrual products to homeless women.[3] Menstrual leave—already the law in South Korea, Japan, and Taiwan—was seriously considered (but not ultimately adopted) in Italy in 2017.[4] In many countries, menstruation-related matters continue to provide a lens for evaluating issues of gender equality.

This chapter turns its focus to five countries on four continents, providing a snapshot of menstrual advocacy in varied economic, social, and political contexts. For example, women in India face a variety of cultural taboos surrounding menstruation and have led transformative legal challenges to taxes on menstrual products. In Kenya, the first country to lift the tampon tax, getting menstrual supplies to schoolchildren in need remains a significant challenge, despite a law that provides for their availability in public schools. Kenyan women such as activist Scheaffer

Okore were among the first to use social media to call attention to the health hazards posed by menstrual products.[5] Kenyan women are also part of "by women, for women" efforts to produce reusable menstrual pads that expand access to sustainable menstrual products to those in need.[6] In Australia and New Zealand, governments have taken steps to provide free menstrual products in schools and to more broadly address poverty, especially among women and children. Scotland presently is the world leader in enacting reforms to address period poverty. In November 2020, it became the first country to make period products free to all who need them.[7] Developments in each of these five countries illuminate the challenges and possibilities for making law and society more responsive to the needs of all people.

India

Cultural taboos around menstruation in India came to international attention in 2018 when India's Supreme Court declared unconstitutional certain laws that prohibited all girls and women between the ages of ten and fifty from visiting the Lord Ayyappa Temple at Sabarimala in the southern state of Kerala.[8] This temple, one of the world's largest pilgrimage sites, attracts millions of devotees each year from India and abroad.[9] In 1993, the High Court in Kerala had upheld laws banning most girls and women from the temple, on the grounds that these visitors "are not in a position to observe penance . . . due to physiological reasons" of menstruation and the "impurity" of menstruation.[10] The High Court had reasoned that these prohibitions were permissible because they were "in accordance with the usage prevalent from time immemorial," and that there was no discrimination against women as a class but rather "women of a particular age group," i.e., women of menstruating age.[11]

When brought before the India Supreme Court in 2018, the case pitted women's groups against each other. One group calling itself "Happy to Bleed" advocated for the right of women to enter the temple. This group was represented by a female attorney, Indira Jaising, who had previously served as India's additional solicitor general. She argued that the exclusion of women violated Article 14 of the Constitution of India, which guarantees the right to equality. The other group, calling itself "Ready to Wait," claimed that the demand for women's entry into the temple reflected Western values, not Indian ones; these women said they were willing to wait until the age of fifty to enter the temple.[12]

The Supreme Court ruled, by a four-to-one vote, that the exclusionary practice was unconstitutional. It reasoned that "[r]eligion ... cannot become a cover to exclude and to deny the basic right to find fulfillment in worship to women. ... To treat women as children of a lesser god is to blink at the Constitution itself."[13] Menstrual taboos, according to the Court, had the effect of limiting "the ability of menstruating women to attain the freedom of movement, the right to education and the right of entry to places of worship and, eventually, their access to the public sphere." For that reason, the Court reasoned, women have a "constitutional entitlement that their biological processes must be free from social and religious practices, which enforce segregation and exclusion."[14]

The *Sabarimala* decision, as it is commonly known, set off significant protests. After the Supreme Court's decision, numerous women who tried to enter the temple ended up turning back, due to threats and physical intimidation from protestors.[15] For this reason, although the Court issued its decision in September 2018, it was not until early January 2019 that two women finally made their way into the inner sanctum of the temple.[16] This, in turn, prompted the head priest to shut down the temple for an hour to perform a purification ritual.[17] In response to the pushback and protests that the *Sabarimala* decision engendered, the Indian Supreme Court agreed in February 2020 to review its own decision, referring it to a larger nine-judge bench to consider the issue in the context of larger questions about religious freedoms.[18] In a recent article, human rights advocates Divya Srinivasan and Bharti Kannan explained that this referral has put the *Sabarimala* verdict "in jeopardy."[19] Indeed, the future course of the decision is uncertain.

As in many countries, menstrual taboos are prevalent in many parts of India. In some communities, menstruating girls are not permitted to live or have meals with their families, and they are not permitted to touch cooking materials or drinking water.[20] For some religious people, there are restrictions on participation in everyday life during menstruation, with "purification" required before resumption of daily rituals.[21] In certain parts of India, some common myths are that menstruating women will contaminate food, or that menstrual blood is a mechanism by which women can impose their will on men.[22]

In 2015, Procter & Gamble won a global industry award for its "Touch the Pickle" advertising campaign for Whisper brand menstrual pads in India. This campaign responded to the superstition, held in some parts of the country, that a menstruating woman can cause a pickle to rot if she touches it.[23] The ad shows a teenager dressed in white who touches a pickle jar and pronounces, "I touched the pickle jar," to the applause of gathered women. Bollywood actress Parineeti Chopra joined the campaign, endorsing the pledge of over 2.9 million consumers in India to "touch the pickle jar."[24]

Menstrual taboos in India and elsewhere are fueled in part by lack of education, as well as by how families and teachers themselves treat menstruating students. A 2006 study conducted in the state of Rajasthan found that 56% of girls received no information about menstruation before their first periods.[25] In a survey of five hundred mothers from five different districts, 70.4% of respondents reported that they believed that menstruation was "dirty and polluting."[26] These stigmas carry over to the educational arena. In 2017, a school warden at the Kasturba Gandhi Junior Residential School in the state of Uttar Pradesh became irate after finding menstrual blood on a toilet door and forced seventy girls ages twelve to fourteen to strip naked in class so that she could check if they were menstruating. The warden, who was fired from the job, defended her actions by saying, "I still say what I did was right because I believe in cleanliness and discipline."[27]

Relatedly, menstruation sometimes functions as an obstacle to continued attendance at school for students in India and elsewhere; this is particularly true in those schools that lack separate toilet facilities and places where girls can dispose of used menstrual products and wash their hands. Girls report skipping school because of menstrual-related pain, fear of staining their clothes, and general embarrassment. In India, several government-sponsored interventions have focused on education, access to menstrual products, and proper disposal of menstrual products. In some studies, product availability seems correlated with reduced rates of school absenteeism in certain geographic regions of India,[28] but other scholars suggest the relationship between access to menstrual pads and school attendance may be attenuated.[29]

According to the National Family Health Survey 2015, during menstruation an estimated 57.6% of all Indian girls and women ages fifteen through twenty-four use some form of what researchers called a "hygienic method," meaning tampons (2.4%), commercially produced sanitary napkins (41.85%), or locally produced napkins (16.25%); approximately 62.2% use cloth protection. (The sum exceeds 100% because some respondents reported using multiple methods for menstrual management.)[30] According to other sources, however, 88% of menstruating girls and women in India have no access to either commercial or locally produced napkins, using grass or other materials instead.[31] This is slowly changing, in part because of the work of entrepreneur Arunachalam Muruganantham, profiled in the Oscar-winning film *Period. End of Sentence* and the Bollywood film *Pad Man*.[32] Muruganantham's pad-making machine allows multiple nonprofits, job-training organizations, and women's microfinance groups to supply low-cost pads to underserved communities in India and elsewhere.[33]

India is also one of the countries that recently repealed its tampon tax. In 2017, India's federal government introduced a comprehensive goods and services tax (GST), with rates ranging from zero to 28%, based on the category of goods. In the "zero rate" bracket were kohl eyeliner (*kajal*), red hand dye (*alta*), plastic and glass bracelets, condoms, and other contraceptives. A 12% bracket was for "luxury products," such as toys, leather goods, mobile phones, and processed foods. Menstrual products were initially classified as luxury products.[34] The law inspired an immediate negative reaction from activists, students, lawmakers, and others. Sushmita Dev, a member of Parliament, started a petition urging the minister of finance to reduce or abolish the tax. Her petition, which she posted on Change.org, emphasized that "[w]omen are being taxed 12 months a year, for about 39 years on a process they have no control over" and urged the government to "make sanitary napkins tax free (like condoms and contraceptives) as it is an essential item which is a necessity for every woman."[35] Over four hundred thousand people signed the petition, which also received support from the minister for women and child development.[36] Activists began using the phrase "*Lahu ka Lagaan*," or "blood tax," in calling for the law's repeal.[37]

India's tax on menstrual products was the subject of two court challenges. Zarmina Israr Khan, a doctoral student at Jawaharlal Nehru University, brought a public-interest litigation in the High Court of Delhi. Indian law permits this type of suit for the purpose of effectuating change in the name of society as a whole, as opposed to on behalf of individual plaintiffs or even a class of plaintiffs.[38] Khan alleged that the GST classification of menstrual products violated multiple human-rights provisions of the Constitution of India, as well as constitutional prohibitions against discrimination on the basis of sex.[39] At a hearing in the case, the court publicly questioned the absence of women from the Goods & Services Tax Council, the thirty-one-member constitutional body charged with making recommendations to the federal and state governments.[40] Similarly, a nonprofit organization called the Shetty Women Welfare Foundation brought a public-interest litigation in the High Court of Bombay, challenging the tax on menstrual products as a violation of the constitutional rights to life and personal liberty, saying that "over 80 per cent of women" did not use sanitary napkins, either because they were unaware of them or because they are too expensive.[41] At hearings in that case, the court asked the government in the state of Maharashtra what had been "done to increase and spread awareness about the use of sanitary napkins" and urged the state to lower the prices on menstrual products.[42]

These two cases became moot when India's GST Council agreed to place sanitary napkins in the "nil rate" (or 0%) bracket for GST purposes, making the products tax exempt.[43] Women's rights advocates hailed the action as "a most-awaited and necessary step to help girls and women to stay in school, their jobs, to practise proper menstrual hygiene. This will help them to grow, to show their true potential."[44] India's elimination of the GST on menstrual products was indeed an important step in making products more accessible. Women's rights advocates in India continue to work for elimination of menstrual taboos, comprehensive menstrual education, access to safe menstrual products, and improvements in sanitation to ensure that menstruation does not prevent full participation in public life.[45]

Kenya

Kenya has been one of the global leaders in the menstrual movement. In 2004, Kenya became the first country to eliminate the tampon tax, when Kenya moved menstrual products into the zero bracket for purposes of the value-added tax, essentially exempting them from taxation.[46] Just five years after that reform, local reporters estimated that 35% of Kenyan women were using commercial menstrual products, compared to 16% in Uganda and Tanzania.[47] (Without more analysis, though, it is not clear whether the elimination of the tax directly impacted usage rates.)

International companies like Procter & Gamble have taken a particular interest in developing the Kenyan market for commercial menstrual products, through give-away programs aimed at young school girls.[48] Still, these products remain out of financial reach for most; 65% of Kenyan girls and women are unable to afford commercial products.[49] One study of girls attending rural schools in Nyanza Province of Western Kenya found that while most of the girls preferred commercial menstrual pads, they could not afford them. These girls instead reported that they managed menstruation through a variety of "make do" methods, including creating their own pads from rags or bunched pieces of old cloth, mattress cuttings, or dried grass.[50] The girls reported dissatisfaction with using cloth scraps, because the cloth could easily fall to the ground, leak through, feel wet, or emit an undesirable odor.[51] Girls also reported deploying a variety of other strategies for managing menstruation when attending school, such as wearing multiple layers consisting of underwear, shorts, and a skirt; wearing dark clothes; avoiding sitting while at school; waiting to be the last one to leave the class, for fear of displaying stained clothing; or simply leaving school when they get their period.[52]

For some girls in Kenya and elsewhere, difficulties in managing menstruation may be so insurmountable that they decide not to attend school for multiple days each month. For example, in 2011, thirteen-year-old Dorothy Akinyi of Kibera, Kenya, said that she stayed home every month during her period: "Without sanitary pads, life at school is difficult. We are subjected to very embarrassing and humiliating incidences, especially from the boys. Tying a pullover around your waist to hide the soiled patch behind your uniform in case the tissue leaks is a dead giveaway. We choose to stay at home."[53] To address the issue of school absenteeism, beginning in 2011, the Kenyan government implemented a "Sanitary Towels programme" administered by the Ministry of Education. The goal of the program was to provide free menstrual pads to students in schools in low-income areas, but the program was unsuccessful in reaching all students who needed pads.[54] The Kenya Ministry of Public Service and Gender reported in 2013 that girls from poor families continued to miss up to 20% of all school days because of lack of access to menstrual products.[55]

In 2017, President Uhuru Kenyatta signed into law the Basic Education Amendment Act, which moved responsibility for the Sanitary Towels program from the Ministry of Education to the Ministry of Public Service, Youth, and Gender Affairs. The law also mandated the provision of free products to girls in all Kenyan schools nationwide: it is the duty of the cabinet secretary to "provide free, sufficient and quality sanitary towels to every girl child registered and enrolled in a public basic education institution who has reached puberty and provide a safe and environmentally sound mechanism for disposal of the sanitary towels."[56] Unfortunately, this program has not been entirely successful, due to problems in supply and distribution chains, as well as corruption.[57] For example, in 2020, in a building under construction in Juja, Kiambu County, police seized over three hundred thousand menstrual pads that seemed to have been destined for free distribution in schools based on the packaging, but were being repackaged for illegal sale.[58] One NGO official commented that "[t]he cartels in this country are hijacking government projects."[59] Local leaders have called for increased monitoring and surveillance of the government's menstrual-product distribution program.[60]

In 2019, the Kenyan government approved a National Menstrual Hygiene Management policy that aims to make menstrual health part of "the mainstream of the country's health and development agenda by considering the prevailing social, economic, cultural and demographic contexts of women and girls."[61] The program contemplates expanding the distribution of menstrual products—currently targeted for students attending schools—to also include refugees, homeless individuals, and those living in crowded urban conditions.[62] The program also aims to integrate menstrual-hygiene programming into existing government programs to decrease gender-based violence and childhood marriages.[63] There is some optimism that this program will have positive results in Kenya, but the COVID-19 pandemic dealt a significant blow to these efforts.[64]

Indeed, during the pandemic, schools in Kenya were initially closed from March 2020 until June 2020; they began to partially reopen in late

2020.[65] During the initial period of school closures, the Kenya Institute of Curriculum took to radio, television, and the internet to broadcast educational programming.[66] The international humanitarian organization Plan International recommended "integrating menstrual hygiene management into remote and online learning curriculums," so that "people, including adolescent girls[,] have the knowledge that they need on their first period and safely manage their menstrual health during this time."[67] Menstrual education is a pressing need: according to one study, only 12% of girls in Kenya are comfortable receiving information about menstrual hygiene from their mothers, preferring to receive information from other sources instead.[68] But the lack of electricity, the cost of internet access, and the expense of technology are insurmountable obstacles for many Kenyan students in rural communities, refugee camps, and elsewhere, suggesting that few students were able to access menstruation-related education during pandemic-era remote instruction.[69]

Because of the ways that menstruation contributes to gender inequality in schooling, and because of a past pattern of governmental inactions, a variety of nongovernmental organizations have invested in learning more about how Kenyan girls experience menstruation. These organizations have as their ultimate goal girls' continued attendance at school, which in sub-Saharan Africa has been found to contribute to reduced incidences of early marriage, sexually transmitted diseases, including HIV, and teen pregnancy.[70] One NGO-funded study from 2013 drew on focus-group conversations with 120 Kenyan girls ages fourteen to sixteen in Siaya County in the rural part of western Kenya, as well as separate focus groups with parents. One of the main themes to emerge from these focus groups was the girls' lack of preparation for menarche, with many girls reporting having no knowledge of menstruation before getting their first period.[71] One student reported, "When I first started my lower abdomen was stretching painfully and when I went back to the classroom everybody was asking me what was on my clothes, then I told them I don't know."[72] A parent reflected, "[T]hese girls are scared because they think that they are the only ones experiencing monthly period. And also it is our fault as parents not to share with our girls of the changes they will be undergoing. They are not aware that all females undergo the same."[73] The girls participating in the focus groups did not necessarily understand the biology of menstruation, as evidenced by one girl's explanation of menstruation: "The blood comes from the ovary, then it comes and breaks into the uterus. Then it becomes blood and that is the monthly period."[74] Focus-group participants also reported using menstrual products longer than recommended, leading to chafing, as well as soreness from using rags or grass as absorbent materials. Some participants reported that "other girls" did not attend school while menstruating because of lack of access to menstrual products, and that "other girls" received menstrual pads from boyfriends or exchanged sex for menstrual pads.[75] The possibility that some girls engage in sexual behavior in return for pads supplied by men echoes the findings of a later study, published in 2015, which found a low, but not trivial (1.3% incidence), level of females ages thirteen to twenty reporting engaging in transactional sex to obtain menstrual pads.[76]

In addition to the obstacles impeding the government program to distribute menstrual products to all students, menstrual shaming and taboos are still common in Kenya. According to some news reports, a teacher in Kabiangek, Bomet County allegedly called a fourteen-year-old girl "dirty" and expelled her from class when the girl got her period during class and then menstrual blood stained her clothes. The girl later killed herself, setting off a protest of over two hundred parents that authorities dispersed with tear gas.[77] An investigation by the Ministry of Education, however, found that the teacher had not shamed the student.[78] Even so, the incident sparked female members of Kenya's parliament to draw new attention to the failure of the government's Sanitary Towels program and the culture of period shaming in Kenya.[79]

Another significant menstruation-related challenge in Kenya is the nexus between waste management and water safety. The Dandora Estate Sewerage Treatment Plant, located thirty kilometers from Nairobi, is the largest wastewater stabilization pond in Africa; it treats 80% of all of Nairobi's wastewater.[80] In 2019, an official for the Nairobi Water & Sewerage system reported that the majority of solids that clog the plant are plastics, condoms, menstrual products, and wet wipes.[81] Similarly, the Mavoko Water and Sewerage Company, located in Eastern Kenya, has reported that menstrual pads represent 40% of the solid material retrieved from blocked sewers. Blockages are so frequent and widespread that the company often is unable to respond in a timely manner; delays can lead to sewage backup that flows into homes.[82]

Cultural taboos and attitudes about menstruation may help explain why so much menstrual waste—including rags, menstrual pads, and tampons—gets thrown into sewers.[83] In some parts of Kenya, there may be a general desire to hide the evidence of menstruation, because of shame and secrecy associated with it. And in some pockets of Kenyan society, as in other places, there are associations between used menstrual products and curses.[84]

In addition to creating problems for traditional sewer systems, non-degradable products pose a particular challenge in areas served by pit latrines. As explored in chapter 7, commercial menstrual pads may take up to one year to decay (with their plastic liners possibly never decaying), and rags take even longer to do so. If rags are comprised of synthetic material or wrapped in polythene, a practice reported by one study in Kenya, they may not decay at all.[85] The undecomposed materials then can coalesce into larger balls that cannot be removed through the suction hoses typically used to empty urban latrines (rural latrines are typically covered over).[86]

In the nation's capital, the Nairobi River is used in poorer areas for cleaning homes and for bathing; but it is also a repository for industrial, household, and human waste, meaning the river contains harmful levels of bacteria such as *E. coli*. These bacteria can lead to typhoid, cholera, dysentery, and other water-borne diseases. Heavy metals found in the river can lead to kidney damage and are linked to cancer.[87] Kenyan commentators have observed that massive change is needed to improve the health of the river and the communities living around it; there is an urgent need to clean the water, monitor industrial waste, improve human sanitation in poor communities along the river, and provide better wastewater treatment.[88] The availability, use, and disposal of menstrual products has an enormous impact on everyday life in Kenya, as well as the health and well-being of the overall population.

Australia and Aotearoa New Zealand

Because Australia and Aotearoa New Zealand have shared histories, intramobile populations, geographic proximity, and ongoing financial, cultural, and political ties, it is useful to consider in tandem both countries' recent initiatives to increase the affordability and accessibility of menstrual products. On the issue of affordability, the most salient difference between the two countries is that Australia eliminated its goods and services tax on menstrual products in 2018, while New Zealand continues to tax menstrual products at a rate of 15%.[89] In 2018, Australia's treasurer, Josh Frydenberg, proudly pronounced that "[c]ommon sense ha[d] prevailed" when the state treasurers agreed to repeal the 10% goods and services tax on menstrual products.[90] As recently as 2015, Australian states and territories had voted to retain the tax, but women's rights groups—which had long targeted the tampon tax—brought continued pressure through demonstrations, public opinion, and a popular online campaign.[91] The tax repeal is not popular in all corners, however. Australian feminist tax scholar Miranda Stewart has critiqued the elimination of the GST on menstrual products as increasing complexity and weakening the overall tax base. Instead, Stewart and some others favor a broad tax base with no exemptions, increased tax rates, and increased spending on public health and other government functions.[92]

New Zealand also had a tampon-tax-repeal campaign of its own, with a Change.org petition started by two university students in 2017.[93] The petition received over forty thousand signatures, but did not succeed in prompting legislative action. In 2018, one tax partner at Deloitte New Zealand, Allan Bullot, predicted—correctly, as it turned out—that New Zealand would be "extremely unlikely" to follow Australia's lead, given the two countries' different philosophical taxation frameworks.[94] He explained that New Zealand tends to approach tax issues with a bedrock presumption of a large tax base (such as that endorsed by scholars like Stewart), whereas Australia's tax debates tend to focus on "evening things up" through rates and exemptions. "While there are sections of society for whom [menstrual] products are expensive, GST is not the best way to deal with it," Bullot opined, stating his preference for approaches that ensure people receive sufficient welfare payments to afford such products.[95]

Consistent with maintaining a broad tax base, New Zealand has begun taking steps to address period poverty by means other than the tax system, with a particular focus on schools. In 2020, Prime Minster Jacinda Ardern launched a $2.6 million NZ (approximately $1.7 million US) program to provide free period products in fifteen schools in the Waikato region starting with the school term beginning in July 2020.

In 2021, Ardern extended that program to all state and state-integrated schools (i.e., former private schools, including Catholic schools) beginning in June 2021. In making the announcement, Ardern explained, "Young people should not miss out on their education because of something that is a normal part of life for half the population."[96]

Ardern's concerns about menstruation-related absences were supported by data from the Youth19 Survey sponsored by the Health Research Council of New Zealand, which found that 12% of secondary school students who menstruate reported difficulty affording menstrual products and that 8% of students missed school because of lack of access to menstrual products, with rates as high as 21% in schools with the largest percentage of students from low socioeconomic communities.[97] Associate education minister Jan Tinetti reported that after the country's 2020 menstrual-product pilot program, students provided the government with feedback about which products to offer and how to do so. Tinetti said that students "wanted information about periods, period products, and other practical elements of managing their period such as tracking and knowing when and who to reach out to for assistance."[98] These responses of the New Zealand students reinforce the conclusions in chapter 3 about the importance of providing both menstrual products and menstrual education in schools.

Australia also has increasingly moved toward providing free menstrual products in schools. In 2019, the Australian state of Victoria became the first state in the nation to provide free sanitary pads and tampons in all government schools. The initiative's press release proclaimed that "[s]anitary items are a necessity, not a luxury, and the free sanitary pads and tampons in public schools initiative will support tens of thousands of students across the state."[99] The state of South Australia followed, with a trial in fifteen schools in 2020, announcing in February 2021 that free products would become available in all public schools.[100] In March 2021, the Australian state of New South Wales announced that it, too, was developing a pilot program with an eye toward the same result.[101]

As in many other countries, period poverty is a pervasive issue outside Australia's and New Zealand's schools. In a survey of five thousand New Zealand women, 23.6% reported missing school or work because of a lack of access to menstrual products; over 33% reported purchasing food over needed menstrual products; and 53% reported difficulty in purchasing menstrual products because of cost.[102] In Australia, an estimated one in eight adults and one in six children are living below the poverty line.[103] The organization Homelessness Australia estimates that 44% of the Australian homeless population are women, and that women are at a greater risk of homelessness due to several factors, including greater rates of part-time employment compared to men, absence from the workforce due to family care responsibilities, and family violence. Especially vulnerable groups include the Aboriginal and Torres Strait Islanders, the elderly, people with disabilities or mental illness, and those living in rural or remote locations.[104] In 2015, it was national news when police in Western Australia fined an Aboriginal woman five hundred dollars for shoplifting a package of tampons worth $6.45. In response to public criticism, though, the police minister doubled down, stating that "[s]tealing of any kind is an offence which the community has no tolerance for and this Government doesn't apologise for handing out swift punishment of actual consequence." Women's rights advocates critiqued the fine as both disproportionate to the offense and tone-deaf to the fact that many people do not have the basic supplies they need in order to manage menstruation, given that food pantries, shelters, and other charitable organizations do not routinely receive donations of menstrual products.[105] In 2019, the Australian government announced that it was committing $6 billion AUS (approximately $4.27 billion US) to housing support and homeless services, with states and territories to provide matching funding, with women and children among the priority cohorts for programmatic funding.[106]

Private actors have also played a role in addressing period poverty. In July 2018, the New Zealand supermarket Countdown made the astute business decision to lower prices on its store-brand menstrual products. "Sanitary products are a necessity for all women, no matter who you are or where you come from. The fact that not all women and girls can access them is something Countdown felt we wanted to help address by making good quality products more affordable for all women," the store's spokesperson said in a press release.[107] As discussed in chapter 6, Countdown made news again in 2020 when it relabeled menstrual products on its online shopping platform, dropping the label "personal care and sanitary products" (as well as "continence products") in favor of "Period and Continence Care."

Scotland

Around the globe, Scotland stands out as the nation that has most prioritized reducing period poverty. During protracted debates over the United Kingdom's elimination of the tampon tax (which finally happened once Brexit took effect on January 1, 2021), Scotland already had begun pursuing expansive strategies for addressing period poverty. In 2016, Monica Lennon, a member of the Scottish Labour Party, was elected as a member of the Scottish Parliament (MSP). She quickly made menstruation-related issues a core part of her legislative agenda. On International Women's Day in March 2017, Lennon announced that she would be introducing legislative proposals for free menstrual products in Scotland. She also led the first Member's Debate on period poverty in the Scottish Parliament. Later that year, the Scottish government announced a pilot program to provide free menstrual products to low-income women and girls in the city of Aberdeen.[108] Thus, in her very first term as a legislator, Monica Lennon showed how the law can be an effective tool for addressing menstrual inequities.

Parallel with Lennon's efforts, other Scottish legislators such as Danielle Rowley—a Scottish member of the British Parliament (and thus an MP, rather than an MSP)—also drew attention to period poverty. During a 2018 discussion in the House of Commons about the tampon tax, Rowley announced, "[T]oday I'm on my period—and it's cost me this week already [twenty-five pounds]."[109] Her remarks sparked heated discussion on social media, with some posters praising her and others asserting that she should not have been so frank about "private" matters. "I knew I was breaking a taboo, but I could not have imagined the huge reaction there has been, not just in the UK but from news organisations around the world," Rowley subsequently reflected, concluding that "[i]t helps if lots of women are talking about it and sharing their varied experiences. It becomes something that isn't a taboo anymore. I hope I have played my part in doing just that."[110] By mentioning menstruation during a formal legislative session, Rowley paved the way for others to talk about a topic that has otherwise been treated "out of sight, out of mind" by most lawmakers for centuries.

In August 2018, Scotland became the first country in the world to provide free menstrual products to students at all schools, colleges, and universities, at an initial cost of approximately £5.2 million,[111] and an annual ongoing cost of approximately £24 million ($32 million US).[112] Two different studies highlighted the need for this program: a Plan International UK survey found that between 10% and 15% of young girls surveyed had struggled to afford sanitary products;[113] a survey of two thousand students in Scotland found that 25% of them had trouble accessing menstrual products.[114] In the Scottish government's press release about the new legislation, communities secretary Aileen Campbell spoke emphatically about the need to address period poverty. "In a country as rich as Scotland it's unacceptable that anyone should struggle to buy basic sanitary products. I am proud that Scotland is taking this world-leading action to fight period poverty," she declared.[115] As described in chapter 3, members of a diverse working group (including local government leaders, university representatives, and students) had collaborated to create guiding principles for the delivery of such products in Scotland's schools, including "[p]rotecting students' dignity, avoiding anxiety, embarrassment and stigma," "[m]aking a range of products and different qualities available, giving students choice," "[e]nsuring sanitary products are easily accessible," and "[g]ender equality, ensuring anyone who menstruates can access products, including transgender men and non-binary individuals, and that language is gender neutral."[116] Students are important voices in designing programs that deliver menstrual products to them.

Following on the heels of the announcement regarding free products in schools, North Ayrshire, a council area within Scotland, announced that it would begin providing free menstrual products in all public buildings, such as libraries and community centers.[117] The leader of North Ayrshire, Joe Cullinane, explicitly linked the action to the new availability of menstrual products in the country's schools. "When you've got that kind of momentum in schools, you think that periods don't stop at the school gates, so what about their sister or mother? . . . How can we normalise this even further, so that it's like providing toilet paper or handwash?" he commented.[118] Cullinane's remarks echo the discussion in chapter 4 about free menstrual products available in public buildings as a parallel avenue for addressing period poverty.

Scotland's efforts against period poverty reached their apex in November 2020, when the Period Products (Free Provision) (Scotland) Bill passed unanimously in the Scottish Parliament. The bill included three main components: (1) requiring the Scottish government to set up a country-wide program for allowing anyone who needs menstrual products to get them free of charge; (2) requiring schools, colleges, and universities to make a range of menstrual products available for free; and (3) giving the Scottish government the power to require other public bodies to provide free menstrual products as well. The draft bill had received initial approval in February 2020, just before the COVID-19 pandemic hit. Between February and November 2020, the economic and social havoc wreaked by the pandemic only heightened the need for the Period Products (Free Provision) (Scotland) Bill.

Monica Lennon, who had initially introduced the bill in 2017 and had been promoting it for several years, said in Parliament, "It matters now more than ever, because periods don't stop in a pandemic."[119] Before the bill's passage, Lennon also spoke at length with the *Scotsman* about the next menstruation-related policy steps that she would pursue, once the bill was passed. Notably, she singled out several of the topics that are discussed in earlier chapters of this book: providing "menstrual education" to all students, ending "all stigma around menstruation," and working with trade unions to "improve period dignity in all workplaces."[120] She added that Scotland could serve as an example of best practices for the rest of the world to follow, stating that "there is an opportunity for other countries around the world to learn from what we have achieved on period poverty in just a few short years."[121]

The two-hour discussion of the draft bill in the Scottish Parliament in February 2020 notably had covered a range of period-poverty issues, including which products would and would not be provided on a complimentary basis in restrooms, as well as which types of products would work best for people with heavy bleeding.[122] A male member of the Scottish Parliament, Neil Findlay, commented that the bill had broken down "our inability to discuss such serious issues about our health and well-being in the media or in public without embarrassment, reticence and discomfort," adding that "[i]t was absolutely fantastic to see male industrial workers from Unite the union—members of my own union; I see some of them in the gallery—out there campaigning on period poverty. Long may that continue."[123]

When the bill passed unanimously in November 2020, Lennon credited collaboration among legislators, adding that "[i]n these dark times, we can bring light and hope to the world this evening."[124] Cabinet secretary Aileen Campbell added that the bill made it "clear that everyone in this chamber agrees that no one in our society should have to suffer the indignity of not having the means to meet their basic needs and that being able to access period products is fundamental to equality and dignity."[125] First Minister Nicola Sturgeon, in turn, stated that she was "proud to vote for this groundbreaking legislation."[126] The Scottish example suggests that once discussing menstruation becomes destigmatized, legislators and others can recognize the multiple ways that menstruation can be an obstacle to some people's full participation in public life. It also opens the door for robust discussion of how the law can eliminate those obstacles.

Indeed, the menstruation-related developments in the five countries discussed in this chapter provide lenses for evaluating issues of political, economic, and social equality of all people. Each country supplies examples of the challenges faced by those who menstruate, as well as strategies for addressing these obstacles. Some challenges and approaches are place-specific (such as Kenya's open-pit toilets); others are universal (such as the need for access to menstrual products in schools). Some successes have been achieved through litigation, as with India's *Sabarimala* case, while most have been achieved through legislative reform, most dramatically with the Period Products (Free Provision) (Scotland) Bill.

A common theme that emerges from the activities in all of these countries is that when an empowered and vocal citizenry meets willing and engaged political leadership (and vice versa), the law can achieve meaningful change that makes a difference in the lives of all who menstruate. The ability of half the population to worship, attend school, go to work, and otherwise participate in public life without shame or stigma is a necessary precondition for human flourishing. Open and informed discussion of menstruation must become the norm. Menstruating individuals must be empowered to advocate for their own needs, and leaders in government, religious institutions, schools, businesses, and community organizations must respond to these needs. Only then will law and society be able to fully achieve menstrual equity.

Conclusion

In 2021, two men pitched their idea for a new menstruation-related product on the German reality television show *Die Höhle der Löwen* (translation: The Lion's Den) with the hope of attracting investors from among the television judges. Over forty versions of this show air in at least 186 countries, including the United States (*Shark Tank*) and Canada (*Dragons' Den*).[1] The products pitched in these programs rarely make the news, unless they ultimately hit it big. But in April 2021, word spread fast that the two men had gotten the nod from *Die Höhle der Löwen* investor Ralf Dümmel for a menstrual product called "Pinky Gloves."

The Pinky Gloves were, indeed, pink gloves—to be used for both removal and disposal of a used tampon or pad. As several bloggers put it, the concept was akin to a "dog poo bag."[2] When it was time to remove a tampon or pad, the user would theoretically put a Pinky Glove on one hand, remove the used menstrual product with the gloved hand, use the other hand to peel off the glove and turn the glove inside-out to become a disposal bag, and then place the bag (with the used menstrual product now inside) in the trash can. Why might such a product be necessary? According to the company's website,

> Every woman knows the problem: You are a guest in another household, at festivals or when traveling and there is no rubbish bin in the local toilet for the proper disposal of used tampons and sanitary towels. In order to eliminate the resulting discomfort, Pinky is the ideal companion on all your journeys.[3]

The internet reaction was international, swift, and overwhelmingly negative. Across the globe, people pointed out that these products were unnecessary, created extra environmental waste, and perpetuated menstrual stigmas and "period shaming."[4] They also mocked the entrepreneurs as "mansplaining" the supposed need for this product.[5] Shortly thereafter, Dümmel and the Pinky Gloves founders publicly apologized for the product and took it off the market.[6]

The Pinky Gloves firestorm connects in interesting ways to the menstrual advocacy movement and the underlying project of this book. On the one hand, attention to menstruation is often welcome, given the culture of silence that typically surrounds it. But Pinky Gloves were precisely the *wrong* kind of attention. Rather than addressing genuine menstrual needs, the gloves played off pernicious menstrual stigmas, suggesting that used tampons and pads are so dirty, unhygienic, and embarrassing that they cannot even be touched with a bare hand or disposed of by ordinary means. The Pinky Gloves undermined—rather than advanced—the goal of ensuring that menstruation does not preclude anyone from fully participating, without shame, in all aspects of private and public life.

Notably—but not surprisingly—the means by which the negative reaction to the Pinky Gloves spread so quickly were social media and the internet. These mechanisms, of course, are what have fueled the growth of the larger menstrual advocacy movement, too. From chapter 2's discussion of the various nation-specific internet petitions to repeal the tampon tax to chapter 3's accounts of how students have used social media to raise awareness about the need for free menstrual products in their schools to chapter 4's description of how the founders of numerous menstruation-related charities first learned about period poverty from the internet, this book has shown that today's successful movement is truly a product of the digital age.

Also notable is that, as with other menstrual activism, the reaction to the Pinky Gloves included commentary from people of all ages.[7] Speaking out against menstrual injustice or stigma is not limited by age or position. Laura Coryton was a twenty-one-year-old university student when she launched the UK tampon-tax petition that then snowballed around the world.[8] It was a high school senior whose newspaper article led Brookline, Massachusetts, to pass a law requiring free menstrual products in all of its town-owned buildings.[9] Even middle schoolers have gotten involved, at times leading the charge to require their schools to provide free menstrual products.[10]

Law's Successes and Limitations

On the menstrual-equity front, law has been a successful tool in numerous ways. Legislative reform and (actual or threatened) litigation have worked in tandem to end the tampon tax in several countries and in multiple states, as chapter 2 details. Numerous cities and states have passed laws requiring free menstrual products to be made available in school restrooms, as described in chapter 3. Thanks to legislative initiatives by Representative Grace Meng (D-NY), menstrual products can now be purchased with Flexible Spending Accounts, Health Savings Accounts, Health Reimbursement Accounts, and by federal agencies responding to disaster relief.[11] These products eventually may become available in all federal public buildings, if the Menstrual Equity for All Act advances.[12] The law has also been successful in making menstrual products available in some state and city jails and homeless shelters.[13] The First Step Act mandates access to menstrual products for those in federal prisons.[14]

These types of issues, along with menstruation-related employment discrimination explored in chapter 5, and even the health and environmental concerns associated with menstrual products detailed in chapter 8, are ones that the law is well poised to address. Both ordinary citizens and lawyers can harness the power of law to achieve greater gender equity, whether by persuading legislative bodies to adopt new laws, urging administrative agencies to provide more complete guidance on existing laws, or bringing litigation.

As cognizant as we are about what the law has accomplished already and can achieve in the future, it is also important to acknowledge law's limitations. Compliance can be a challenge, both in the United States and abroad, particularly in the context of mandates to provide free products in schools or prisons. Similarly, strong cultural practices may be resistant to legal change. In the case of the Lord Ayyappa Temple at Sabarimala in the southern state of Kerala, India, discussed in chapter 9, many celebrated the India Supreme Court's decision allowing women to enter the temple as a victory. But the decision also set off days of violent protests by those who saw the decision as an attack on their Hindu religious values, and the Court ultimately agreed to rehear the case.[15]

So while the law is one important lever to achieve menstrual equity, this book has also identified several problems that do not lend themselves to ready legal solutions. Systemic poverty, corporations that profit from menstrual stigma and shame, and negative cultural attitudes about menstruation are not easily addressed through lawsuits or legislation. Indeed, there may be little present consensus that any of these issues *should* be addressed through law. Nevertheless, bringing menstruation—and all who menstruate—into the mainstream of public discourse is the first step in raising awareness. In turn, public conversation and opinion can shape social and political policies aimed at eliminating the tangible and intangible obstacles that menstruation can impose for some people, especially those who are vulnerable because of their age (e.g., students), their economic status (e.g., the poor or economically precarious), or their relationship with the state (e.g., prisoners and detainees).

In many ways, there is nothing new about menstruation. It is an ordinary part of life for approximately half the world's population, after all. Menstruation affects some people significantly and others not very much at all. What *is* new about menstruation is that the topic is finally emerging from the shadows of stigma and shame to take its place in legal and social discourse in the United States and other places around the globe. This book has shown that, in recent years, menstruation has become publicly visible and *speakable* in a way that it never has been before.

Speaking frankly about menstruation furthers the goals of the menstrual advocacy movement on several levels. It raises awareness about specific problems that need to be addressed, like the tampon tax or vulnerable populations' needs for free menstrual products. It enhances the long-term project of reducing menstrual stigma and expectations of concealment. And, somewhat ironically, frank talk leverages the existing taboos surrounding discussion of menstruation to achieve political gains. "Sometimes when [Representative Grace Meng] tries to pitch Democratic colleagues on her bill, they get squeamish," observed a 2019 *USA Today* article about the Menstrual Equity for All Act, quoting Meng as saying, "Some of them have said that to my face: 'I'll sign on, and you don't need to explain anymore.' I think that's hilarious . . . [H]owever I can get them to be a co-sponsor if that's part of our strategy, I'm fine with that."[16] Meng's reflection echoes the experience of state legislators like Ohio representative Brigid Kelly, who—in successfully shepherding through a bill to repeal the state's tampon tax—found that although her colleagues had been professional, "it's definitely not something they are eager to discuss over the lunch table."[17] Indeed, just as expectations of menstrual silence have allowed injustice and discrimination to flourish, subverting those expectations can help achieve menstrual equity.

All of these successes, small and large, are cause for celebration and optimism about the future of the menstrual advocacy movement. At the same time, as foundational as menstruation is to human experience, and as much as menstruation touches multiple legal issues, it is only a small part of the larger project of gender justice. Broader efforts must also address other menstruation-related issues such as menopause, discrimination related to pregnancy and breastfeeding, and reproductive justice. Menstruation, then, is a threshold justice issue—one that has been present throughout human history, and one that the law is only beginning to acknowledge. Recognizing the many ways that *menstruation matters* is the first step in making law and society more responsive to human needs.

Let us begin.

ACKNOWLEDGMENTS

We have received support from multiple people in many corners. Our project would not be possible without the visionary work of Laura Strausfeld, Jennifer Weiss-Wolf, and others who continue to draw attention to the many ways that menstruation matters. We are grateful for the inspiration and support of Judy Blume, Elizabeth B. Cooper, Martha Fineman, Jamal Hakim, Indira Jaisring, Margaret Johnson, Marcy Karin, Monica Lennon, Dahlia Lithwick, Carolyn Maloney, Grace Meng, Neville Okwaro, and Nicola Sturgeon.

For helpful comments and conversations, we thank Michele Anglade, Noa Ben-Asher, Anita Bernstein, Jason J. Czarnezki, Michele E. Gilman, Victoria J. Haneman, Anthony C. Infanti, Lolita Buckner Inniss, Katrina Fischer Kuh, Colin J. Lingle, Margot J. Pollans, Claudia Polsky, Carla Spivack, Laura Strausfeld, James F. Theis, and Jennifer Weiss-Wolf. We thank participants in faculty workshops and symposia at Columbia Law School, Florida International University College of Law, and the Elisabeth Haub Law School at Pace University.

We received technical and administrative support from Jennifer Chin and Judy Jaeger.

We are grateful for the research assistance from multiple students at the Elisabeth Haub School of Law at Pace University: Matt Califano '21, Giovanni Hernandez '21, Jacqueline Jonczyk '21, Bhumi Patel '21, and Robert Rosenberg '21. Joanna P. Jensen, Parinita Pradeep Kare, June Moon, James F. Theis, and Daphne Tsapalas provided additional research support.

We thank Clara Platter for her enthusiastic collaboration at every stage of this project, as well as guidance and assistance throughout the publication process.

The preparation of the book's index was supported by a Faculty Book and Performance Completion Award from the Pace University Provost's Office. Portions of chapters 1 and 2 draw on our work published in the

Washington Law Review and the *University of Richmond Law Review*, respectively. Chapter 3 builds on our article, coauthored with Margaret Johnson, published in the *Harvard Journal of Law & Gender*.

Finally, we thank those who have supported and inspired us throughout our work on this book, including Horace Anderson, Ann Bartow, Naomi Cahn, Michelle Simon, and Leslie Tenzer. Bridget Crawford adds special personal thanks to Aurora and Seiji for productive car rides in the summer of 2016; and to Barry Burland and Wendy Gerzog. Emily Gold Waldman adds special personal thanks to Dan, Arielle, and Benjamin Waldman, Janet and Sandy Gold, and Joan and Larry Waldman.

NOTES

INTRODUCTION

1 See Bridget Crawford, *Origins of "Are You There, Law? It's Me, Menstruation"* (Columbia Journal of Gender & Law Symposium, April 2021), FEMINIST L. PROFESSORS (Apr. 26, 2021), https://perma.cc/MAH8-RB4L; JUDY BLUME, ARE YOU THERE GOD? IT'S ME, MARGARET (1970).
2 See Chris Bobel, *From Convenience to Hazard: A Short History of the Emergence of the Menstrual Activism Movement, 1971–1992*, 29 HEALTH CARE FOR WOMEN INT'L 738, 740–41 (2008).
3 See Ashley Fetters, *The Tampon: A History*, THE ATLANTIC (June 1, 2015), https://perma.cc/68UC-ELHC.
4 See Bobel, supra note 2, at 743.
5 *Id.* at 743–49.
6 See *A Message About the Future of Our Bodies Ourselves*, OUR BODIES OURSELVES (Apr. 2, 2018), https://perma.cc/V9X7-8JEB.
7 See Bobel, supra note 2, at 739.
8 Pub. Citizen Health Rsch. Grp. v. Comm'r, Food & Drug Admin., 724 F. Supp. 1013 (D.D.C. 1989).
9 *Id.* at 1022.
10 Geary v. Dominick's Finer Foods, Inc., 544 N.E.2d 344 (Ill. 1989).
11 *Id.* at 353–57.
12 Anna Maltby, *The 8 Greatest Menstrual Moments of 2015*, COSMOPOLITAN (Oct. 13, 2015), https://perma.cc/DP2H-5E6U.
13 *Id.*
14 See Petition, *No Tax on Tampons: Stop Taxing Our Periods! Period.*, CHANGE.ORG (Oct. 10, 2015), https://perma.cc/D38W-DR4G.
15 See, e.g., Rebecca Walker, *Becoming the 3rd Wave*, MS. MAG., Jan./Feb. 1992, reprinted in MS. MAG., Spring 2002, at 86–87; JENNIFER BAUMGARDNER & AMY RICHARDS, MANIFESTA: YOUNG WOMEN, FEMINISM, AND THE FUTURE 17–18 (2000).
16 See Bridget J. Crawford, *Toward a Third-Wave Feminist Legal Theory: Young Women, Pornography, and the Praxis of Pleasure*, 14 MICH. J. GENDER & L. 99, 116–24 (2007).
17 See CHRIS BOBEL, NEW BLOOD, THIRD-WAVE FEMINISM AND THE POLITICS OF MENSTRUATION (2010).

18 *See* Camilla Mørk Røstvik, *Blood Works, Judy Chicago and Menstrual Art Since 1970*, 42 OXFORD ART J. 335 (2019).
19 *But see* Crawford, *supra* note 16, at 104 (noting lack of third-wave feminist engagement with the law).
20 Bridget Crawford, *Interview with Jennifer Weiss-Wolf, New York Attorney and Menstrual Equity Advocate*, FEMINIST L. PROFESSORS (Nov. 22, 2016) [hereinafter *Interview with Jennifer Weiss-Wolf*], https://perma.cc/FFY9-E6BN.
21 *Mission & History*, PERIOD EQUITY, https://perma.cc/A45M-NM84.
22 *Interview with Jennifer Weiss-Wolf*, *supra* note 20.
23 *See* Margaret E. Johnson et al., *Title IX & Menstruation*, 443 HARV. J. L. & GENDER 225 (2020).
24 *See* Crawford, *supra* note 16, at 116–24.
25 Anna Druet, *Menstrual Equity Is the Ground We All Need to Stand on*, CLUE (Sept. 19, 2018), https://perma.cc/9XUL-4P8G (quoting Jennifer Weiss-Wolf) (alteration in original).
26 Jen Bell & Silvia Maggi, *What's All the Fuss About Free Bleeding, and Why Does It Matter?*, CLUE (July 16, 2019), https://perma.cc/B6QE-XGDY.
27 *See* Chelsey Sanchez, *Brooklyn Girl Scouts Find City Isn't Fully Implementing Menstrual Equity Law*, GOTHAM GAZETTE (Dec. 28, 2018), https://perma.cc/97MJ-R427.
28 *See* Alexis Morillo, *Middle School Students Baked Tampon Cookies to Prove Menstrual Products Should Be Free in Schools*, DELISH (Nov. 7, 2019), https://perma.cc/C3UE-HDEM.
29 *See, e.g.*, Crawford, *supra* note 16, at 118–19; JENNIFER WEISS-WOLF, PERIODS GONE PUBLIC: TAKING A STAND FOR MENSTRUAL EQUITY xvii–ix (2017).
30 Verified Class Action Complaint, Seibert v. New York State Dep't of Tax'n & Fin., Index No. 151800/2016 (Albany Cnty. Ct. 2016), NYSCEF No. 1.
31 Bridget Crawford, *Interview with Zoe Salzman, New York Attorney Challenging the "Tampon Tax,"* FEMINIST L. PROFESSORS (July 28, 2016), https://perma.cc/DQ3W-T6MX.
32 *See* Bridget J. Crawford & Emily Gold Waldman, *Period Poverty in a Pandemic: Harnessing Law to Achieve Menstrual Equity*, 98 WASH. U. L. REV. 1569 (2021).
33 *See* Bridget J. Crawford & Emily Gold Waldman, *The Unconstitutional Tampon Tax*, 53 U. RICH. L. REV. 439 (2019).
34 *See* Johnson et al., *supra* note 23.
35 First Step Act of 2018, Pub. L. No. 115-391, 132 Stat. 5194.
36 *See* Sanchez Manning, *Transgender Lobby Forces Sanitary Towel-Maker Always to Ditch Venus Logo from Its Products*, DAILY MAIL (U.K.) (Oct. 19, 2019, 7:39 PM), https://perma.cc/55EX-Q3BP.
37 *See* Michele Estrin Gilman, *Periods for Profit and the Rise of Menstrual Surveillance*, 41 COLUM. J. GENDER & L. 100, 102–03 (2021).
38 *See* Katie Kindelan, *How Tracking Their Periods Helped USA Women's Soccer Team Win the World Cup*, GOOD MORNING AMERICA (Aug. 8, 2019), https://perma.cc/R54P-H8Q2 (quoting Dawn Scott).

39 See Katie Dupere, *Trans Artist Destroys Period Stigma with One Seriously Bold Facebook Post*, MASHABLE (July 22, 2017), https://perma.cc/JD83-BZR6; *see also* Jen Bell, *Menstruating While Trans: Meet Artist and Educator Cass Clemmer*, CLUE (July 30, 2017), https://perma.cc/6CRR-S5K9.
40 *Compare, e.g.*, ELI R. GREEN & LUCA MAURER, THE TEACHING TRANSGENDER TOOLKIT: A FACILITATOR'S GUIDE TO INCREASING KNOWLEDGE, DECREASING PREJUDICE & BUILDING SKILLS 53–57 (2015), https://perma.cc/PJY2-P47C (*Glossary of Transgender Terms, Avoiding Outdated & Offensive Terminology*), *with Glossary of Terms—Transgender*, GLAAD, https://perma.cc/6W4Q-EX93.
41 These definitions are borrowed from, and the quoted language comes from, the GLAAD Media Reference Guide. *See Glossary of Terms—Transgender*, GLAAD, https://perma.cc/6W4Q-EX93.
42 *Id.*
43 Trina Grillo, *Anti-Essentialism and Intersectionality: Tools to Dismantle the Master's House*, 10 BERKELEY WOMEN'S L.J. 16, 21 (1995).

CHAPTER 1. MENSTRUAL STIGMA, SHAME, AND PERIOD POVERTY

1 *See* Judith Vonberg, *She Had No Sanitary Pads. No One Knew and No One Helped*, CNN (Oct. 3, 2018), https://perma.cc/5M4L-ZMBK.
2 Amarica Rafanelli, *Rags Instead of Tampons. Here's What Period Poverty Looks Like in the U.S.*, DIRECT RELIEF (Oct. 23, 2019, 6:07 AM), https://perma.cc/TL5X-EU5V (transcript of podcast) (quoting Nancy and Jorie Nilson).
3 *See* JESSICA SEMEGA ET AL., U.S. CENSUS BUREAU, INCOME AND POVERTY IN THE UNITED STATES: 2019, at 12–15 (2020), https://perma.cc/3379-KQ4T.
4 Anne Sebert Kuhlmann et al., *Unmet Menstrual Hygiene Needs Among Low-Income Women*, 133 OBSTETRICS & GYNECOLOGY 238 (2019), https://perma.cc/4WKX-S5VB.
5 *See, e.g.*, Seth Freed Wessler, *Timed Out on Welfare, Many Sell Food Stamps*, TYPE INVESTIGATIONS (Feb. 16, 2010), https://perma.cc/X59A-QXWR (describing one woman's experience).
6 42 U.S.C. §§ 601–19.
7 *Id.*
8 Gene Falk & Patrick A. Landers, *The Temporary Assistance for Needy Families (TANF) Block Grant: Responses to Frequently Asked Questions*, CONG. RSCH. SERV. (July 16, 2020), https://perma.cc/K5WG-73NC.
9 *See* Kimberly Yam, *Free Tampons, Pads Now Stocked in Bathrooms Across Brown University Campus*, HUFFINGTON POST (Sept. 7, 2016, 6:01 PM), https://perma.cc/AK8R-H9QA.
10 THINX & PERIOD, STATE OF THE PERIOD: THE WIDESPREAD IMPACT OF PERIOD POVERTY ON US STUDENTS 1, 2, https://perma.cc/9A4J-KETE [hereinafter STATE OF THE PERIOD]; *see also* Margaret E. Johnson et al., *Title*

IX & Menstruation, 43 HARV. J.L. & GENDER 225, 233–34 (2020) (discussing same study).

11 Christopher A. Cotropia, *Menstruation Management in United States Schools and Implications for Attendance, Academic Performance, and Health*, 6 WOMEN'S REPROD. HEALTH 289, 295 (2019).

12 STATE OF THE PERIOD, *supra* note 10.

13 *See, e.g.*, Erica Sanchez & Leah Rodriguez, *Period Poverty: Everything You Need to Know*, GLOBAL CITIZEN (Feb. 5, 2019), https://perma.cc/C8UM-KLAF.

14 *See, e.g., About Us*, SAHAYOG, https://perma.cc/7FVL-4UWT.

15 *See, e.g., Our History*, WATERAID, https://perma.cc/8J6W-CCWX.

16 *See infra* chapter 8.

17 *See* Subeta Vimalarajah, *Stop Taxing My Period!*, https://perma.cc/A6HL-DLMM (Australia petition); Jill Piebiak, *Government of Canada—No Tax on Tampons: A Campaign to Remove the GST Charged on Menstruation Products*, https://perma.cc/5UYS-ZXHL (Canada petition); Jennifer Weiss-Wolf, *No Tax on Tampons: Stop Taxing Our Periods! Period.*, https://perma.cc/FJ8A-TF8T (US petition); Laura Coryton, *Stop Taxing Periods. Period. #EndTamponTax*, https://perma.cc/PQW3-H94T (UK petition).

18 JENNIFER WEISS-WOLF, PERIODS GONE PUBLIC: TAKING A STAND FOR MENSTRUAL EQUITY xvi (2017).

19 *Mission & History*, PERIOD EQUITY, https://perma.cc/PE6U-4CWD.

20 *What Does Menstrual Equity Mean to You?*, WOMEN'S VOICES FOR THE EARTH, https://perma.cc/J5X4-E6YP.

21 *See* Margaret E. Johnson, *Menstrual Justice*, 53 U.C. DAVIS L. REV. 1, 8–9 (2019).

22 *Every Woman's Right to Water, Sanitation and Hygiene*, U.N. OFF. OF THE HIGH COMM'R FOR HUM. RTS. (Mar. 14, 2014), https://perma.cc/R7JN-342F.

23 *Women's Menstrual Health Should No Longer Be a Taboo*, U.N. OFF. OF THE HIGH COMM'R FOR HUM. RTS. (Mar. 5, 2019), https://perma.cc/VQ65-R9CE.

24 *See Time to Tampax with Amy Schumer*, TAMPAX, https://perma.cc/J8CV-HG23.

25 *Id.*

26 Brittney McNamara, *6 Period Myths and the Truth About Them*, TEEN VOGUE (May 28, 2019), https://perma.cc/594Z-AK9Z.

27 STATE OF THE PERIOD, *supra* note 10, at 2; *see also* Johnson et al., *supra* note 10, at 233–34.

28 *See* Tomi-Ann Roberts et al., *"Feminine Protection": The Effects of Menstruation on Attitudes Towards Women*, 26 PSYCH. WOMEN Q. 131, 136–38 (2002).

29 *See* Ma Luisa Marván et al., *Stereotypes of Women in Different Stages of Their Reproductive Life: Data from Mexico and the United States*, 29 HEALTH CARE FOR WOMEN INT'L 673 (2008).

30 TÁIN BÓ CÚAILNG FROM THE BOOK OF LEINSTER 269 (Cecile O'Rahilly ed., 1970).

31 *Leviticus* 15:19–22.

32 See, e.g., Ilana S. Cristofar, *Blood, Water and the Impure Woman: Can Jewish Women Reconcile Between Ancient Law and Modern Feminism?*, 10 S. CAL. REV. L. & WOMEN'S STUD. 451, 452 (2001); Channa Lockshin Bob, *A Detailed Explanation of Niddah, or "Family Purity" Laws*, MY JEWISH LEARNING, https://perma.cc/V9ZZ-RG5M.
33 Tova Mirvis, *Personal Narrative: Out of the Mikvah, into the World*, LENNY LETTER (Sept. 19, 2017), *reprinted in* THE PALGRAVE HANDBOOK OF CRITICAL MENSTRUATION STUDIES 131, 131 (Chris Bobel et al. eds., 2020).
34 See, e.g., *Menstruation and Human Rights—Frequently Asked Questions*, U.N. POPULATION FUND (May 2020), https://perma.cc/QZP6-MCY6.
35 See id.
36 See id.
37 *See* SARAH HOUSE ET AL., WATER AID, MENSTRUAL HYGIENE MATTERS: A RESOURCE FOR IMPROVING MENSTRUAL HYGIENE AROUND THE WORLD 27 (2012), https://perma.cc/77JH-BW25.
38 See, e.g., Catherine Kansiime et al., *Menstrual Health Intervention and School Attendance in Uganda (MENISCUS-2): A Pilot Intervention*, 10 BMJ OPEN 1, 11 n.16 (2020); *see* House et al., *supra* note 37, at 56–57.
39 Shannon A. McMahon et al.,*"The Girl with Her Period Is the One to Hang Her Head": Reflections on Menstrual Management Among Schoolgirls in Rural Kenya*, 11 BMC INT'L HEALTH & HUM. RTS. 1 (2011), https://perma.cc/3XQ5-5U2H.
40 Teketo Kassaw Tegegne & Mitike Molla Sisay, *Menstrual Hygiene Management and School Absenteeism Among Female Adolescent Students in Northeast Ethiopia*, 14 BMC PUB. HEALTH 1, 7 (2014), https://perma.cc/F2N8-EY39.
41 *Id.* at 8.
42 Maureen C. McHugh, *Menstrual Shame: Exploring the Role of "Menstrual Moaning"*, in THE PALGRAVE HANDBOOK OF CRITICAL MENSTRUATION STUDIES 409, 409 (Chris Bobel et al. eds., 2020).
43 See, e.g., Christina Cauterucci, *Embracing "the Blob"—and Other Period Euphemisms*, SLATE (Mar. 1, 2016, 2:52 PM), https://perma.cc/QD76-RFH6; *Top Euphemisms for "Period" by Language*, CLUE (Mar. 10, 2016), https://perma.cc/4VVK-VL98.
44 *See* Erin Laskis, *Period Slang & Funny Euphemisms: Great Code Words for Aunt Flo*, KNIXTEEN (June 6, 2018), https://perma.cc/PBM2-MRZF.
45 Alma Gottlieb, *Menstrual Taboos: Moving Beyond the Curse*, in THE PALGRAVE HANDBOOK OF CRITICAL MENSTRUATION STUDIES 143, 145 (Chris Bobel et al. eds., 2020).
46 *Id.*
47 *See* Roberts et al., *supra* note 28, at 138.
48 *Id.*
49 Gloria Steinem, *If Men Could Menstruate*, MS. MAG., October 1978, *reprinted in* THE PALGRAVE HANDBOOK OF CRITICAL MENSTRUATION STUDIES 353, 353–54 (Chris Bobel et al. eds., 2020).

50 *See, e.g.*, Laura Bennett, *What Trump Really Meant When He Said That Megyn Kelly Had "Blood Coming Out of Her Wherever,"* SLATE (Aug. 10, 2015, 7:33 PM), https://perma.cc/KFE6-6CUP.
51 haley (@haleyp), TWITTER (Aug. 8, 2015, 11:08 AM), https://twitter.com/haleyp/status/630229206753017857.
52 Tara Dublin, Untapped Writing Goldmine #SignTara (@taradublinrocks), TWITTER (Aug. 10, 2015, 2:54 PM), https://twitter.com/taradublinrocks/status/630829492475293696.
53 *See* Rachel Dicker, *Women Are Calling the Indiana Governor to Tell Him About Their Periods*, U.S. NEWS & WORLD REP. (Apr. 6, 2016), https://perma.cc/AFR2-GPW9 (reproducing Facebook posts from the account Periods for Politicians/Periods for Pence).
54 *See* Allison Carter, *Periods for Pence Evolves into Tampons for Trump*, INDY STAR (July 19, 2016, 5:27 PM), https://perma.cc/M5NX-9R2K.
55 JUDY BLUME, ARE YOU THERE GOD? IT'S ME, MARGARET (1970).
56 Judy Blume, *Judy Blume on the 50th Anniversary of Are You There God? It's Me, Margaret*, BOOKS & BOOKS, https://perma.cc/6R8W-8AK6.
57 *See* Jen Bell, *What Advertising Teaches Us About Periods*, CLUE (Sept. 11, 2017), https://perma.cc/6SVN-BP35.
58 Jessica Henderson, *Haute Heritage: 6 Vintage Johnson & Johnson Ads Shot by Famous Fashion Photographers*, JOHNSON & JOHNSON (Sept. 5, 2018), https://perma.cc/F7MM-HLU6.
59 *See Olympic Gymnast Cathy Rigby and Stayfree Menstrual Pads*, MUSEUM OF MENSTRUATION & WOMEN'S HEALTH, https://perma.cc/L2GS-3ZCX (showcasing the May 1982 ad).
60 *See, e.g.*, Maggie Mertens, *Great Moments in Menstrual History*, THE CUT (Sept. 14, 2015), https://perma.cc/X439-PLH4.
61 *See* Arti Patel, *Kotex Breaks Tradition and Uses Blood-Like Liquid in New Ad*, GLOBAL NEWS (Jan. 24, 2020, 2:59 PM), https://perma.cc/7LBF-7WYK.
62 *See* Julie Bort, *Amazon and Other Sellers Have Run Out of Tampons as Coronavirus Fears Sell Out Online Stores*, BUS. INSIDER (Mar. 20, 2020, 4:11 PM), https://perma.cc/YMY5-EC5K.
63 Emma Goldberg, *Periods Don't Stop for Pandemics, So She Brings Pads to Women in Need*, N.Y. TIMES (Apr. 5, 2020), https://perma.cc/XK84-YRL4.
64 I Support The Girls (@I_Support_Girls), TWITTER (Mar. 21, 2020, 9:31 AM), https://twitter.com/I_Support_Girls/status/1241371856030044161.
65 Goldberg, *supra* note 63.
66 *See* PLAN INTERNATIONAL, PERIODS IN A PANDEMIC: MENSTRUAL HYGIENE MANAGEMENT IN THE TIME OF COVID-19, at 4 (2020), https://perma.cc/J32R-5SM3 (quoting "Young woman, Indonesia").
67 *Id.* (quoting "Young woman, Australia").

68 *See id.* at 3. In addition to surveying professionals, Plan International also surveyed people who menstruate in Australia, Ireland, Fiji, the Solomon Islands, Papua New Guinea, Indonesia, and Vanuatu. *Id.*
69 *See* Jeffrey Gettleman & Kai Schultz, *Modi Orders 3-Week Total Lockdown for All 1.3 Billion Indians*, N.Y. TIMES (Mar. 24, 2020), https://perma.cc/V4MV-TAUH (quoting Prime Minister Modi).
70 *See* Puja Awasthi, *These UP Girls Are Reminding Us Periods Don't Stop During a Pandemic*, THE WEEK (May 28, 2020, 11:52 AM), https://perma.cc/WEC5-64M7.
71 *See Access to Menstrual Health Supplies During COVID-19: What Have We Learnt?*, REPROD. HEALTH SUPPLIES COAL. (June 12, 2020), https://perma.cc/3DKN-8768.
72 *See* PLAN INTERNATIONAL, *supra* note 66, at 7 (quoting "Program Facilitator, Zimbabwe").
73 *Id.* (quoting "Young woman, Fiji").
74 *See* Sophia Chang, *City Has Handed Out Nearly 14 Million Meals During Outbreak, Adding Tampons and Pads to Distribution Sites After Push*, GOTHAMIST (May 16, 2020, 1:40 PM), https://perma.cc/2GNU-ZECL.
75 *See, e.g.,* Goldberg, *supra* note 63.
76 *See, e.g.,* Caren Lissner, *Periods Don't Stop in a Pandemic, Say Westfield and Summit Women*, PATCH (July 20, 2020, 5:41 AM), https://perma.cc/PKM8-K47J.
77 *See Periods in the Pandemic: 9 Things We Need to Know*, UNICEF (May 27, 2020), https://perma.cc/824V-GDP2.
78 *See* UNICEF, COVID-19 EMERGENCY RESPONSE: MONITORING AND MITIGATING THE SECONDARY IMPACTS OF THE COVID19 EPIDEMIC ON WASH SERVICES AVAILABILITY AND ACCESS 1–3 (Mar. 11, 2020), https://perma.cc/9EKZ-MFRH.
79 *See* PLAN INTERNATIONAL, *supra* note 66, at 6.
80 *See, e.g.,* Alan Nicol, *The Pandemic Is Laying Bare a Global Water Crisis*, FOREIGN POL'Y (May 12, 2020, 3:44 PM), https://perma.cc/K67N-GPJF.
81 *See* Anouk Ride & Georgina Kekea, *Together or Apart Against COVID-19? The Solomon Islands State of Emergency*, ASIA & THE PAC. POL'Y SOC'Y (June 5, 2020), https://perma.cc/6SZL-Q92P.
82 *See* PLAN INTERNATIONAL, *supra* note 66, at 9 (quoting "Young woman, Solomon Islands").
83 *Id.* (quoting "Young woman, Fiji").
84 *Id.* at 9 (quoting "Program Facilitator from Zimbabwe").
85 *See* Shobhita Rajagopal & Kanchan Mathur, *"Breaking the Silence Around Menstruation": Experiences of Adolescent Girls in an Urban Setting in India*, 25 GENDER & DEV. 303, 306–7 (2017).
86 PLAN INTERNATIONAL, *supra* note 66, at 5 (quoting "Young woman, Australia").
87 *Id.* (quoting "Woman 30+, Australia").

88 See, e.g., Yelena Dzhanova, *Sanitation Workers Battle Higher Waste Levels in Residential Areas as Coronavirus Outbreak Persists*, CNBC (May 16, 2020, 9:15 AM), https://perma.cc/7NQH-ALQC; see PLAN INTERNATIONAL, *supra* note 66, at 9 ("Without access to rubbish disposal systems, people often burn or bury pads some distance from home.").
89 See, e.g., Marni Sommer et al., *Girls' and Women's Unmet Needs for Menstrual Hygiene Management (MHM): The Interactions Between MHM and Sanitation Systems in Low-Income Countries*, 3 J. WATER, SANITATION & HYGIENE FOR DEV. 283, 287–88 (2013).
90 See PLAN INTERNATIONAL, *supra* note 66, at 10 (alteration in original) (quoting "Young woman, Papua New Guinea").
91 See *id.* at 10.
92 *Id.*
93 See Pınar Yalçın Bahat et al., *The Covid-19 Pandemic and Patients with Endometriosis: A Survey-Based Study Conducted in Turkey*, 151 INT'L J. GYNECOL. OBSTETS. 249 (2020).
94 *Id.*
95 See, e.g., Lori Beail-Farkas, *The Human Right to Water and Sanitation: Context, Contours, and Enforcement Prospects*, 30 WIS. INT'L L.J. 761, 762–68 (2013).
96 See Caroline Kabiru, *Periods in a Pandemic: Women and Girls in Low-Income Settlements Need More Support*, THE CONVERSATION (May 28, 2020, 3:58 AM), https://perma.cc/J9GD-53Q6.
97 *Id.*
98 CARES Act, Pub. L. No. 116-136, 137 Stat. 281 (2020).
99 CARES Act § 3702, Pub. L. No. 116-136, 137 Stat. 281 (2020); IRC § 223(d)(2).
100 See Selena Simmons-Duffin, *Save Those Pharmacy Receipts! New Payment Flexibility, Courtesy of COVID Rescue Act*, NPR (Apr. 1, 2020, 4:30 PM), https://perma.cc/8J8U-QE8D (quoting Jennifer Berman).
101 See Leah Rodriguez, *US Government Acknowledges Period Products Are Necessities in COVID-19 Stimulus Bill*, GLOBAL CITIZEN (Apr. 10, 2020), https://perma.cc/QCH3-GT9Q (quoting Jennifer Weiss-Wolf).
102 See, e.g., Bridget J. Crawford & Emily Gold Waldman, *Tampons and Pads Should Be Allowed at the Bar Exam*, N.Y.L.J. (July 22, 2020, 2:09 PM), https://perma.cc/SXU8-8GAT; see also Bridget J. Crawford, *Menstruation and the Bar Exam: Unconstitutional Tampons Bans*, 41 COLUM. J. GENDER & L. 63, 64–65 (2021); Elizabeth B. Cooper et al., *Menstrual Dignity and the Bar Exam*, 55 U.C. DAVIS L. REV. 1, 14–15 (2021).
103 ARIZONA SUPREME COURT, INSTRUCTIONS AND INFORMATION: ARIZONA UNIFORM BAR EXAMINATION (2020), https://perma.cc/5RPA-9WN8.
104 *Id.*
105 See Crawford & Waldman, *supra* note 102. Professor Cat Moon is the originator of the #bloodybarpolcalypse hashtag, at least in the context of menstrual products at

the bar exam. *See* Cat Moon (@inspiredcat), TWITTER (July 16, 2020, 4:27 PM), https://twitter.com/inspiredcat/status/1283875875273007104.
106 *See* Letter from a group of professors, lawyers, recent law school graduates, and law students to Judith Gunderson, President & CEP of the National Conference of Bar Examiners (July 20, 2020), https://perma.cc/G9MF-SQPD.
107 *See* Stephanie Francis Ward, *Do Some States Really Prohibit Bringing Tampons and Pads to the Bar Exam?*, ABA J. (July 23, 2020, 12:47 PM), https://perma.cc/2C7N-MKP5.
108 WEST VIRGINIA BOARD OF LAW EXAMINERS, FREQUENTLY ASKED QUESTIONS—EXAM APPLICANTS 3, https://perma.cc/L2QX-GJM6.
109 *See* Ward, *supra* note 107.
110 *See, e.g.*, Megan Specia, *Tackling "Period Poverty," Scotland Is First Nation to Make Sanitary Products Free*, N.Y. TIMES (Nov. 24, 2020), https://perma.cc/4GGZ-CLZN.
111 *Id.*

CHAPTER 2. THE TAMPON TAX
1 *See, e.g.*, Alice Hearing, *Tampon Tax: How Laura Coryton Started the "Stop Taxing Periods" Campaign While a Student*, INDEPENDENT (Feb. 23, 2016, 3:28 PM), https://perma.cc/3T9J-TNC9; Rebecca Holman, *Q: Why Are We Getting Taxed for Tampons but Not Crocodile Meat?*, GRAZIA DAILY UK (June 6, 2014), https://perma.cc/2PDS-86DS.
2 Laura Coryton, *Stop Taxing Periods. Period. #EndTamponTax*, https://perma.cc/PQW3-H94T.
3 *Id.*
4 Holman, *supra* note 1.
5 Indeed, by the end of 2014, there were already an estimated 2.3 billion broadband subscribers, a figure that has only increased in subsequent years. INT'L TELECOMM. UNION, ICT FACTS AND FIGURES 2014, at 6 (2014) https://perma.cc/B7W2-G6MS (estimating 44% of global households have internet access in 2014); INT'L TELECOMM. UNION, MEASURING DIGITAL DEVELOPMENT: FACTS AND FIGURES 2020, at 6 (2020), https://perma.cc/VY35-MJA8 (estimating 57% percent of global households with internet access at home in 2019).
6 *See* Elke Asen, *2021 VAT Rates in Europe*, TAX FOUND. (Jan. 7, 2021), https://perma.cc/2SRE-JN7A.
7 Council Directive 2006/112, art. 99, of the Council of the European Union of 28 Nov. 2006 on the Common System of Value Added Tax, 2006 O.J. (L. 347) 1, 24.
8 *See* Gail Cole, *Tampons Aren't Essential, Crocodile Meat Is. Wacky Tax Wednesday*, AVALARA (Aug. 20, 2014), https://perma.cc/5UWD-SRRQ.
9 *See* Christina Morales, *U.K. Eliminates Tax on Tampons and Other Sanitary Products*, N.Y. TIMES (Jan. 1, 2021), https://perma.cc/XNM6-VDTY.
10 *See* Geary v. Dominick's Finer Foods, Inc., 520 N.E.2d 968 (Ill. App. Ct.) (striking part of claim), *perm. app. granted*, 535 N.E.2d 401 (Ill. 1988), *and rev'd and remanded*, 544 N.E.2d 344 (Ill. 1989).

11 *Geary*, 520 N.E.2d 968.
12 See Robin Levinson King, *The Unsung History of the Fight to End the Tax on Tampons*, TORONTO STAR (May 12, 2015), https://perma.cc/NRU8-4D2Z.
13 See Vicky Hallett, *What Kenya Can Teach the U.S. About Menstrual Pads*, NPR (May 10, 2016, 9:00 AM), https://perma.cc/M2GP-7BQ5.
14 Jill Piebiak, *Government of Canada—No Tax on Tampons: A Campaign to Remove the GST Charged on Menstruation Products*, https://perma.cc/5UYS-ZXHL.
15 See Morales, *supra* note 9.
16 See *About the Campaign*, CANADIAN MENSTRUATORS, https://perma.cc/9CH2-3U3D; Jason Fekete, *Federal Government Taking the Tax off Tampons, Effective July 1*, OTTAWA CITIZEN (June 2, 2020), https://perma.cc/29KY-KSL9.
17 See Michele Henry, *Toronto Woman Behind Campaign to Kill Tampon Tax "Ecstatic" over Victory*, TORONTO STAR (June 4, 2015), https://perma.cc/PWD5-RNMV (quoting Jill Piebiak).
18 See Subeta Vimalarajah, *Stop taxing my period!*, https://perma.cc/39NE-JFN4 (petition to Australia's state and territory treasurers).
19 *"Tampon Tax" Scrapped in Australia After 18-Year Controversy*, BBC (Oct. 3, 2018), https://perma.cc/QZ5V-GE2N.
20 See Steve George, *Australia Scraps Controversial Tampon Tax*, CNN (Oct. 3, 2018, 11:57 AM), https://perma.cc/8AJ8-3PT8.
21 JENNIFER WEISS-WOLF, PERIODS GONE PUBLIC: TAKING A STAND FOR MENSTRUAL EQUITY 133 (2017).
22 *Id.*
23 A. 7555A, 2015–2016 Legis. Sess. (N.Y. 2016); S. 7838, 2015–2016 Legis. Sess. (N.Y. 2016).
24 Jennifer Weiss-Wolf, *No Tax on Tampons: Stop Taxing Our Periods! Period.*, https://perma.cc/D38W-DR4G (petition to US state legislators).
25 *Id.*
26 See Bridget J. Crawford & Emily Gold Waldman, *The Unconstitutional Tampon Tax*, 53 U. RICH. L. REV. 439, 455–56 (2019).
27 *Id.* at 447.
28 Bridget Crawford, *Interview with Laura Strausfeld, New York Attorney Challenging the "Tampon Tax,"* FEMINIST L. PROFESSORS (Nov. 15, 2016), https://perma.cc/8ZNB-423X.
29 *Id.*; see also Verified Class Action Complaint, Seibert v. N.Y. State Dep't of Tax'n & Fin., No. 151800/2016 (N.Y. Sup. Ct. Mar. 3, 2016), NYSCEF No. 1, *transferred under* No. 904075–16 (N.Y. Sup. Ct. 2016), https://perma.cc/G6CU-3X9U.
30 N.Y. TAX LAW § 1105(a).
31 Verified Class Action Complaint, *supra* note 29, at paras. 2–4.
32 *Id.* at paras. 31, 5.
33 *Id.* at para. 6.
34 Linda B. Rosenthal (@LindaBRosenthal), TWITTER (July 21, 2016, 11:10 AM), https://twitter.com/LindaBRosenthal/status/756189723937439744.

35 Press Release, Office of the Governor, Governor Cuomo Signs Legislation to Exempt Sales and Use Taxes on Feminine Hygiene Products (July 21, 2016), https://perma.cc/H9VT-9SBM.
36 Class Action Complaint at paras. 40, 34, Wendell v. Fla. Dep't of Revenue, No. 2016 CA 001526 (Fla. Leon County Ct. 2016).
37 Order Granting Motion of California Department of Tax & Fee Administration for Summary Judgment & Denying Motion of Plaintiffs for Summary Judgment at 4–8, Disimone v. Cal. Dep't of Tax and Fee Admin., No. CGC-16-552458, 2018 Cal. Super. LEXIS 1814 (Jan. 29, 2018), https://perma.cc/F458-MTDP.
38 *See* Leah Rodriguez, *California Just Officially Eliminated Its "Tampon Tax,"* GLOBAL CITIZEN (Jan. 9, 2020), https://perma.cc/3JH5-3GG4.
39 Rowitz v. McClain, 138 N.E.3d 1241 (Ohio Ct. App. 2019).
40 *Id.* at 1252–58.
41 *Id.* at 1268.
42 U.S. CONST. amend. XIV, § 1.
43 Personnel Adm'r of Mass. v. Feeney, 442 U.S. 256 (1979).
44 *Id.* at 259, 261–63, 270, 276–79, 281 (1979).
45 Bray v. Alexandria Women's Health Clinic, 506 U.S. 263, 270 (1993).
46 Geduldig v. Aiello, 417 U.S. 484 (1974).
47 *Id.* at 487–89, 493–94.
48 *Id.* at 496 n.20.
49 General Elec. Co. v. Gilbert, 429 U.S. 125 (1976).
50 Pregnancy Discrimination Act of 1978, Pub. L. No. 95-555, 92 Stat. 2076 (codified as amended at 42 U.S.C. § 2000e(k)).
51 *Id.*
52 Craig v. Boren, 429 U.S. 190 (1976).
53 Frontiero v. Richardson, 411 U.S. 677 (1973) (four justices applied strict scrutiny in a case involving laws that automatically granted spousal benefits to married men but not married women in the Air Force).
54 Obergefell v. Hodges, 576 U.S. 644 (2015).
55 Holning Lau & Hillary Li, *American Equal Protection and Global Convergence*, 86 FORDHAM L. REV. 1251, 1261–63 (2017).
56 Geduldig v. Aiello, 417 U.S. 484, 496 n.20 (1974) (emphasis added).
57 *Id.* (citations omitted).
58 *See* Moritz v. Comm'r, 469 F.2d 466, 470 (10th Cir. 1972) (finding unconstitutional the denial of a tax deduction to a never-married man that was otherwise available to similarly situated widowers, married men, divorced men, and all women).
59 Totes-Isotoner Corp. v. United States, 594 F.3d 1346, 1355 (Fed. Cir.), *cert. denied*, 562 U.S. 830 (2010) (emphasis added).
60 Daily Mail, *President Obama Is Shocked to Learn About Tampon Tax in the US—Daily Mail*, YOUTUBE (March 15, 2018), https://www.youtube.com/watch?v=Wgu4RXCkJLE.

61 *Totes-Isotoner Corp.*, 594 F.3d at 1358 (quoting Bray v. Alexandria Women's Health Clinic, 506 U.S. 263, 270 (1993)).
62 United States v. Virginia, 518 U.S. 515, 531 (1996).
63 *Id.* at 533–34 (last alteration added) (quoting Califano v. Webster, 430 U.S. 313, 320 (1977) (per curiam); Cal. Fed. Sav. & Loan Ass'n v. Guerra, 479 U.S. 272, 289 (1987)).
64 U.S. Dep't of Agric. v. Moreno, 413 U.S. 528 (1973).
65 *Id.*
66 *See Exit Polls for Nevada Question 2: Repeal Pink Tax*, CNN (Dec. 21, 2018), https://perma.cc/V2T8-3YXE.
67 *See India Scraps Tampon Tax After Campaign*, BBC (Jul. 21, 2018), https://perma.cc/P45R-Z6NJ.
68 Corte Constitucional [C.C.] [Constitutional Court], noviembre 14, 2018, Sentencia C-117/18, https://perma.cc/HGY5-C2PR.
69 *See* Yvonne Wabai, *Rwanda Removes Tax on Sanitary Pads*, THE AFRICAN EXPONENT (Dec. 14, 2019), https://perma.cc/F7BD-CVVT.
70 *See* Rachel Epstein, *The Current State of the Tampon Tax—and How We're Going to Eliminate It*, MARIE CLAIRE (Oct. 18, 2019), https://perma.cc/CJ58-PW9V (quoting D.C. councilmember Anita Bonds).
71 *DiPalma Legislation to End "Tampon Tax" Gets House Approval*, NEWPORT (RI) DAILY NEWS (Jun. 24, 2019, 3:06 PM), https://perma.cc/4UR4-8XEH.
72 *See* Ema Sagner, *More States Move to End "Tampon Tax" That's Seen As Discriminating Against Women*, NPR (Mar. 25, 2018, 7:01 AM), https://perma.cc/25L2-VWL5.
73 *See* Becky Jacobs, *Utah Eliminates Tampon Tax with Sweeping Reform Package*, SALT LAKE TRIB. (Dec. 19, 2019, 2:55 PM), https://perma.cc/72AS-53FQ (quoting Utah State Representative Robert McCormick (R-Sandy)).
74 *See id.* (quoting Emily Bell McCormick).
75 *See About Tax Free. Period.*, TAXFREE. PERIOD., https://perma.cc/4FJ4-JKJQ; *Explore Our Interactive Map*, TAXFREE. PERIOD., https://perma.cc/TJ7H-ZWCU.
76 42 U.S.C. § 2000e(k).
77 Young v. United Parcel Serv., Inc., 135 S.Ct. 1338 (2015).
78 *Id.*
79 42 U.S.C. § 2000e(k).
80 *Young*, 135 S.Ct. at 1344, 1342 (alteration in original).
81 *Id.* at 1349–50 (emphasis in original).
82 *Id.* at 1350–53.
83 McDonnell Douglas Corp. v. Green, 411 U.S. 792 (1973).
84 *Young*, 135 S.Ct. at 1342–43.
85 *See Sales Tax Exemptions for Healthcare Items*, COMPTROLLER.TEXAS.GOV (May 2020), https://perma.cc/PXA8-76B2 (listing products eligible for sales tax exemption).

86 See, e.g., Arwa Mahdawi, *Tennessee Republicans Worry Women Will Go on Tampon-Buying Frenzy*, GUARDIAN (U.K.) (Feb. 14, 2020, 5:00 PM), https://perma.cc/3GLV-CT2K (citing economic reasons given by states for maintaining tampon tax).
87 See, e.g., Bridget J. Crawford & Emily Gold Waldman, *Tampons and Pads Should Be Allowed at the Bar Exam*, N.Y.L.J. (July 22, 2020, 2:09 PM).
88 See Press Release, *supra* note 35.
89 Press Release, Office of Senator Lynda Wilson, Wilson Bill to End State Tax on Menstrual Products Passes Legislature (Mar. 10, 2020), https://perma.cc/G7MC-2TF5.
90 *Id.*
91 See Sagner, *supra* note 72 (quoting Ohio State Representative Brigid Kelly).
92 United States v. Windsor, 570 U.S. 744 (2013); Obergefell, 576 U.S. 644.

CHAPTER 3. SCHOOLS AND MENSTRUATION
1 Yilu Zhao, *Beyond "Sweetie,"* N.Y. TIMES (Nov. 7, 2004), https://perma.cc/9NDN-FTM5. This chapter is based in part on a journal article written by the authors and Margaret Johnson. See Margaret E. Johnson et al., *Title IX & Menstruation*, 43 HARV. J.L. & GENDER 225 (2020).
2 See Annual Report of the Number and Percentage of Public School Students Eligible for Free or Reduced-Price Lunch by State in Selected Years from 2000–01 through 2017–18, NAT'L CTR. FOR EDUC. STAT. (Feb. 2020), https://perma.cc/7TB6-TNGS.
3 JENNIFER WEISS-WOLF, PERIODS GONE PUBLIC: TAKING A STAND FOR MENSTRUAL EQUITY 148 (2017).
4 See, e.g., *Funding Our Schools*, N.Y.C. DEP'T OF EDUC., https://perma.cc/Q32H-CYHX (explaining that for the 2020–2021 academic year, New York City will provide 57% of the total $34 billion budget for the Department of Education, separate and apart from the capital budget).
5 WEISS-WOLF, *supra* note 3, at 148–52.
6 Jennifer Gerson Uffalussy, *First Free Tampon Machine Comes to New York City School*, YAHOO NEWS (Sept. 23, 2015), https://perma.cc/ER35-L7KL.
7 *NYC Schools Provide Free Feminine Hygiene Products from Harlem to Hollis*, HARLEM WORLD MAG. (Mar. 14, 2016), https://perma.cc/D3WL-RU9S.
8 Katie Honan, *Corona High School Offers Free Feminine Hygiene Products in Pilot Program*, DNAINFO (Sept. 22, 2015, 6:09 PM), https://perma.cc/2XXQ-YDQT.
9 Uffalussy, *supra* note 6.
10 *Id.*
11 See Janaki Chadha, *For First Time Ever, Free Feminine Care to Arrive in 25 NYC Public Schools*, OBSERVER (Mar. 14, 2016, 4:29 PM), https://perma.cc/Z76G-9HSD.
12 *Free Feminine Hygiene Products Coming to 25 NYC Public Schools*, NONWOVENS INDUS. (Mar. 15, 2016), https://perma.cc/YZ4C-TFEG.

13 Eillie Anzilotti, *How New York Is Easing Access to Menstrual Hygiene Products*, BLOOMBERG CITYLAB (June 21, 2016, 1:45 PM), https://perma.cc/L7WX-WSZS.

14 *See* Katie Mettler, *"They're As Necessary as Toilet Paper": New York City Council Approves Free Tampon Program*, WASH. POST (June 23, 2016, 3:48 AM), https://perma.cc/4AXX-S5U5 (reprinting posts by Mayor de Blasio to Twitter and Facebook).

15 *"Tampons for All": A Poem by First Lady of NYC Chirlane McCray*, WOMEN YOU SHOULD KNOW (Mar. 28, 2016), https://perma.cc/8VNL-8EGZ.

16 Anzilotti, *supra* note 13.

17 Press Release, Assemblymember Cristina Garcia, Menstrual Product Access Bill Advances Unanimously (Apr. 5, 2017), https://perma.cc/D8UW-QBT3.

18 *Menstrual Products, School Districts, and COVID-19*, THE PAD PROJECT (Sept. 24, 2020), https://perma.cc/E5MC-AB9Z.

19 Melanie Mason & Mina Corpuz, *Free Tampons in Schools and Expanded Family Leave for Small Businesses Are Coming to California*, L.A. TIMES (Oct. 12, 2017, 8:35 PM), https://perma.cc/35N8-ZL5Q; *see also* Story Hinckley, *California Keeps Girls in School by Providing Feminine Products*, CHRISTIAN SCI. MONITOR (Jan. 19, 2018), https://perma.cc/29JL-F8TH.

20 2017 Ill. Legis. Serv. 100-0163 (West) (codified at 105 ILL. COMP. STAT. 5/10-20.60, 27A-5, 34-18.53 (2018)). The relevant portion of the Learn with Dignity Act here, relating to the availability of menstrual products, was first codified at 105 Ill. Comp. Stat. 5/10-20.60 (2018). It was later renumbered and is now codified at 105 Ill. Comp. Stat. 5/10-20.63 (2018).

21 Press Release, Office of the Governor, Governor Cuomo Reminds Schools of New Law Requiring School Districts to Provide Free Feminine Hygiene Products in Restrooms (Sept. 10, 2018), https://perma.cc/T29P-C87F.

22 Maya T. Prabhu, *Georgia OKs Providing Menstrual Products to Low-Income Girls, Women*, ATLANTA J.-CONST. (April 10, 2019), https://perma.cc/P2G5-BMZQ.

23 Jill Nolin, *Opponents of Ga. "Tampon Tax" Vow to Press Lawmakers in 2020*, GA. RECORDER (Sept. 9, 2019) (second alteration in original), https://perma.cc/E3X4-PU2X.

24 *Id.*

25 Prabhu, *supra* note 22.

26 *See* Hannah Ellis-Petersen, *Tampon Tax: £15m Raised to Be Spent on Women's Charities*, GUARDIAN (U.K.) (Nov. 25, 2015, 8:31 AM), https://perma.cc/JG77-VUB9.

27 *See* Bridget Crawford, *How Much Do "Free" Tampons Cost? #MenstrualCapitalism and Examples from New York State*, FACULTY LOUNGE (Sept. 14, 2018, 12:58 PM), https://perma.cc/7GXS-F8PS.

28 *See* Bridget Crawford, *How Much Do "Free" Tampons Cost Schools? $2.48 Per Student Per Year in Cambridge, MA*, FEMINIST L. PROFESSORS (May 10, 2020), https://perma.cc/S97H-83YW.

29 Katie Mettler, *Free Tampons for All at Brown University This School Year—Even in the Men's Room*, WASH. POST (Sept. 9, 2016, 3:44 AM), https://perma.cc/G7QC-SSLY.
30 *Id.*
31 Melanie Pincus, *Facilities Takes over Project Tampon*, BROWN DAILY HERALD (Nov. 11, 2018), https://perma.cc/5J5R-MQFE.
32 *See* Leah Willingham, *Students Seeking Free Access to Tampons and Pads at N.H. Schools*, VALLEY NEWS (Feb. 5, 2019, 10:08 PM), https://perma.cc/8EAP-267B (quoting seventeen-year-old Caroline Dillon).
33 *See* Jordyn Brown, *The Menstrual Movement: How 4 Eugene Students Got Free Menstrual Products in School Bathrooms*, REG.-GUARD (Nov. 30, 2019, 5:00 AM), https://perma.cc/PT9H-57GA.
34 *Id.*
35 Ignite National, *It's Been Three Years in the Making but When Young Women Speak Up, We WIN!*, FACEBOOK (Nov. 12, 2019), https://www.facebook.com/IGNITEnational/posts/2633701160043730.
36 Roni Caryn Rabin, *Free the Tampons*, N.Y. TIMES (Feb. 29, 2016, 2:20 PM) (emphasis added), https://perma.cc/FUJ3-Q85D.
37 *Id.*
38 Shannon Barbour, *Middle Schoolers Protest After Their Principal Said They'd "Abuse the Privilege" of Free Tampons*, COSMOPOLITAN (Oct. 30, 2019), https://perma.cc/NP7W-XA2Y.
39 Ayana Harry, *City Councilwoman Looks to Bring Free Tampons to High School Bathrooms*, PIX11 (June 10, 2015, 9:26 PM), https://perma.cc/JX7M-JEE2.
40 20 U.S.C. §§ 1681–1688 (1972).
41 U.S. DEP'T OF JUST., EQUAL ACCESS TO EDUCATION: FORTY YEARS OF TITLE IX, at 1 (June 23, 2012), https://perma.cc/3GFD-74YX.
42 Society of Women's Health Research, *Survey of School Nurses Reveals Lack of Bathroom Policies and Bladder Health Education*, MED. EXPRESS (Nov. 26, 2018), https://perma.cc/4QD3-J7LX; *see also* Johnson et al., *supra* note 1, at 241–44.
43 THINX & PERIOD, STATE OF THE PERIOD: THE WIDESPREAD IMPACT OF PERIOD POVERTY ON US STUDENTS 1, 2, https://perma.cc/9A4J-KETE.
44 Christopher A. Cotropia, *Menstruation Management in United States Schools and Implications for Attendance, Academic Performance, and Health*, 6 WOMEN'S REPROD. HEALTH 289 (2019).
45 *Id.* at 289.
46 *Id.* at 294.
47 Jill M. Wood, *(In)Visible Bleeding: The Menstrual Concealment Imperative, in* THE PALGRAVE HANDBOOK OF CRITICAL MENSTRUATION STUDIES 319, 322 (Chris Bobel et al. eds., 2020).
48 Cotropia, *supra* note 44, at 294.
49 *Id.* at 295.

50 Seth Galanter, U.S. Dep't of Educ., Off. for Civil Rights, Dear Colleague Letter: Supporting the Academic Success of Pregnant and Parenting Students (June 25, 2013), https://perma.cc/7SRG-J8FL; U.S. Dep't of Educ., Supporting the Academic Success of Pregnant and Parenting Students under Title IX of the Education Amendments of 1972 (2013), https://perma.cc/L9DW-T5YY.
51 U.S. Dep't of Educ., *supra* note 50, at 9 (emphasis added).
52 Press Release, Office of the Governor, Governor Chris Sununu Signs SB 142 into Law (July 17, 2019), https://perma.cc/67RE-XTUX.
53 Samantha Cooney, *Brown University Will Provide Free Tampons and Pads to All Gender Identities*, Time (Sept. 9, 2016, 9:14 AM), https://perma.cc/9K7P-3NX9.
54 Scottish Gov't, Access to Free Sanitary Products Programme for Government Commitment: Business and Regulatory Impact Assessment 4 (Sept. 2018), https://perma.cc/HMC4-SWRV.
55 N.H. Rev. Stat. Ann. § 189:16-a (2019).
56 105 Ill. Comp. Stat. 5/10–20.63 (2018).
57 Cal. Educ. Code § 35292 (West 2018).
58 N.Y. Pub. Health Law § 267 (McKinney 2018).
59 Va. Code Ann. § 22.1–6.1 (West 2020).
60 Angie Leventis Lourgos, *Tampons in Men's Restrooms? Activists, Schools and Businesses Are Serving the Menstrual Needs of Those Who Don't Identify as Women*, Chicago Trib. (Nov. 12, 2019) (emphasis added), https://perma.cc/DHZ2-BREA.
61 *Id.*
62 Catherine E. Lhamon, U.S. Dep't of Educ., Off. for Civil Rights & Vanita Gupta, U.S. Dep't of Just., Civil Rights Div., Dear Colleague Letter: Transgender Students (May 13, 2016), https://perma.cc/7BS3-NBRL.
63 Sandra Battle, U.S. Dep't of Educ., Off. for Civil Rights & T.E. Wheeler, II, U.S. Dep't of Just., Civil Rights Div., Dear Colleague Letter, at 1 (Feb. 22, 2017), https://perma.cc/EBQ7-6XHN.
64 Eric T. Schneiderman, State of N.Y., Off. of the Att'y Gen. & MaryEllen Elia, N.Y. State Educ. Dep't, U.S.N.Y., Letter as Reminder to Schools: New York State Protects Transgender Students (Feb. 28, 2018), https://perma.cc/7K9W-S8HT.
65 Grimm v. Gloucester Cnty. Sch. Bd., 972 F.3d 586 (4th Cir. 2020).
66 *Id.*
67 Bostock v. Clayton Cnty., 140 S.Ct. 1731 (2020).
68 *Grimm*, 972 F.3d at 616.
69 *Id.* at 619–20.
70 Exec. Order No. 13988, 86 Fed. Reg. 7023 (Jan. 20, 2021).
71 Memorandum from the Principal Deputy Assistant Att'y Gen. Pamela S. Karlan, Civ. Rights Div., to the Fed. Agency Civil Rights Dirs. and Gen. Couns., at 2 (Mar. 26, 2021), https://perma.cc/TUL5-9GAN ("Application of *Bostock v. Clayton County* to Title IX of the Education Amendments of 1972").

72 Society of Women's Health Research, *supra* note 42.
73 Dusty Rhodes, *Feedback: Noble Charter Schools Story Hit a Nerve*, NPR ILL. (Apr. 30, 2018), https://perma.cc/KA8F-9VZ7.
74 Nathan Baca, *What Some Kids Who Get One Bathroom Pass a Week Say They Face Daily at a DC Charter School*, WJLA.COM (July 19, 2018).
75 *Sssh! Periods: Marshmallow* (Oct. 16, 2019) (downloaded using Soundcloud).
76 *Id.*
77 Kristi Pahr, *Period Shaming: A Not-So-New Type of Bullying Parents Need to Know About*, YAHOO NEWS PARENTS (Nov. 4, 2019), https://perma.cc/VJV4-749B.
78 *Id.*
79 Anna North, *Schools Don't Know How to Handle Girls' Menstrual Periods, and Their Education Is Suffering Because of It*, VOX (May 4, 2018, 6:20 AM), https://perma.cc/QUQ6-Y293.
80 Droll Embiid. (@GeeDee215), TWITTER (Apr. 30, 2018, 10:13 PM), https://twitter.com/GeeDee215/status/991153704089849856.
81 Rhodes, *supra* note 73.
82 Mohsen Gul, *MHM Supportive Schools in Pakistan: Dark Tale of Pale Coloured Uniforms*, MEDIUM (Nov. 12, 2019), https://perma.cc/5R98-M594.
83 34 C.F.R. § 106.40(b)(5) (1980).
84 U.S. DEP'T OF EDUC., *supra* note 50, at 9 (emphasis added).
85 *Id.* at 15 (emphasis added).
86 *Id.* at 16.
87 *Id.*
88 LAURA FINGERSON, GIRLS IN POWER: GENDER, BODY, AND MENSTRUATION IN ADOLESCENCE 119–27 (2006).
89 Katherine R. Allen et al., *More Than Just a Punctuation Mark: How Boys and Young Men Learn About Menstruation*, 32 J. FAM. ISSUES 129 (2011).
90 *Id.* at 145–52.
91 Anja Benshaul-Tolonen et al., *Period Teasing, Stigma and Knowledge: A Survey of Adolescent Boys and Girls in Northern Tanzania*, 15(10) PLOS ONE 1 (2020).
92 Davis *ex rel.* LaShonda D. v. Monroe Cnty. Bd. of Educ., 526 U.S. 629 (1999).
93 *Id.* at 633, 645, 647.
94 U.S. DEP'T OF EDUC., REVISED SEXUAL HARASSMENT GUIDANCE: HARASSMENT OF STUDENTS BY SCHOOL EMPLOYEES, OTHER STUDENTS, OR THIRD PARTIES (2001), https://perma.cc/S7BA-FDUY.
95 34 C.F.R. § 106.44 (2020).
96 Ann C. Herbert et al., *Puberty Experiences of Low-Income Girls in the United States: A Systematic Review of Qualitative Literature from 2000 to 2014*, 60 J. OF ADOLESCENT HEALTH 363, 364–67 (2017).
97 *Id.* at 369–76; *see also* Johnson et al., *supra* note 1, at 258–61.
98 Herbert et al., *supra* note 96, at 367.
99 Allen et al., *supra* note 89, at 152.
100 *Id.* at 153.

101 *Break This Down: Period Teasing*, BARNARD COLL. (Nov. 2, 2020), https://perma.cc/GNE5-SF6K.
102 Benshaul-Tolonen et al., *supra* note 91, at 17.
103 34 C.F.R. § 106.34(a)(3) (2006).

CHAPTER 4. PERIODS IN PUBLIC
 1 *See, e.g.*, Press Release, Office of the Mayor, Mayor de Blasio Signs Legislation Increasing Access to Feminine Hygiene Products for Students, Shelter Residents and Inmates (July 13, 2016), https://perma.cc/R7NJ-Y7TS.
 2 Eillie Anzilotti, *How New York Is Easing Access to Menstrual Hygiene Products*, BLOOMBERG CITYLAB (June 21, 2016, 1:45 PM), https://perma.cc/6QQN-LRF8 (quoting Jennifer Weiss-Wolf).
 3 *See* Emily Pietras, *Homeless Period Project Provides Feminine Hygiene Products to Women, Girls in Need*, GREENVILLE J. (May 5, 2017), https://perma.cc/UE8T-R7LS (quoting Sharron Phillips (now Sharron Champion)).
 4 *See* Katie Kindelan, *This Congresswoman Nicknamed "Period Lady" Is on a Mission to Give All Women Access to Period Products*, GMA (Oct. 18, 2019), https://perma.cc/YGX2-9AD7.
 5 *Id.*
 6 Letter from Grace Meng, U.S. Rep. from New York 6th Dist., to Jeh Johnson, U.S. Sec'y of Homeland Sec. (Jan. 7, 2016) (citations omitted), https://perma.cc/C3S8-NUWR.
 7 Press Release, Congresswoman Grace Meng, FEMA to Permit Homeless Assistance Providers to Purchase Feminine Hygiene Products—Such as Tampons and Pads—With Federal Grant Funds (Mar. 1, 2016), https://perma.cc/J9VQ-3TCA.
 8 *See* MD. CODE ANN., HOUS. & CMTY. DEV. § 4-2401 (West 2021).
 9 H.R. 7054, 116th Cong. (2020).
 10 *Id.* at § 2(a)-(c).
 11 *See* Bill Emerson Good Samaritan Food Donation Act, Pub. L. No. 104-210, 110 Stat. 3011, 3011 (1996) (codified at 42 U.S.C. § 1791).
 12 Press Release, Congresswoman Grace Meng, Meng Introduces Legislation to Improve Access to Menstrual Products as Nation Marks Menstrual Hygiene Day and National Period Poverty Awareness Week (May 28, 2020), https://perma.cc/BC63-BFHA.
 13 *See* JACOB KANG-BROWN ET AL., VERA INST., PEOPLE IN PRISON IN 2019, at 1 (May 2020), https://perma.cc/NJ5E-8R3Z.
 14 First Step Act of 2018, Pub. L. No. 115-391, § 611, 132 Stat. 5194, 5247 (2018); *see also* Eleanor Goldberg, *Women Often Can't Afford Tampons, Pads in Federal Prisons. That's About to Change*, HUFFPOST (Dec. 20, 2018, 11:22 AM), https://perma.cc/HX22-EXGB.
 15 First Step Act of 2018, *supra* note 14, at § 611.

16 *See* S. 1524, 115th Cong. § 2 (2017); *see also* Michael Alison Chandler, *The Once-Whispered Topic of Women's Menstruation Now Has Political Cachet*, WASH. POST (Aug. 7, 2017), https://perma.cc/84Q8-8KQD.
17 Press Release, Congresswoman Grace Meng, Meng Renews Effort to Make Menstrual Hygiene Products More Accessible and Affordable to Women (Feb. 13, 2017), https://perma.cc/8NXA-XW7L.
18 Letter from Grace Meng, U.S. Rep. from New York 6th Dist., & Julissa Ferreras-Copeland, New York City Council Member, to Loretta E. Lynch, Att'y Gen. of the United States (Jul. 19, 2016), https://perma.cc/9BCA-T3G7.
19 Operations Memorandum on the Provision of Feminine Hygiene Products from the U.S. Dep't of Just., Fed. Bureau Prisons (Aug. 1, 2017), https://perma.cc/7HFU-KG6Q.
20 *Id.*
21 *Id.*
22 Commissary Shopping List Form, U.S. DEP'T OF JUST., FED. BUREAU OF PRISONS (Feb. 23, 2016), https://perma.cc/G8BR-JWKN.
23 *Work Programs*, U.S. DEP'T OF JUST., FED. BUREAU OF PRISONS, https://perma.cc/D3UG-SXSE; Derek Gilna, *New Policies for Federal and State Prisoners Guarantee Feminine Hygiene Products*, PRISON LEGAL NEWS (Apr. 2, 2018), https://perma.cc/AJ28-QFZT.
24 Gilna, *supra* note 23; *see also* BRAWS & DCSL LEGIS. CLINIC, PERIODS, POVERTY, AND THE NEED FOR POLICY: A REPORT ON MENSTRUAL INEQUITY IN THE UNITED STATES 20 (2018), https://perma.cc/W7TJ-6LXD.
25 Press Release, Congresswoman Grace Meng, Meng Secures Provisions to Improve Access to Menstrual Hygiene Products (Aug. 27, 2019) [hereinafter Meng Press Release to Improve Access], https://perma.cc/J2DM-G45Q.
26 *Id.*
27 *See* ALA. CODE §§ 14-3-44, 14-6-19 (2019); CAL. PENAL CODE § 3409 (West 2021); COLO. REV. STAT. ANN. § 26-1-136.5 (West 2019); CONN. GEN. STAT. ANN. § 18–69e (West 2018); FLA. STAT. § 944.242 (2019); KY. REV. STAT. ANN. § 441.055 (2018); LA. STAT. ANN. § 15:892.1 (2018); MD. CODE ANN., CORR. SERVS. §§ 9–616, 4–214 (West 2018); N.Y. CORRECT. LAW § 625 (McKinney 2019); TENN. CODE ANN. § 41-21-206 (West 2019); TEX. GOV'T CODE ANN. § 501.0675 (2019); VA. CODE ANN. § 53.1–32 (2018).
28 *See* Ann E. Marimow, *A New Law Promised Maryland's Female Inmates Free Tampons. They're Still Paying*, WASH. POST (June 5, 2019, 5:00 AM), https://perma.cc/3UWJ-VNBB.
29 *Id.*
30 *Id.* (quoting Maryland Public Safety and Correctional Services Secretary Robert Green).
31 Kalia White, *Arizona Legislator Kills Bill That Would Have Given Female Inmates Free Feminine Products*, AZCENTRAL (Feb. 12, 2018, 6:27 PM).

32 Jimmy Jenkins, *"Pads and Tampons and the Problems with Periods": All-Male Committee Hears Arizona Bill on Feminine Hygiene Products in Prison*, KJZZ (Apr. 8, 2020, 12:04 PM), https://perma.cc/A8GP-6M8B (quoting Representative Salman and Representative Lawrence).
33 *Id.*
34 *See* Kaila White, *Arizona Prisons Will Now Give Female Inmates Free Tampons*, AZCENTRAL (Feb. 21, 2018, 7:04 PM), https://perma.cc/JCW5-UR7F.
35 *See* Raheem F. Hosseini, *Menstruating in Captivity*, SACRAMENTO NEWS & REV. (Feb. 28, 2019), https://perma.cc/8RAA-PZ6Y (quoting Paula Canny).
36 *Id.*
37 Chandra Bozelko, *Prisons That Withhold Menstrual Pads Humiliate Women and Violate Basic Rights*, GUARDIAN (U.K.) (June 12, 2015, 6:30 AM), https://perma.cc/Q8MJ-VFT6.
38 Zoe Greenberg, *In Jail, Pads and Tampons as Bargaining Chips*, N.Y. TIMES (Apr. 20, 2017), https://perma.cc/E2L4-HPA8.
39 *Id.*
40 *Id.*
41 Tomi-Ann Roberts, *Bleeding in Jail: Objectification, Self-Objectification, and Menstrual Injustice*, in THE PALGRAVE HANDBOOK OF CRITICAL MENSTRUATION STUDIES 53, 57–58 (Chris Bobel et al. eds., 2020).
42 *Id.*
43 Plaintiff's Original Complaint at ¶ 25, Simms v. City of San Antonio, No. 5:18-CV-00211, 2019 WL 1369942 (W.D. Tex. Nov. 25, 2019).
44 *Id.* at ¶¶ 17, 20, 25; *see* Nicole Einbinder, *A Woman Is Suing the City of San Antonio After a Police Officer Pulled Out Her Tampon in Public*, INSIDER (Oct. 16, 2019, 8:37 PM), https://perma.cc/UHD3-PRVU.
45 Plaintiff's Original Complaint, *supra* note 43, at ¶ 23.
46 *Id.* at ¶ 35.
47 Stipulation of Dismissal with Prejudice, Simms v. City of San Antonio, No. 5:18-CV-00211 (W.D. Tex. Nov. 25, 2019).
48 Einbinder, *supra* note 44.
49 Tom Nash, *Deny, Delay, Release: Virginia DOC Finally Issues Tampon Ban Memo*, MUCKROCK (Dec. 5, 2018), https://perma.cc/837E-BDZX (featuring a Twitter post by user Jana #VACFSY, who attached an image of the policy).
50 Christina Caron, *After Outcry, Virginia Reverses Tampon Ban for Visitors to Prisons*, N.Y. TIMES (Sept. 25, 2018), https://perma.cc/KBK4-N8KE.
51 Memorandum from A. David Robinson, Corr. Operations Chief, to Commonwealth of Virginia Dep't of Corr. Reg'l Operations Chiefs, Reg'l Adm'rs, and Wardens (Sept. 17, 2018), https://perma.cc/QFX9-2Y2Y; *see also* Nash, *supra* note 49.
52 Del. Kaye Kory (@KayeKory), TWITTER (Sept. 25, 2018, 3:37 PM), https://twitter.com/KayeKory/status/1044687282970734595.
53 Caron, *supra* note 50 (quoting Bill Farrar of the American Civil Liberties Union of Virginia).

54 Tom Jackman, *Update: Va. Suspends Ban on Tampons in Prison*, WASH. POST (Sept. 25, 2018, 3:12 PM), https://perma.cc/5GW3-6ZHX.
55 *Id.*
56 Saffeya Ahmed, *Virginia Panel Wants Prisons to Modify Tampon Ban*, WTKR NEWS 3 (Jan. 25, 2019, 6:31 PM), https://perma.cc/3M7F-PDBR.
57 H. 1884, 2019 Sess. (Va. 2019).
58 Second Amended Complaint, Doe v. Corr. Corp. of Am., No. 3:15-cv-68 (M.D. Tenn. Mar. 6, 2017).
59 *See* Consent Order of Dismissal, Doe v. Corr. Corp. of Am., No. 3:15-cv-68 (M.D. Tenn. Mar. 6, 2017).
60 *See* Jonathan Mattise, *Private Prisons Reach Deal with Women Forced to Show Tampons*, ASSOCIATED PRESS (Mar. 7, 2017), https://perma.cc/5T2Q-MVKU.
61 H.R. 1882, 116th Cong. § 3(a) (2019).
62 Meng Press Release to Improve Access, *supra* note 25.
63 *See* Paulina Cachero, *Woman Denied Period Products in Policy Custody Files Lawsuit Against NYPD: "I Felt Humiliated,"* YAHOO LIFE (Oct. 29, 2019), https://perma.cc/MN73-7B5X.
64 Flores v. City of New York, No. 1:19-CV-05763, 2021 WL 663977 (E.D.N.Y. Apr. 18, 2021); Stipulation and Order of Settlement and Discontinuance, Flores v. City of New York, No. 1:19-CV-05763 (E.D.N.Y. June 4, 2021).
65 Houglin v. Rodden, No. 1:16-CV-01331 (S.D. Ind. Apr. 18, 2017).
66 First Amended Complaint, Houglin v. Rodden, No. 1:16-CV-01331 (S.D. Ind. Apr. 18, 2017).
67 Order of Dismissal with Prejudice, Houglin v. Rodden, No. 1:16-CV-01331 (S.D. Ind. Apr. 18, 2017).
68 Darnell v. Pineiro, 849 F.3d 17, 38 (2d Cir. 2017) (alteration in original), *aff'g in part, vacating in part* Cano v. City of New York, 119 F.Supp.3d 65 (E.D.N.Y. 2015).
69 *See id.*
70 Stipulation and Order of Settlement & Dismissal, Cano v. City of New York, 119 F.Supp.3d 65 (E.D.N.Y. 2015) (No. 1:13-cv-03341), https://perma.cc/NA2Q-8CA8.
71 Chavarriaga v. N.J. Dep't of Corr., 806 F.3d 210, 229 (3d Cir. 2015), *aff'g in part, rev'g in part* Chavarriaga v. New Jersey, No. 3:12-CV-04313, 2014 WL 1276345 (D.N.J. Mar. 27, 2014).
72 *Id.* at 230.
73 Chavarriaga v. N.J. Dep't of Corr., No. 3:12-CV-04313, 2016 WL 5796864 (D.N.J. Sept. 30, 2016).
74 Johnson v. Blaukat, 453 F.3d 1108 (8th Cir. 2006).
75 First Amended Complaint at ¶¶ 108–29, 261, Semelbauer v. Muskegon Cnty., No. 1:14-CV-01245, 2015 WL 9906265 (W.D. Mich. July 24, 2017).
76 Semelbauer v. Muskegon Cnty., No. 1:14-CV-01245, 2015 WL 9906265 (W.D. Mich. July 24, 2017).
77 Turano v. County of Alameda, No. 4:17-CV-06953, 2018 WL 5629341, at *1, *5, *6 (N.D. Cal. Aug. 20, 2019).

78   *Id.* at *6 n.2; *see also* Margaret E. Johnson, *Menstrual Justice*, 53 U.C. DAVIS L. REV. 1, 44–57 (2019).
79   *See* Complaint for Declaratory & Injunctive Relief, California v. McAleenan, No. 2:19-cv-07390, 2019 WL 4017654 (C.D. Cal. Apr. 19, 2021), https://perma.cc/U846-AUBQ.
80   *See* Antonia Blumberg, *19 States, D.C. to Challenge Trump Administration's Detention of Migrant Children*, HUFFPOST (Aug. 26, 2019, 1:33 PM), https://perma.cc/J4VC-MGAQ; *see also* Declaration of Alma Poletti, Investigations Supervisor, Wash. State Off. of the Att'y Gen., Civ. Rights Div., at 6 (Aug. 23, 2019), https://perma.cc/HNT9-2958.
81   Declaration of Alma Poletti, *supra* note 80, at 6.
82   *See also* Valeria Gomez & Marcy Karin, *Menstrual Justice in Immigration Detention*, 41 COLUM. J. OF GENDER & LAW 123, 123–24 (2021).
83   Letter from Grace Meng, U.S. Rep. from New York 6th Dist., et al., to Kevin McAleenan, Acting Sec'y, U.S. Dep't of Homeland Sec. (Sept. 13, 2019), https://perma.cc/C9DD-JGT7.
84   H.R. 1882, 116th Cong. § 3(f) (2019).
85   *See* Molly Redden, *No Water, No Toilet Paper, No Tampons: How the US Treats Border Detainees*, MOTHER JONES (June 5, 2014), https://perma.cc/4ZVL-GP3H.
86   *See* Complaint, Flores v. United States, 142. F.Supp.3d 279 (E.D.N.Y. 2014) (No. 1:14-cv-03166); *see also* Press Release, Ams. for Immigrant Just., AI Justice Wins Landmark Settlement for Asylum Seeker Detained by Customs and Border Protection (Feb. 19, 2016), https://perma.cc/69MV-A86C.
87   *See* HARRIS INTERACTIVE & FREE THE TAMPON FOUND., THE MURPHY'S LAW OF MENSTRUATION (2013), https://perma.cc/ZYE9-ZK4B.
88   Press Release, Rep. Sean Patrick Maloney, Maloney Hits Back Against House Administration Committee's Lies Regarding Tampon Purchase, Releases Text of Email (June 29, 2018), https://perma.cc/2XT5-DLBN; *see also* Eleanor Goldberg, *This Congressman Is Fighting to Bring Free Tampons to the Hill*, HUFFPOST (Aug. 16, 2018), https://perma.cc/KA2E-3S7G.
89   Goldberg, *supra* note 88.
90   *Id.*
91   Katherine Tully-McManus, *Tampons to Be Stocked in House Supply Store: Allowed for Purchase with Office Funds*, ROLL CALL (Feb. 12, 2019, 11:16 AM), https://perma.cc/83QL-BE8T.
92   *See* Ally Jarmanning, *Brookline to Offer Free Tampons and Pads in All Its Public Buildings*, WBUR NEWS (June 5, 2019), https://perma.cc/V8QQ-3428.
93   Sarah Groustra, *Stigma Around Periods Produces Undue Shame*, SAGAMORE (Apr. 26, 2018), https://perma.cc/G6N8-9HHE.
94   Jarmanning, *supra* note 92.
95   *See id.*
96   Press Release, Salt Lake City Council, City Council Approves Free Hygiene Products (June 18, 2019), https://perma.cc/K2P3-NFXQ.

97 *Id.* (quoting Valdemoros).
98 *Id.*
99 Taylor Stevens, *Tampons, Pads Will Now Be Free at a Number of Salt Lake City–Run Facilities*, SALT LAKE TRIB. (June 18, 2019, 5:46 PM), https://perma.cc/C7QS-ZCP7.
100 Press Release, Columbus City Council, What's Missing in Public Restrooms?, https://perma.cc/743E-DZDF.
101 *Id.*
102 *Id.*
103 Lori Kurtzman, *Free the Tampons: Nancy Kramer Inspires a Movement*, COLUMBUS MONTHLY (Feb. 20, 2017), https://perma.cc/H35N-9LPV.
104 Jake Flynn, *Blumenfield's Free Feminine Hygiene Products Proposal Advanced by City Council*, Post on *Newsroom*, BOB BLUMENFIELD: COUNCILMEMBER, (Feb. 5, 2020), https://perma.cc/DQ4M-WDE3.
105 *Id.* (quoting Blumenfield).
106 *See* Madeleine Keck, *Melbourne Will Fight Period Poverty by Introducing Free Pads & Tampons Across the City*, GLOB. CITIZEN (Apr. 28, 2021), https://perma.cc/9UWJ-HET3 (quoting Nicholas Reece but incorrectly identifying him as the "Deputy Lord Mayor," instead of the former Lord Mayor); Jamal Hakim (@thejamalhakim), TWITTER, https://perma.cc/4YED-T3J9 (sporting the label "Proud Feminist" in his profile bio).
107 H.R. 1882, 116th Cong. (2019); *see also* Katherine Tully-McManus, *This Democrat Wants Free Tampons and Pads Available in All Federal Buildings*, ROLL CALL (Mar. 26, 2019, 4:12 PM), https://perma.cc/8FDS-L59M.
108 Meng Press Release to Improve Access, *supra* note 25.

CHAPTER 5. PERIODS AT WORK
1 Flores v. Va. Dep't of Corr., No. 5:20-cv-00087, 2021 WL 668802 (W.D. Va. Feb. 22, 2021); Complaint, Flores v. Va. Dep't of Corr., No. 5:20-cv-00087, 2021 WL 668802 (W.D. Va. Feb. 22, 2021).
2 Coleman v. Bobby Dodd Inst., No. 4:17-CV-00029, 2017 WL 2486080 (M.D. Ga. Nov. 6, 2017); Initial Brief of Plaintiff-Appellant, Coleman v. Bobby Dodd Inst., No. 4:17-13023, 2017 WL 3500308, at *4 (11th Cir. Nov. 6, 2017), https://perma.cc/6X4L-SQEG.
3 Alisha Coleman, *I Was Fired from My Job as a 911 Call Taker for Getting My Period at Work*, ACLU (Aug. 25, 2017, 12:00 PM), https://perma.cc/A84N-CEPC.
4 Margaret E. Johnson, *Menstrual Justice*, 53 U.C. DAVIS L. REV. 1, 33 (2019).
5 42 U.S.C. § 2000e-2(a)(1).
6 42 U.S.C. § 2000e(k).
7 *Id.*
8 Coleman v. Bobby Dodd Inst., No. 4:17-CV-00029, 2017 WL 2486080, at *2 (M.D. Ga. Nov. 6, 2017).
9 *Id.*

10 *Id.*
11 Raisa Habersham, *Woman Settles with Employer She Says Fired Her for Getting Period at Work*, ATLANTA J.-CONST. (Nov. 16, 2017), https://perma.cc/E297-WJL2.
12 42 U.S.C. § 2000e(k).
13 Flores v. Va. Dep't of Corr., No. 5:20-cv-00087, 2021 WL 668802, at *6 (W.D. Va. Feb. 22, 2021) (emphasis in original).
14 *Id.* at *5.
15 *Id.* at *5 n.6 (emphasis in original).
16 Deborah A. Widiss, *Menstruation Discrimination and the Problem of Shadow Precedents*, 41 COLUM. J. GENDER & LAW 235, 236 (2021).
17 *Compare, e.g.*, EEOC v. Hous. Funding II, Ltd., 717 F.3d 425, 428 (5th Cir. 2013) (recognizing lactation as a "related medical condition" under the PDA); Hall v. Nalco Co., 534 F.3d 644, 647–48 (7th Cir. 2008) (recognizing infertility and the need for infertility treatments as covered by the PDA); Harper v. Thiokol Chem. Corp., 619 F.2d 489, 491–92 (5th Cir. 1980) (holding that a policy requiring women on pregnancy leave to have a normal menstrual cycle before returning to work violated Title VII), *with* Jirak v. Fed. Express Corp., 805 F. Supp. 193, 195 (S.D.N.Y. 1992) (holding that menstrual cramps were not a medical condition related to pregnancy or childbirth).
18 OXFAM AM., NO RELIEF: DENIAL OF BATHROOM BREAKS IN THE POULTRY INDUSTRY (2016), https://perma.cc/3BTL-RCJX.
19 *Id.* at 2.
20 *Id.* at 4, 7 (alteration in original).
21 Memorandum from John B. Miles, Jr., Dir., Directorate of Compliance Programs, to the Reg'l Adm'rs & State Designees, Interpretation of 29 CFR 1910.141(c)(1)(i): Toilet Facilities (Apr. 6, 1998), https://perma.cc/98F5-YAF3.
22 42 U.S.C. § 2000e-(2)(k).
23 Susanna Kim, *Company Limits Worker Bathroom Use to 6 Minutes a Day, Union Claims*, ABC NEWS (July 16, 2014, 1:25 PM), https://perma.cc/RKF2-AY9X.
24 Flores v. Va. Dep't of Corr., No. 5:20-cv-00087, 2021 WL 668802, at *7 (W.D. Va. Feb. 22, 2021).
25 42 U.S.C. § 12112(b)(5)(A); 42 U.S.C. § 12111(10)(A).
26 42 U.S.C. § 12102 (1).
27 *See* Munoz v. Selig Enters., Inc., 981 F.3d 1265, 1273 (11th Cir. 2020) (holding that there was not enough evidence to determine whether plaintiff's endometriosis rendered her disabled under the ADA, but suggesting that more evidence about its "timing, frequency, and duration" might have sufficed).
28 Pregnancy Discrimination Act of 1978, Pub. L. No. 95-555, 92 Stat. 2076.
29 Young v. United Parcel Serv., Inc., 135 S.Ct. 1338, 1354 (2015).
30 H.R. 1065, 117th Cong. (2021).
31 *See, e.g.*, Jessica Silver-Greenberg & Natalie Kitroeff, *Miscarrying at Work: The Physical Toll of Pregnancy Discrimination*, N.Y. TIMES (Oct. 21, 2018), https://perma.cc/HF37-WDAT.

32 H.R. 1065, 117th Cong. § 2(1) (2021).
33 Julia Hollingsworth, *Should Women Be Entitled to Period Leave? These Countries Think So*, CNN BUS. (Nov. 20, 2020, 6:13 PM), https://perma.cc/L7JP-SBX8; Alice J. Dan, *The Law and Women's Bodies: The Case of Menstruation Leave in Japan*, 7 HEALTH CARE FOR WOMEN INT'L 1 (1986).
34 Dan, *supra* note 33, at 9.
35 Hollingsworth, *supra* note 33.
36 *Id.*
37 Justin McCurry & Stuart Leavenworth, *Period Policy in Asia: Time Off "May Be Seen as a Sign of Weakness*," GUARDIAN (U.K.) (Mar. 4, 2016, 4:38 AM), https://perma.cc/QQ58-7TUX.
38 *Id.*
39 Yang Lan, *Menstrual Leave Could Cost Chinese Women Their Career*, GLOB. TIMES (Feb. 29, 2016, 5:58 PM), https://perma.cc/2QMK-M453.
40 Anna Momigliano, *Giving Italian Women "Menstrual Leave" May Backfire on Their Job Prospects*, WASH. POST (Mar. 24, 2017, 11:53 PM), https://perma.cc/Z3HZ-MPEQ.
41 *Id.*
42 MARTHA CHAMALLAS, *Thinking Like a Feminist*, *in* INTRODUCTION TO FEMINIST LEGAL THEORY 10 (3d ed. 2012).
43 Muller v. Oregon, 208 U.S. 412 (1908).
44 *Id.* at 421–23.
45 Arianne Renan Barzilay, *Women at Work: Towards an Inclusive Narrative of the Rise of the Regulatory State*, 31 HARV. J. L. & GENDER 169, 175 (2008).
46 Ruth Bader Ginsburg, Muller v. Oregon: *One Hundred Years Later*, 45 WILLAMETTE L. REV. 359, 379 (2009).
47 Cal. Fed. Sav. & Loan Ass'n v. Guerra, 479 U.S. 272, 289–90 (1987).
48 *Id.* at 290.
49 Jessica L. Barnack-Tavlaris et al., *Taking Leave to Bleed: Perceptions and Attitudes Toward Menstrual Leave Policy*, 40 HEALTH CARE FOR WOMEN INT'L 1355 (2019).
50 *Id.* at 1365–66.
51 Rachel B. Levitt & Jessica L. Barnack-Tavlaris, *Addressing Menstruation in the Workplace: The Menstrual Leave Debate*, *in* THE PALGRAVE HANDBOOK OF CRITICAL MENSTRUATION STUDIES 561, 570–71 (Chris Bobel et al. eds., 2020).
52 *Nike, Inc., Code of Conduct, March 1997*, UNIV. OF MINN. HUM. RTS. LIBR., https://perma.cc/H7U5-C7HL.
53 *See Nike, Inc., Code of Conduct*, Nov. 2020, https://perma.cc/YC9A-U4ZZ; *Nike Code Leadership Standards* 124, Nov. 2021, https://perma.cc/H2WN-Y2CY.
54 Bex Baxter, *Ending a Workplace Taboo. Period.*, TEDxBRISTOL (Nov. 2017), https://www.ted.com/talks/bex_baxter_ending_a_workplace_taboo_period/up-next.

55 Deepinder Goyal, *Introducing Period Leaves for Women*, ZOMATO (Aug. 8, 2020) (emphasis in original), https://perma.cc/S6DK-JZQB.
56 Nancy Kramer & TEDxColumbus, *Free the Tampons*, YOUTUBE (Oct. 16, 2013), https://www.youtube.com/watch?v=tE_1KjHvuAk.

CHAPTER 6. MENSTRUATING WHILE MALE

1 See Marni Sommer et al., *Opinion: Creating a More Equal Post-COVID-19 World for People Who Menstruate*, DEVEX (May 28, 2020), https://perma.cc/VHM8-QWZB.
2 J. K. Rowling (@jk_rowling), TWITTER (June 6, 2020, 4:35 PM), https://twitter.com/jk_rowling/status/1269382518362509313.
3 Daniel Radcliffe, *Daniel Radcliffe Responds to J.K. Rowling's Tweets on Gender Identity*, THE TREVOR PROJECT (June 8, 2020), https://perma.cc/SR7Z-EBBX.
4 Emma Watson (@EmmaWatson), TWITTER (June 10, 2020, 4:15 PM), https://twitter.com/EmmaWatson/status/1270826851070619649.
5 See Aja Romano, *Harry Potter and the Author Who Failed Us*, VOX (June 11, 2020, 1:10 PM), https://perma.cc/KL5P-QYJB.
6 J. K. Rowling, *J.K. Rowling Writes About Her Reasons for Speaking Out on Sex and Gender Issues*, JKROWLING.COM (June 10, 2020), https://perma.cc/TVX7-X4YR.
7 Meghan Murphy, *Are We Women or Are We Menstruators?*, FEMINIST CURRENT (Sept. 7, 2016), https://perma.cc/DK3H-XM8N.
8 Anna Hummer, Comments to Murphy, *supra* note 7.
9 JBWodehousian, Comment to Murphy, *supra* note 7.
10 Anonymous, Comment to Murphy, *supra* note 7.
11 Press Release, City of New York, NYC Commission on Human Rights Announces Strong Protections for City's Transgender and Gender Non-Conforming Communities in Housing, Employment and Public Spaces (Dec. 21, 2015), https://perma.cc/K2NY-HCNB.
12 *Glossary of Terms—Transgender*, GLAAD, https://perma.cc/6W4Q-EX93.
13 ANDREW R. FLORES ET AL., THE WILLIAMS INST., HOW MANY ADULTS IDENTIFY AS TRANSGENDER IN THE UNITED STATES? (2016), https://perma.cc/5U2F-MB8S.
14 *Id.* at 3–4.
15 See Allie Shah, *Almost 3 Percent of Minnesota Teens Identify as Transgender or Gender Nonconforming*, STAR TRIB. (July 28, 2017, 4:32 PM), http://perma.cc/V4N7-FZU4.
16 GLAAD & HARRIS POLL, ACCELERATING ACCEPTANCE 2017 (2017), https://perma.cc/5BM5-2T2D.
17 See ANDREW R. FLORES ET AL., *supra* note 13, at 2 (finding that "18 to 24 year olds . . . [are] more likely than older age groups to identify as transgender").
18 See *supra* notes 2–6 and accompanying text.
19 ACLU (@ACLU), TWITTER (Nov. 19, 2019, 1:46 PM), https://twitter.com/ACLU/status/1196877415810813955.

20 *See, e.g.*, CHRIS BOBEL, THE MANAGED BODY: DEVELOPING GIRLS AND MENSTRUAL HEALTH IN THE GLOBAL SOUTH 76 (2018) (discussing "menstruators' (private) material needs during the menstrual period").
21 Wiley Reading, *My Period and Me: A Trans Guy's Guide to Menstruation*, EVERYDAY FEMINISM (Nov. 4, 2014), https://perma.cc/9TYE-EG2R.
22 *Id.* (emphasis in original).
23 Sarah E. Frank, *Queering Menstruation: Trans and Non-Binary Identity and Body Politics*, 90 SOCIO. INQUIRY 371, 371 (2020), https://onlinelibrary.wiley.com/doi/pdf/10.1111/soin.12355.
24 *Id.* at 386 (quoting interviewee "Peter").
25 *Id.*
26 *Id.* at 382 (quoting interviewee "Chase").
27 MARTHA CHAMALLAS, INTRODUCTION TO FEMINIST LEGAL THEORY 9 (3d ed. 2012).
28 Klara Rydström, *Degendering Menstruation: Making Trans Menstruators Matter*, in THE PALGRAVE HANDBOOK OF CRITICAL MENSTRUATION STUDIES 945, 945–95 (Chris Bobel et al. eds., 2020).
29 Frank, *supra* note 23, at 387 (quoting interviewee "Peter").
30 *Id.*; *Only Women Bleed?*, PERIOD! (Aug. 7, 2017), https://perma.cc/N73C-H98Q (critiquing advertising of menstrual products).
31 Frank, *supra* note 23, at 387.
32 Rydström, *supra* note 28, at 953.
33 a garden gnome (@sartoninwho), TWITTER (Mar. 31, 2019, 5:47 PM), https://twitter.com/sartoninwho/status/1112486599139475462.
34 *See* Sanchez Manning, *Transgender Lobby Forces Sanitary Towel-Maker Always to Ditch Venus Logo from Its Products*, DAILY MAIL (U.K.) (Oct. 19, 2019, 6:13 PM), https://perma.cc/55EX-Q3BP; Emily Zanotti, *Transgender Activists Force Menstrual Products Brand Always to Remove "Woman" Symbol from Packaging*, DAILY WIRE (Oct. 20, 2019), https://perma.cc/53QX-A2ZS; Harron Walker, *No, Trans Activists Didn't Force a Period Brand to Change Its Packaging*, VICE (Oct. 23, 2019, 1:40 PM), https://perma.cc/AF85-SPS2.
35 Dan MacGuill, *Did Trans Activists "Force" Procter & Gamble to Remove Female Symbol from Some Period Products?*, SNOPES (Oct. 21, 2019), https://www.snopes.com/fact-check/pg-venus-symbol-removed.
36 Manning, *supra* note 34 (quoting "leading feminist campaigner" Julie Bindel).
37 Reading, *supra* note 21.
38 Georgina Tait, *Period Packaging: The Damaging Taboo*, REDBRICK (July 22, 2020, 12:30 PM), https://perma.cc/WE9M-75Q5.
39 Press Release, Countdown, Countdown Calls It What It Is. Period. (June 26, 2020), https://perma.cc/4AD2-HGJU ("General Manager Corporate Affairs, Safety and Sustainability, Kiri Hannifin, says this is another step Countdown is taking to help remove a stigma that many women and girls continue to face around periods and their bodies.").

40 *Id.*
41 Charlotte Graham-McLay, *New Zealand Supermarket Chain Becomes First to Use "Period" Label on Menstrual Products,* GUARDIAN (U.K.) (June 25, 2020, 8:17 PM), https://perma.cc/J4CA-AMBT (quoting The Period Place cofounder Sarah Mikkelsen).
42 N.Y.C. DEP'T OF CONSUMER AFFS., FROM CRADLE TO CANE: THE COST OF BEING A FEMALE CONSUMER: A STUDY OF GENDER PRICING IN NEW YORK CITY (2015), https://perma.cc/9SKY-73JH.
43 *Id.* at 75.
44 *See* CAL. CIV. CODE § 51 (West 2016).
45 *See* Gender Tax Repeal Act of 1995, S.B. 899, 2015–2016 Reg. Sess. (Cal. 2016), https://perma.cc/6M8A-DYK9.
46 *See* Press Release, Office of the Governor, Governor Cuomo Reminds New Yorkers "Pink Tax" Ban Goes into Effect Today (Sept. 30, 2020), https://perma.cc/FBJ7-SQ76.
47 JENNIFER WEISS-WOLF, PERIODS GONE PUBLIC: TAKING A STAND FOR MENSTRUAL EQUITY 234 (2017).
48 Gabriel Arkles & Jennifer Weiss-Wolf, *Menstruation-Related Discrimination Is Sex Discrimination—We Don't Need to Erase Trans or Non-Binary People to Make That Point,* ACLU (Dec. 17, 2019), https://perma.cc/8R9V-QZA3.
49 Complaint at ¶ 34, Flores v. Va. Dep't of Corr., No. 5:20-cv-00087, 2021 WL 668802 (W.D. Va. Feb. 22, 2021).
50 *Flores,* 2021 WL 668802, at *6, *3 n.1.
51 Bostock v. Clayton Cnty., 140 S. Ct. 1731 (2020).
52 Memorandum from the Principal Deputy Assistant Att'y Gen. Pamela S. Karlan, Civ. Rights Div., to the Fed. Agency Civil Rights Dirs. and Gen. Couns. (Mar. 26, 2021), https://perma.cc/C7TE-N6PK.

CHAPTER 7. MENSTRUATION, HEALTH, AND THE ENVIRONMENT
1 *See* Textile Fiber Products Identification Act, 15 U.S.C. §§ 70–70k; Wool Products Labeling Act of 1939, 15 U.S.C. §§ 68–68j; 16 C.F.R. pt. 303 (Rules and Regulations Under the Textile Fiber Products Identification Act); 16 C.F.R. pt. 300 (Rules and Regulations Under the Wool Products Labeling Act of 1939). However, there is no requirement that the manufacturer reveal whether any hazardous dyes or other chemicals are used in the fabrication process. *See, e.g., Threading Your Way Through the Labeling Requirements Under the Textile and Wool Acts,* FED. TRADE COMM'N (Jan. 2021), https://perma.cc/S6WV-DNPN; Andrea Plell, *There Are Hidden Chemicals in Our Clothing,* REMAKE (Jan. 5, 2018), https://perma.cc/NK5T-52JA.
2 *See* PRESIDENT'S COUNCIL ON SUSTAINABLE DEV., SUSTAINABLE AMERICA: A NEW CONSENSUS FOR PROSPERITY, OPPORTUNITY, AND A HEALTHY ENVIRONMENT FOR THE FUTURE iv (1996) ("A sustainable United States will have a growing economy that provides equitable opportunities for

satisfying livelihoods and a safe, healthy, high quality of life for current and future generations . . . [It] will protect its environment, its natural resource base, and the functions and viability of natural systems on which all life depends.").
3   See *About Organic Labeling*, U.S. DEP'T OF AGRIC., https://perma.cc/5KLQ-ETUR.
4   Elizabeth Peberdy et al., *A Study into Public Awareness of the Environmental Impact of Menstrual Products and Product Choice*, 11 SUSTAINABILITY 1, 1–2 (2019).
5   *See id.*
6   WOMEN'S VOICES FOR THE EARTH, CHEM FATALE: POTENTIAL HEALTH EFFECTS OF TOXIC CHEMICALS IN FEMININE CARE PRODUCTS 6 (2013), https://perma.cc/8JRQ-76R6.
7   Francesca Branch et al., *Vaginal Douching and Racial/Ethnic Disparities in Phthalates Exposures Among Reproductive-Aged Women: National Health and Nutrition Examination Survey 2001–2004*, 14 ENV'T HEALTH 1 (2015), https://perma.cc/5Y3H-AYLE.
8   Amy Hait & Susan E. Powers, *The Value of Reusable Feminine Hygiene Products Evaluated by Comparative Environmental Life Cycle Assessment*, 150 RES., CONSERVATION & RECYCLING 1, 2 (2019) (citing Feminine Hygiene Market, Statista (2019)), https://perma.cc/5D65-G6MD.
9   *See* Alejandra Borunda, *How Tampons and Pads Became So Unsustainable*, NAT'L GEOGRAPHIC (Sept. 6, 2019), https://perma.cc/4KGR-HANN.
10 Medical Device Amendments of 1976, Pub. L. No. 94–295, 90 Stat. 539 (1976) (codified as amended in scattered sections of 21 U.S.C.). *See* 21 U.S.C. § 360k(a) (giving the Food and Drug Administration jurisdiction over any "device intended for human use" by preempting state laws); *id.* at § 321(h)(1) (defining "device"); *id.* at § 360c(a)(1)(B) (definition of Class II device intended for human use).
11 21 U.S.C.A. § 360c(a)(1)(A).
12 *Id.* at § 360c(a)(1)(B).
13 *See, e.g.*, Roni Caryn Rabin, *Period Activists Want Tampon Makers to Disclose Ingredients*, N.Y. TIMES (May 24, 2017), https://perma.cc/Z5S9-97P7.
14 21 U.S.C.A. § 360c(1)(C)(i)–(ii).
15 *Classify Your Medical Device*, FOOD & DRUG ADMIN., https://perma.cc/8JQ4-DT4T; 21 U.S.C. §§ 360c(a)(1)(B)–(C) (manufacturers of Class II medical devices must follow performance standards set by the FDA, and premarket approvals are required for Class III medical devices); Robert Fenton, *What Are the Differences in the FDA Medical Device Classes?*, QUALIO (Oct. 27, 2020), https://perma.cc/2S72-FUX8.
16 Armand Lione & Jon Kapecki, *Testing Tampons in Rochester: Just What Can You Rely On?*, ROCHESTER (N.Y.) PATRIOT, July 23–Aug. 5, 1975, at 1, https://perma.cc/36LX-KFEG.
17 *See* Ashley Fetters, *The Tampon: A History*, ATLANTIC (June 1, 2015), https://perma.cc/444D-B7VD (describing uses of carboxymethylcellulose, including in Rely tampons).

18 Lione & Kapecki, *supra* note 16.
19 *See* Fetters, *supra* note 17 (quoting NYU microbiologist Philip Tierno).
20 James Todd et al., *Toxic-Shock Syndrome Associated with Phage-Group-I Staphylococci*, 312 LANCET 1116 (1978).
21 *See Toxic-Shock Syndrome—United States*, 29 MORBIDITY & MORTALITY WKLY. REP. 229 (1980), https://perma.cc/8KUT-MM2A.
22 *See Company Found Negligent in Toxic Shock Disease Suit*, N.Y. TIMES (Mar. 20, 1982), https://perma.cc/MG7F-S26X.
23 *See* Fetters, *supra* note 17.
24 Rana A. Hajjeh et al., *Toxic Shock Syndrome in the United States: Surveillance Update, 1979–1996*, 5 EMERGING INFECTIOUS DISEASES 807, 808 (1999), https://perma.cc/B964-MZP6.
25 *See* Michael T. Osterholm & Jan C. Forfang, *Toxic-Shock Syndrome in Minnesota: Results of an Active-Passive Surveillance System*, 145 J. INFECTIOUS DISEASES 458, 459 (1982).
26 *See* Fetters, *supra* note 17.
27 *See Company Found Negligent in Toxic Shock Disease Suit*, *supra* note 22.
28 *See* Hajjeh et al., *supra* note 24.
29 *See* Donald E. Low, *Toxic Shock Syndrome: Major Advances in Pathogenesis, but Not Treatment*, 29 CRITICAL CARE CLINICS 651, 651 (2013).
30 *See id.* at 656.
31 *See* Susan Dudley et al., *Tampon Safety*, NAT'L CTR. FOR HEALTH RSCH., https://perma.cc/S4G8-SBWS (summarizing views of Dr. Rana Hajjeh of the CDC).
32 Pub. Citizen Health Rsch. Grp. v. Comm'r, Food & Drug Admin., 724 F. Supp. 1013 (D.D.C. 1989).
33 *See* 21 C.F.R. § 801.430 (prescribing language that must appear in labeling); *see also* Fetters, *supra* note 17.
34 *See Pub. Citizen Health Rsch. Grp.*, 724 F. Supp 1013.
35 *See Toxic-Shock Syndrome—United States*, *supra* note 21.
36 Tampon Safety and Research Act of 1997, H.R. 2900, 105th Cong. (1997).
37 H.R. 2416, 115th Cong. (2017).
38 H.R. 2900 § 2 (referring to report by the Environmental Protection Agency).
39 *See* Sherry Rier & Warren G. Foster, *Environmental Dioxins and Endometriosis*, 70 TOXICOLOGICAL SCIS. 161 (2002) (finding plausible link between dioxin exposure and endometriosis in rodents). *But see* Jeffrey C. Archer et al., *Dioxin and Furan Levels Found in Tampons*, 14 J. WOMEN'S HEALTH 311, 312 (2005).
40 H.R. 2900 § 2.
41 Ann Borowski, Are American Women Turning to Reusable and Greener Menstrual Products Due to Health and Environmental Pollution Concerns?, at 11 (2011) (M.S. thesis, Rochester Institute of Technology), https://perma.cc/RP89-T5B3.

42 *The Facts on Tampons—and How to Use Them Safely*, FOOD & DRUG ADMIN. (Sept. 12, 2018), https://perma.cc/WYF5-F3JR.
43 See Chris Bobel, *"Our Revolution Has Style": Contemporary Menstrual Product Activists "Doing Feminism" in the Third Wave*, 54 SEX ROLES 331, 333 (2006) (describing a "Dioxin Out of Tampons" campaign started by a group of environmentally minded students in 1999).
44 Dudley et al., *supra* note 31; *see also* Michael J. DeVito & Arnold Schecter, *Exposure Assessment to Dioxins from the Use of Tampons and Diapers*, 110 ENV'T HEALTH PERSPS. 23 (2002), https://perma.cc/RG3K-XWZY; Archer et al., *supra* note 39.
45 See Nadia Kounang, *What's in Your Pad or Tampon?*, CNN (Nov. 13, 2015, 10:19 AM), https://perma.cc/FM6W-RMJB (reporting on WVE's tests of Procter & Gamble's Always pads).
46 Press Release, Women's Voices for the Earth, Hidden Nanosilver in Period Products Is a Concern, Says Health Organization (Apr. 18, 2019), https://perma.cc/GH6C-X7RQ.
47 *Id.*
48 Walter G. Larsen, *Sanitary Napkin Dermatitis Due to the Perfume*, 115 ARCHIVES DERMATOLOGY 363 (1979).
49 See Erica L. Eason & Perle Feldman, *Contact Dermatitis Associated with the Use of Always Sanitary Napkins*, 154 CAN. MED. ASS'N J. 1173 (1996).
50 Jason D. Williams et al., *Allergic Contact Dermatitis from Methyldibromo Glutaronitrile in a Sanitary Pad and Review of Australian Clinic Data*, 56 CONTACT DERMATITIS 164 (2007).
51 See Chan Jin Park et al., *Sanitary Pads and Diapers Contain Higher Phthalate Contents Than Those in Common Commercial Plastic Products*, 84 REPROD. TOXICOLOGY 114, 115 (2019).
52 *Id.* at 117–19.
53 See Ákos Kuki et al., *Rapid Mapping of Various Chemicals in Personal Care and Healthcare Products by Direct Analysis in Real Time Mass Spectrometry*, 192 TALANTA 241, 241–43 (2019).
54 U.S. DEP'T OF HEALTH & HUMAN SERVS., GUIDANCE FOR INDUSTRY AND FDA STAFF, MENSTRUAL TAMPONS AND PADS: INFORMATION FOR PREMARKET NOTIFICATION SUBMISSIONS (510(K)S), at 10 (2005), https://perma.cc/SQ5H-MFLQ.
55 WOMEN'S VOICES FOR THE EARTH, *supra* note 6.
56 *See id.* at 9–10.
57 See Kounang, *supra* note 45.
58 Nicole Wendee, *A Question for Women's Health: Chemicals in Feminine Hygiene Products and Personal Lubricants*, 122 ENV'T HEALTH PERSPS. A70 (2014), https://perma.cc/E2N2-DNJQ; *see also* Margaret E. Johnson, *Menstrual Justice*, 53 U.C. DAVIS L. REV. 1 (2019).

59 Michael A. Mitchell et al., *A Confirmed Case of Toxic Shock Syndrome Associated with the Use of a Menstrual Cup*, 26 CAN. J. INFECTIOUS DISEASES & MED. MICROBIOLOGY 218 (2015), https://perma.cc/5LDP-Q97E.

60 *See* Louis Nonfoux et al., *Impact of Currently Marketed Tampons and Menstrual Cups on* Staphylococcus Aureus *Growth and Toxic Shock Syndrome Toxin 1 Production* In Vitro, 84 APPLIED & ENV'T MICROBIOLOGY (2018), https://perma.cc/AYB3-28LB. *But see* Stephanie Soucheray, *New Toxic Shock Study Touts Bad Tampon Advice, Expert Says*, CTR. FOR INFECTIOUS DISEASE RSCH. & POL'Y (Apr. 24, 2018), https://perma.cc/M9SU-HHFX (critiquing study by Nonfoux et al.).

61 *See The Facts on PFAS*, 3M (2019), https://perma.cc/UZ27-BJGJ (describing the company 3M's decision to phase out production of PFOA and PFOS, two types of PFAS, because of potential adverse health and environmental impacts).

62 *See* Jessian Choy, *What You Need to Know About "Nontoxic" Menstrual Underwear*, SIERRA MAG. (Mar. 18, 2020), https://perma.cc/666X-ALUG; Elsie M. Sunderland et al., *A Review of the Pathways of Human Exposure to Poly- and Perfluoroalkyl Substances (PFASs) and Present Understanding of Health Effects*, 29 J. EXPOSURE SCI. & ENV'T EPIDEMIOLOGY 131, 138–40 (2019); Kristen M. Rappazzo et al., *Exposure to Perfluorinated Alkyl Substances and Health Outcomes in Children: A Systematic Review of the Epidemiologic Literature*, 14 INT'L J. ENV'T RSCH. & PUB. HEALTH 691 (2017); U.S. DEP'T OF HEALTH & HUM. SERVS., TOXICOLOGICAL PROFILE FOR PERFLUOROALKYLS (2021), https://perma.cc/AVN5-5GUR.

63 Significant New Use Rule: Long-Chain Perfluoroalkyl Carboxylate and Perfluoroalkyl Sulfonate Chemical Substances, 85 Fed. Reg. 45109 (July 26, 2020) (to be codified at 40 C.F.R. pt. 721), https://perma.cc/SZU5-GEVH.

64 *See* Guomao Zheng et al., *Per- and Polyfluoroalkyl Substances (PFAS) in Breast Milk: Concerning Trends for Current-Use PFAS*, ENV'T SCI. & TECH., May 13, 2021, https://doi.org/10.1021/acs.est.0c06978.

65 *How We Ensure Thinx Are Body-Safe*, THINX (Jan. 14, 2020), https://perma.cc/AUY7-GKAR.

66 Choy, *supra* note 62.

67 Alison Potter & Grace Smith, *Period Underwear Review*, CHOICE (May 25, 2020), https://perma.cc/JL8M-X3UZ (quoting Dr. Talat Uppal).

68 Fair Packaging and Labeling Act, 15 U.S.C. §§ 1451–61.

69 DeVito & Schecter, *supra* note 44.

70 *See, e.g.*, Hyun-ju Ock, *Fears Mount over "Toxic" Sanitary Pads*, KOREA HERALD (Aug. 25, 2017, 9:11 AM), https://perma.cc/JCD6-SZ6P.

71 *See id.*; Jae-hyuk Park, *Korean Moms Flex Muscles Across Board*, KOREA TIMES (Aug. 24, 2017, 6:39 PM), https://perma.cc/JFL4-H9Q8; Alex Scranton, *Women in South Korea Moving Market, Decision Makers to Address Toxic Chemicals in Menstrual Pads*, WOMEN'S VOICES FOR THE EARTH (Sept. 25, 2017), https://perma.cc/Z2L9-QHWN.

72 *See* Jung-hee Song, *Amid Sanitary Pad Scare in Korea, Handmade Reusable Pads Are Becoming Popular*, JEJU WKLY. (S. Kor.) (Sept. 29, 2017, 6:18 PM), https://perma.cc/VQ6Q-FYJ9.
73 *Id.*
74 *See* Ock, *supra* note 70; Park, *supra* note 71; Scranton, *supra* note 71.
75 *See* Kayoung Kim, *"Toxic Chemicals Controversy": Lilian Sanitary Pad, 700 Consumers Are Appealing*, SEOUL ECON. NEWS (Oct. 23, 2020, 3:00 PM), https://perma.cc/EDM5-DDPW (translation by Jiyoon Moon); email from Jiyoon Moon to Bridget Crawford (May 14, 2021, 8:36 PM) (on file with authors) (summarizing the newspaper article's description of the holding and reasoning in the case).
76 *See supra* note 49 and accompanying text.
77 *See* Ciku Kimeria, *The Story of How Kenyan Women Are Bringing P&G to Task over the Always "Burning Pads" Saga*, QUARTZ AFR. (Feb. 26, 2020), https://perma.cc/DZ9Y-U2YA.
78 Email from Claudia Polsky to Bridget Crawford (May 13, 2021, 2:21 AM) (on file with authors).
79 *See* Dudley et al., *supra* note 31.
80 *See* Borunda, *supra* note 9.
81 *See* LARA FREIDENFELDS, THE MODERN PERIOD: MENSTRUATION IN TWENTIETH-CENTURY AMERICA 124–25 (2009); Anna Davidson, *Narratives of Menstrual Product Consumption: Convenience, Culture, or Commoditization?*, 32 BULL. SCI., TECH. & SOC'Y 56 (2012).
82 *See* Peberdy et al., *supra* note 4, at 1–2.
83 *See id.*
84 *See id.*
85 *See id.*
86 *See id.*; Dudley et al., *supra* note 31; Potter & Smith, *supra* note 67.
87 *See id.*
88 *See* Maribel Velasco Perez et al., *Waste Management and Environmental Impact of Absorbent Hygiene Products: A Review*, WASTE MGMT. & RSCH., Sept. 2020, at 5.
89 *See* Kelly-Leigh Cooper, *The People Fighting Pollution with Plastic-Free Periods*, BBC NEWS (May 1, 2018), https://perma.cc/J52X-EEBP; Charley Ross, *Why Is There Plastic in Tampons?*, HUFFINGTON POST (U.K.) (Oct. 31, 2018), https://perma.cc/DJK2-RVRU.
90 *See* Rachel Tseng, *The Cost of Tampons*, THE GREEN CIRCLE (Feb. 14, 2019), https://perma.cc/48EY-DZR8.
91 *See* Ross, *supra* note 89; Simon Reddy, *Plastic Pollution Affects Sea Life Throughout the Ocean*, THE PEW CHARITABLE TRS. (Sept. 24, 2018), https://perma.cc/KV9S-6SZ7.
92 *See* Mallory Creveling, *Just How Bad Is It to Flush a Tampon?*, WOMEN'S HEALTH (Sept. 5, 2018), https://perma.cc/T4HB-PNKQ.
93 *See Toilets Are Not Trashcans Campaign*, NAT'L ASSOC. OF CLEAN WATER AGENCIES, https://perma.cc/D7TE-WWUE.

94 *Facts and Stats*, WEN, https://perma.cc/4TAT-PZMG.
95 Peberdy et al., *supra* note 4, at 493.
96 *See Reusable Applicator Set*, DAME, https://perma.cc/8V8T-U3DC.
97 *Rayon*, HOW PRODUCTS ARE MADE, https://perma.cc/D6MR-NALY.
98 *See* Tseng, *supra* note 90; Tampon Safety and Research Act of 1997, H.R. 2900, 105th Cong. § 2 (1997).
99 *See* Annie Dillon, *Planet-Friendly Periods*, STANFORD MAG., May/June 2017, https://perma.cc/62KY-Y85F.
100 *See* Ross, *supra* note 89.
101 *See* Shreya, *The Ecological Impact of Feminine Hygiene Products*, HARV. BUS. SCHOOL DIGIT. INITIATIVE (Nov. 4, 2016), https://perma.cc/YAT2-G6AZ (carbon footprint of tampons and pads); Liza Wood, *A Menstrual Cup? Is That What Is* [sic] *Sounds Like? Gross*, THE ECO GUIDE (Sept. 17, 2015, 11:49 PM), https://perma.cc/EA8N-F6LM (carbon footprint of silicon cups).
102 *See* Shreya, *supra* note 101 (carbon footprint of low-density polyethylene used in tampons and pads).
103 *See, e.g.*, Hait & Powers, *supra* note 8.
104 *See* Laura Parker, *The World Agrees There's a Plastic Waste Crisis—Can It Agree on a Solution?*, NAT'L GEOGRAPHIC (Mar. 25, 2019), https://perma.cc/L3BD-C7JS.
105 *See* Carole Excell, *127 Countries Now Regulate Plastic Bags. Why Aren't We Seeing Less Pollution?*, WORLD RES. INST. (Mar. 11, 2019), https://perma.cc/4ZMU-KZ28.
106 *See* Sarah Gibbens, *A Brief History of How Plastic Straws Took over the World*, NAT'L GEOGRAPHIC (Jan. 2, 2019), https://perma.cc/DX26-59N4; *State Plastic and Paper Bag Legislation*, NAT'L CONF. OF STATE LEGISLATURES (Jan. 24, 2020), https://perma.cc/9RH9-XBJY.
107 *See* Scott Rodd, *Banning the Bans: State and Local Officials Clash over Plastic Bags*, THE PEW CHARITABLE TRS. (Jan. 29, 2019), https://perma.cc/7K3P-9JGK.
108 *Id.*
109 *See, e.g.*, Jude Webber, *Tampons Vanish as Mexico City Takes Aim at Single Use Plastics*, FIN. TIMES (Feb. 12, 2021), https://perma.cc/Z4YR-RLDP (describing impact of Mexico City's ban on single-use plastics and high prices for applicator-free tampons).
110 *Id.*
111 *See* Rachel Abrams, *Under Pressure, Feminine Product Makers Disclose Ingredients*, N.Y. TIMES (Oct. 26, 2015), https://perma.cc/AL3C-JTYE; *Tampax Tampon Ingredients: What Are Tampons Made of?*, TAMPAX, https://perma.cc/RUM8-LWFV.
112 Joan Raymond, *How Safe Is Your Tampon?*, TODAY (Aug. 14, 2018, 1:49 PM), https://perma.cc/MM48-H4SS (reporting email communication from FDA spokesperson Deborah Kotz).
113 *See* S.B. 7838, 2015–2016 Legis. Sess. (N.Y. 2016); Press Release, Office of the Governor, Governor Cuomo Signs Legislation to Exempt Sales and Use Taxes on Feminine Hygiene Products (July 21, 2016), https://perma.cc/H9VT-9SBM.

114 A. 9922, 2015–2016 Legis. Sess. (N.Y. 2016).
115 Press Release, Office of the Governor, On Day of the Girl, Governor Cuomo Signs Legislation to Make New York the First State in the Nation to Require Disclosure of Ingredients in Menstrual Products (Oct. 11, 2019) [hereinafter Cuomo Press Release to Require Disclosure], https://perma.cc/YXN9-6XHX.
116 See What's in Your Tampon? 2018 Tampon Testing Results, WOMEN'S VOICES FOR THE EARTH, https://perma.cc/SJ3B-4RNK.
117 See Cuomo Press Release to Require Disclosure, supra note 115 (quoting Assemblymember Linda Rosenthal).
118 See Press Release, Women's Voices for the Earth, Governor Andrew Cuomo Signs First-in-Nation Period Product Ingredient Disclosure into Law (Oct. 11, 2019), https://perma.cc/7UUN-4S6E.
119 Menstrual Products Right to Know Act of 2020, A.B. 1989, 2019–2020 Sess. § 1.111822.2(a) (Cal. 2020).
120 Id. at §§ 1.111822(d)–(e).
121 Id. at § 1.111822(c)(1)(C).
122 See Reina Gattuso, Are Scented Tampons Bad for You? Why You Should Avoid Them, PUBLIC GOODS (July 7, 2020), https://perma.cc/S2VA-EN43.
123 Cal. A.B. 1989.
124 Press Release, Women's Voices for the Earth, Women's Voices for the Earth's Statement on the Passing of California's AB 1989, Period Product Ingredient Disclosure Bill (Sept. 30, 2020), https://perma.cc/5CH4-B59R.
125 See generally Claudia Polsky & Megan Schwarzman, The Hidden Success of a Conspicuous Law: Proposition 65 and the Reduction of Toxic Chemical Exposures, 47 ECOLOGY L.Q. 823 (2021) (discussing successes under Prop 65).
126 CAL. HEALTH & SAFETY CODE §§ 25249.5–.14 (West 2021).
127 Id. at § 25249.6.
128 See CAL. CODE REGS. tit. 27, § 25701–21 (2021); List of Chemicals Evaluated for Carcinogens and Reproductive Toxicity, OFF. OF ENV'T HEALTH HAZARD ASSESSMENT (Dec. 2020), https://perma.cc/P66W-C5QR.
129 CAL. HEALTH & SAFETY CODE § 25249.7(d) (West 2021).
130 CAL. CIV. PROC. CODE § 1021.5 (West 2021) (attorneys' fees); CAL. HEALTH & SAFETY CODE § 25249.12(b) (West 2021) (penalties).
131 Polsky & Schwarzman, supra note 125, at 833 n.38 (citation omitted).
132 We thank Claudia Polsky for this suggestion. See email from Claudia Polsky to Bridget Crawford, supra note 78.
133 N.Y. EDUC. LAW § 409-i (McKinney 2005).
134 Id. at 3.
135 Id.
136 See Approved Products Listing, N.Y. STATE OFF. OF GEN. SERVS., https://perma.cc/ZE58-24FG.
137 N.Y. Governor Exec. Order No. 202 (Mar. 7, 2020), https://perma.cc/FR4V-TPNT.

138 *See generally* Katherine Fiedler et al., *Life Cycle Costing and Food Systems: Concepts, Trends, and Challenges of Impact Valuation*, 8 MICH. J. ENV'T & ADMIN. L. 1, 4–7 (2018), https://perma.cc/7V9M-FQKX (describing public procurement policies in the European Union and elsewhere).
139 *See* Menstrual Equity for All Act of 2019, H.R. 1882, 116th Cong. (2019).
140 *See* Laura Strausfeld, *Making Tampons Free Can Make Them Safer, Too*, BLOOMBERG (Aug. 31, 2018, 7:00 PM), https://perma.cc/ELE6-XDR3.
141 *See supra* note 36 and accompanying text.
142 *See, e.g.*, Laura Strausfeld, *The Serious Dangers of Tampons—And You Have to Pay Taxes on Them as Well*, ALTERNET (Apr. 24, 2017), https://perma.cc/9SA7-XCCA.
143 *See* Robert B. Cialdini et al., *A Focus Theory of Normative Conduct: A Theoretical Refinement and Reevaluation of the Role of Norms in Human Behavior*, 24 ADVANCES IN EXPERIMENTAL SOC. PSYCH. 201, 203 (1991).
144 *See generally* Fiedler et al., *supra* note 138. Researchers have also explored the potentially transformative impacts of procurement laws in other contexts. *See, e.g.*, Jason J. Czarnezki, Green Public Procurement: Legal Instruments for Promoting Environmental Interests in the United States and European Union 59–63 (Dec. 13, 2019) (Ph.D. dissertation, Uppsala University), https://papers.ssrn.com/sol3/papers.cfm?abstract_id=3504676.
145 *See, e.g.*, Witold Henisz et al., *Five Ways That ESG Creates Value*, MCKINSEY Q., Nov. 2019, at 2, https://perma.cc/4Y5L-Z6EQ.

CHAPTER 8. MENSTRUAL CAPITALISM

1 *See* Hiroko Tabuchi, *Menstruation Joins the Economic Conversation*, N.Y. TIMES (Apr. 21, 2016), https://perma.cc/G44X-B2M5 (providing figure for U.S. menstrual products as $3 billion in 2014).
2 *See Feminine Hygiene Products Market: Global Industry Trends, Share, Size, Growth, Opportunity and Forecast 2020–2025*, IMARC, https://perma.cc/7M76-25ES.
3 *See* Bridget Crawford, *Against Menstrual Capitalism*, FEMINIST L. PROFESSORS (June 25, 2018), https://perma.cc/66L7-8CSD.
4 *See Always/Tampax: Brand Profiles*, ADBRANDS (Sept. 27, 2016), https://perma.cc/8S3X-YN4C.
5 *See* Paul Hiebert, *Tampax Teams Up with Amy Schumer to Bluntly Talk About Periods*, 212ADV, https://perma.cc/LGG3-BF8F.
6 *See* Peggy Truong, *Amy Schumer Gives a Shout Out to Her Tampon at Emmys Red Carpet*, COSMOPOLITAN (Sept. 19, 2016), https://perma.cc/Y759-SUG7.
7 *See Amy Schumer's Top 5 Feminist Comedy Sketches*, HOLLYWOOD REP. (July 19, 2015, 12:30 PM), https://perma.cc/M2D2-3VJ4.
8 Gina Rodriguez, *What My Life Would Have Been Like if I Missed School Because of My Period*, TEEN VOGUE (Aug. 7, 2018), https://perma.cc/T76Y-6DXU.

9 See Mona Nair, *"Jane the Virgin" Gina Rodriguez Is on a Mission to Help Young Women–Here's Why*, NBC NEWS (Aug. 13, 2018, 1:57 PM), https://perma.cc/37VW-3ZJ8.
10 See Olivia Smith, *Sophia Bush Raises Awareness to Help End Period Poverty for Young Women in the US*, GOOD MORNING AM (Sept. 20, 2019), https://perma.cc/CNB4-ZZ28.
11 *Id.*
12 See *2014: Always Unveils Groundbreaking "Like a Girl" Campaign*, THE DRUM (Mar. 31, 2016, 8:09 PM), https://perma.cc/K5Y9-S8K4.
13 Victoria J. Haneman, *Menstrual Capitalism, Period Poverty, and the Role of the B Corporation*, 41 COLUM. J. GENDER & L. 133, 134–35 (2021).
14 Christina Cauterucci, *Ads for Period Underwear Might Be Too Lewd for the NYC Subway*, SLATE (Oct. 21, 2015, 10:32 AM), https://perma.cc/TH7X-LTWC.
15 See *Give Rise!*, THINX, https://perma.cc/22SS-HMP4.
16 *Certification*, CERTIFIED B CORP., https://perma.cc/U9YN-J6AK.
17 See *About B Corps*, CERTIFIED B CORP., https://perma.cc/R5FY-HZSD.
18 See LISA M. FAIRFAX, BUSINESS ORGANIZATIONS: AN INTEGRATED APPROACH 87 (2019).
19 See DIVA INT'L, DIVA CARES: IMPACT REPORT 2019/2020 (2020), https://perma.cc/JZ6S-JNGM.
20 See *Dignity Projects*, AISLE, https://perma.cc/CPP7-EEBR.
21 See *Meet Madeleine Shaw and Suzanne Siemens, Lunapads International Ltd.*, SMALL BUS. B.C., https://perma.cc/B7EQ-7KBT.
22 See Jeff Kroeker, *How to Expand Your Business While Doing Good*, THE GLOBE & MAIL (May 17, 2013), https://perma.cc/PF65-7425.
23 See *Meet the Entrepreneur Whose Company Sparked a Period Revolution*, DAILY-HIVE (Jan. 15, 2020, 1:12 PM), https://perma.cc/4KXT-KZY4.
24 Toby A. Cox, *Corporate Social Responsibility in 2019: Social Issues People Expect Businesses to Support*, CLUTCH (Apr. 3, 2019), https://perma.cc/9WCZ-CHU5.
25 See *id.*
26 Haneman, *supra* note 13, at 144.
27 See Stephanie Castillo, *New Period Tracker Helps Women Track Their Menstrual Cycle in Real Time*, MED. DAILY (May 25, 2016, 4:57 PM), https://perma.cc/DR4A-JGFS.
28 See Gemma Mullin, *PERIOD DRAMA: Controversial Bluetooth Tampon Lets You Know When It Needs Changing—but Has 12ins [sic] String*, U.S. SUN (Jan. 8, 2020, 8:10 AM), https://perma.cc/V5ET-V2N3.
29 See *id.* (quoting Dr. Jennifer Gunter).
30 LOON Lab, Inc., *Can I Trim the Stem of LOONCUP?, Frequently Asked Questions*, KICKSTARTER (July 9, 2019), https://perma.cc/7XSE-7HCP.
31 LOON Lab, Inc., *LOONCUP Receives FCC Certification*, KICKSTARTER (July 9, 2019), https://perma.cc/U4P4-YFH8.

32 LOON Lab, Inc., *Will the LOONCUP Beep at Airport Security?*, *Frequently Asked Questions*, KICKSTARTER (July 9, 2019), https://perma.cc/7XSE-7HCP.
33 See *The Perfect Period Box for All Who Menstruate!*, BONJOUR JOLIE, https://perma.cc/GLV3-MGXB; *see also* Anna, *18 Best Period Boxes [Tampon & Period Subscription Boxes]*, URB. TASTEBUD, https://perma.cc/W3AX-ZZDY.
34 See *The PMS Package: For That Time of the Month!*, THE PMS PACKAGE, https://perma.cc/T5WR-D98W.
35 *See, e.g.*, *Specialty Boxes*, BONJOUR JOLIE, https://perma.cc/WT36-BT7R.
36 See *Why the Kali Teen Box?*, KALI, https://perma.cc/4QJA-GCKJ.
37 See Paisley Gilmour, *This New Blanket Makes Period Sex SO Much Easier*, COSMOPOLITAN (June 25, 2018), https://perma.cc/YZV4-A49X.
38 Amy Boyajian, *Your Guide to Better Period Sex*, THINX (June 22, 2018), https://perma.cc/5MZ3-SQ5X.
39 Gilmour, *supra* note 37.
40 See Kasandra Brabaw, *I Free-Bled on a $369 Period Sex Blanket to See if It's Worth the Price*, REFINERY29 (Aug. 9, 2018, 4:00 PM), https://perma.cc/AGS9-P6GU.
41 See Shannon Palus, *What We Think of Thinx's Period Sex Blanket*, WIRECUTTER (June 28, 2018), https://perma.cc/CWX7-WUFY.
42 See Amy Woodyatt, *Lidl Ireland Becomes First Major Retailer to Offer Free Period Products*, CNN BUS. (Apr. 20, 2021, 6:44 AM), https://perma.cc/WY5P-FTPA.
43 See Lidl Ireland (@lidl_ireland), TWITTER (Apr. 19, 2021), https://twitter.com/HPeriodBelfast/status/1384208290591035398.
44 See Woodyatt, *supra* note 42.
45 See *Lidl Ireland Period Poverty Initiative*, LIDL, https://perma.cc/6FMS-GTNB.
46 Isabella Kwai, *In Ireland, a Grocery Chain Addresses "Period Poverty" with Free Products*, N.Y. TIMES (Apr. 20, 2021), https://perma.cc/ZA9N-V5TQ (quoting Lidl Ireland spokesperson Aoife Clarke).
47 *Id.*
48 *Id.*
49 See *The Homeless Period Ireland* (@homelessperiodIreland), FACEBOOK, https://www.facebook.com/homelessperiodIreland/about/?ref=page_internal.
50 See Sophie Foster, *Morrisons Praised for Giving Out Free Period Products in "Ask for Sandy" Initiative*, DAILY STAR (U.K.) (Apr. 20, 2021, 12:28 PM), https://perma.cc/AWM9-N838.
51 See Emma Batha, *UK and Irish Supermarkets Fight Period Poverty with Free Tampons and Pads*, GLOB. CITIZEN (Apr. 21, 2021), https://perma.cc/Y89M-F7PY.
52 See Chloe Morgan, *Shoppers Praise Morrisons for Handing Out Free Period Products for Those in Need with "Discreet" New "Ask for Sandy" Initiative*, DAILY MAIL (U.K.) (Apr. 20, 2021, 3:42 PM), https://perma.cc/8JVJ-SAU7.
53 See Carina Hsieh, *9 Period Tracking Apps That'll Never Make You Wonder If Your Period's Starting or If It's Just Discharge*, COSMOPOLITAN (Apr. 21, 2020), https://perma.cc/6DJV-QJLG.
54 *Id.*

55 *See* Arwa Mahdawi, *There's a Dark Side to Women's Health Apps: "Menstrual Surveillance,"* GUARDIAN (U.K.) (Apr. 13, 2019, 7:00 AM), https://perma.cc/LX5H-XWVU.
56 Drew Harwell, *Is Your Pregnancy App Sharing Your Intimate Data with Your Boss?*, WASH. POST (Apr. 10, 2019, 2:11 PM), https://perma.cc/JP3M-CCJV.
57 *Id.* (quoting Karen Levy).
58 *See* Mahdawi, *supra* note 55.
59 *See* Michele Estrin Gilman, *Periods for Profit and the Rise of Menstrual Surveillance*, 41 COLUM. J. GENDER & L. 100, 106 (2021).
60 Lori Andrews, *A New Privacy Paradigm in the Age of Apps*, 53 WAKE FOREST L. REV. 421, 430 (2018).
61 Press Release, Fed. Trade Comm'n, Developer of Popular Women's Fertility-Tracking App Settles FTC Allegations That It Misled Consumers About the Disclosure of Their Health Data (Jan. 13, 2021), https://perma.cc/9ZK5-46TJ.
62 FED. TRADE COMM'N, USING A HEALTH APP?, https://perma.cc/YDF4-P6CL.
63 *See* Gilman, *supra* note 59, at 107–09.
64 *Id.* at 111–12.
65 *See* Garri Chaverst, *Dawn Scott's Best Advice for Girls Soccer Players*, GIRLS SOCCER NETWORK (Aug. 13, 2020), https://perma.cc/3TLE-Z4FL.
66 *See Track Your Period & Train Smarter*, FITRWOMAN, https://perma.cc/HYD6-FL2N.
67 *See* Katie Kindelan, *How Tracking Their Periods Helped USA Women's Soccer Team Win the World Cup*, GOOD MORNING AM. (Aug. 8, 2019), https://perma.cc/R54P-H8Q2 (quoting Dawn Scott).
68 *See* Hannah Lichtenstein, *USWNT Tapped into Menstrual Cycle Science on Road to Victory*, GIRLS SOCCER NETWORK (July 25, 2019), https://perma.cc/AQM6-PRVZ.
69 *See* Katie Kindelan, *USWNT Used Innovative Period Tracking to Help Player Performance at World Cup*, ABC NEWS (July 15, 2019, 1:37 PM), https://perma.cc/5BB4-B9EJ.
70 Kieran Pender, *Ending Period "Taboo" Gave USA Marginal Gain at World Cup*, FEMALE COACHING NETWORK (Sept. 19, 2019), https://perma.cc/JPX7-8EAP (quoting Dawn Scott).
71 *See* Emily Feng, *Uninhibited Chinese Swimmer, Discussing Her Period, Shatters Another Barrier*, N.Y. TIMES (Aug. 16, 2016), https://perma.cc/AD7Q-6ABY (quoting Fu Yuanhui).
72 *See* Harvey Araton, *Oudin's Odyssey to Fourth Round Stirs American Optimism*, N.Y. TIMES (June 27, 2009), https://perma.cc/A35M-7MU5 (quoting Jelena Jankovic).
73 *Menstrual Cycle "Last Taboo" for Women in Sport—Annabel Croft*, BBC (Jan. 20, 2015), https://perma.cc/PW6K-6SGG (quoting Heather Watson).
74 *Id.* (quoting Annabel Croft).

75 *See, e.g.*, Sam Carp, *2019 Fifa Women's World Cup Gave French GDP €284m Boost*, SPORTSPRO (July 7, 2020), https://perma.cc/CA2K-KJZL.
76 *See, e.g.*, Ashley Fetters, *What a Time (for Girls) to Be Alive*, ATLANTIC (July 12, 2019), https://perma.cc/8VBZ-DSPT (describing young girls inspired by the US Women's National Team win in the 2019 World Cup).
77 *See, e.g.*, Chris Rael, *US Club Soccer Estimate $4.2 Million Impact*, SOCCER TODAY (June 8, 2016), https://perma.cc/3VEB-PW8S ("Youth soccer is big business in America....").

CHAPTER 9. MENSTRUATION AROUND THE GLOBE

1 *See, e.g.*, Emily Vaughn, *Menstrual Huts Are Illegal in Nepal. So Why Are Women Still Dying in Them?*, NPR (Dec. 17, 2019, 11:59 AM), https://perma.cc/4X4B-R8KN.
2 *See, e.g.*, Melissa Eddy, *Tampons to Be Taxed as Essential, Not Luxury, Items in Germany*, N.Y. TIMES (Nov. 12, 2019), https://perma.cc/JZ38-U6UH (discussing tampon-tax repeal in multiple countries).
3 *See, e.g.*, Monica Arango Olaya, *Blood, Taxes, and Equality*, OXFORD HUM. RTS. HUB (Nov. 17, 2019), https://perma.cc/4RRB-2KMC (describing adoption of Decision T-398 of 2019).
4 *See* Anna Momigliano, *Italy Set to Offer "Menstrual Leave" for Female Workers*, INDEP. (U.K.) (Mar. 27, 2017), https://perma.cc/PXZ9-JD3R.
5 *See* Scheaffer Okore (@scheafferoo), TWITTER (Feb. 14, 2019, 10:56 PM), https://twitter.com/scheafferoo/status/1096302197816610816 (urging users to share "our personal irritations, discomfort and displeasures with Always pads in the Kenyan market").
6 *See, e.g.*, *About Us*, PADMAD, https://perma.cc/6AQF-W8AA (emphasizing that women can "participate meaningfully in local economics and raise their standings within households and communities" by making and using environmentally friendly menstrual pads offered by PadMad); *Padmad, Initiative on Reusable Sanitary Pad in Kenya*, WTERT, https://perma.cc/3TAC-BWLD (describing network of lower-income women who produce over two thousand reusable pads per week).
7 *See Period Products (Free Provisions) (Scotland) Bill*, THE SCOTTISH PARLIAMENT, https://perma.cc/57UP-2WQX; Megan Specia, *Tackling "Period Poverty," Scotland Is 1st Nation to Make Sanitary Products Free*, N.Y. TIMES (Nov. 24, 2020), https://perma.cc/7LXM-AR3N.
8 Indian Young Lawyers Ass'n v. Kerala (2018) 11 SCC 1, https://perma.cc/AW5S-6CNM.
9 *See Sabarimala*, TIMES INDIA (Apr. 18, 2021, 4:04 AM), https://perma.cc/D8FD-H3J9 (reporting "an estimated over 100 million devotees visiting every year").
10 S. Mahendran v. The Secretary, Travancore Devaswom Board, Thiruvananthapuram, AIR 1993 Ker 42, at ¶¶ 43, 38 (Balanarayana, Marar, J.).
11 *Id.* at ¶ 44 (Balanarayana, Marar, J.).

12 Vidhi Doshi, *India's Supreme Court Rules to Allow Women in Ancient Hindu Temple While Menstruating*, NAT'L POST (Sept. 28, 2018), https://perma.cc/784H-T2JH; Adam Withnall, *India's Supreme Court Strikes Down Ban on "Menstruating" Women Entering One of Hinduism's Holiest Sites*, INDEP. (U.K.) (Sept. 28, 2018, 5:23 PM), https://perma.cc/S2GY-SPXW; *Ready to Wait Till 50 to Enter Sabarimala: Women's Group*, HINDU (Dec. 2, 2016, 11:51 AM), https://perma.cc/7DZV-XYR4.
13 *Indian Young Lawyers Ass'n*, 11 SCC at ¶¶ 15, 17 (Dr. Dhananjaya Y. Chandrachud, J.).
14 *Id.* at ¶ 81 (Dr. Dhananjaya Y. Chandrachud, J.).
15 *See, e.g.*, Niha Masih, *In India, Two Women Defy Protests—and Centuries of Tradition—by Entering a Temple*, WASH. POST (Jan. 3, 2019, 9:06 AM), https://perma.cc/ZKT4-PTQR.
16 *Id.*
17 *Id.*
18 *See* Krishnadas Rajagopal, *Sabarimala Case: Supreme Court Upholds Referring Religious Questions to Larger Bench, Frames 7 Questions of Law*, HINDU (Feb. 10, 2020, 12:57 PM), https://perma.cc/UDF2-GH32.
19 Divya Srinivasan & Bharti Kannan, *Establishing the Constitutionality of Menstrual Exclusion Practices in India*, 41 COLUM. J. GENDER & L. 198, 207 (2021).
20 U.S. AGENCY FOR INT'L DEV., KIAWAH TR. & DASRA, SPOT ON! IMPROVING MENSTRUAL HEALTH AND HYGIENE IN INDIA 10 (2015) [hereinafter SPOT ON!], https://perma.cc/SZ8M-RPQT.
21 Suneela Garg & Tanu Anand, *Menstruation Related Myths in India: Strategies for Combating It*, 4 FAM. PRAC. 184, 184 (2015).
22 *Id.*
23 *See* JENNIFER WEISS-WOLF, PERIODS GONE PUBLIC: TAKING A STAND FOR MENSTRUAL EQUITY 28 (2017).
24 *See* thewisewalkers, *How the "Touch the Pickle" Campaign Touched Hearts*, LADY SHRI RAM COLL. FOR WOMEN (Feb. 4, 2019), https://perma.cc/YK2M-W3R3.
25 MARNI SOMMER ET AL., COLUM. UNIV. & UNICEF, WASH IN SCHOOLS EMPOWERS GIRLS' EDUCATION: PROCEEDINGS OF THE MENSTRUAL HYGIENE MANAGEMENT IN SCHOOLS VIRTUAL CONFERENCE 2012, at 17 (2013), https://perma.cc/KYV5-K6G4.
26 INDIA COUNCIL OF MED. RSCH., ANNUAL REPORT 2005-2006, at 74 (2006), https://perma.cc/7Q3P-SCSC.
27 Sandeep Rai, *Warden Forces 70 Schoolgirls to Strip in Class to Check Who's Menstruating*, TIMES INDIA (Apr. 1, 2017, 2:55 PM), https://perma.cc/GVU8-KCKJ.
28 SPOT ON!, *supra* note 20, at 17, 4, 11 (reporting that 25% of schools in India have no toilets, 40% of schools with toilets do not have separate toilets for girls, and a "[l]ack of functioning toilets results in 23% girls [sic] dropping out of school every year").
29 Anna Maria van Eijk et al., *Menstrual Hygiene Management Among Adolescent Girls in India: A Systematic Review and Meta-Analysis*, 6 BMJ OPEN 1, 6, 8–9 (2016), https://perma.cc/EYQ5-4PL3.

30 Int'l Inst. for Population Scis., Ministry of Health & Fam. Welfare, National Family Health Survey (NFHS-4) 2015–16, at 98 (2017), https://perma.cc/TWS7-RZPD (table showing the percentage of women in different groups who use particular types of "menstrual protection," such as cloth or tampons). The local production of menstrual products is the subject of an Oscar-winning film. See Period. End of Sentence. (Netflix 2018).
31 Petition, Zarmina Israr Khan v. Union of India, W.P. (C) No. 6034 of 2017, at ¶ 14, https://perma.cc/J4ZP-S9RT.
32 See Period. End of Sentence., supra note 30; Pad Man (Twinkle Khanna 2018).
33 Weiss-Wolf, supra note 23, at 35.
34 Petition, supra note 31.
35 Sushmita Dev, Petition to Arun Jaitley for Removal of Tax on Sanitary Napkins, Change.org, https://perma.cc/8Y5D-ASFH.
36 Id.; Maneka Gandhi, Maneka Gandhi's Response, Change.org, https://perma.cc/8JBJ-XTDU.
37 India Scraps Tampon Tax After Campaign, BBC News (July 21, 2018), https://perma.cc/5CGN-FFXU.
38 Petition, supra note 31.
39 India Const. arts. 21 (right to life, right to human dignity), 14 (equality before the law and equal protection), 15, cl. 1 (discrimination on the basis of sex).
40 SC Stays Proceedings Challenging GST on Sanitary Napkins in High Courts, Wire (Jan. 23, 2018), https://perma.cc/JKW5-TZLW.
41 Shetty Women Welfare Found. v. Union of India, Public Interest Litigation No. 76 of 2017; Raise Awareness on Sanitary Napkins: HC to Maharashtra Government, Times India (Jan. 16, 2018, 6:35 PM), https://perma.cc/44PR-5VDB.
42 Press Trust of India, Raise Awareness on Sanitary Napkins: HC to Maha Govt, Bus. Standard (Jan. 16, 2018, 6:25 PM), http://perma.cc/JY4R-BMZX.
43 See Press Release, GST Council, On GST Rate on Goods as Recommended by the GST Council in Its 28th Meeting Held on 21.07.2018 (July 21, 2018), https://perma.cc/6B7Y-XXW3.
44 India Scraps Tampon Tax After Campaign, supra note 37.
45 Eradicating Period Poverty in India, Period! Mag. (Jan. 9, 2020), https://perma.cc/B8KD-US6D (describing work of She Wings, an India-based organization focused on female health and hygiene).
46 See, e.g., Macharia Kamau, Sanitary Towel Usage Still Low Despite Tax Cuts, Standard (Kenya) (June 9, 2009), https://perma.cc/93Y4-GCWY.
47 Id.
48 Id.
49 See Alexandra Geertz et al., FSG, Menstrual Health in Kenya: Country Landscape Analysis 1 (2016), https://perma.cc/G8VG-7DYM.

50 Shannon A. McMahon et al., *"The Girl with Her Period Is the One to Hang Her Head": Reflections on Menstrual Management Among Schoolgirls in Rural Kenya*, 11 BMC INT'L HEALTH & HUM. RTS. (2011), https://perma.cc/54UE-DBEP.
51 *Id.*
52 *Id.*
53 Miriam Gathigah, *Kenya: Government Funds Free Sanitary Pads for Schoolgirls*, GUARDIAN (U.K.) (July 29, 2011, 3:48 AM), https://perma.cc/UW4A-S3AH.
54 *Id.*; *see also* Sanitary Towels Programme Information, MINISTRY OF PUB. SERV. & GENDER, STATE DEP'T OF GENDER, https://perma.cc/R5D7-XUHE.
55 Sanitary Towels Programme Information, *supra* note 54.
56 The Basic Education (Amendment) Act, No. 17 (2017), KENYA GAZETTE SUPPLEMENT No. 97 § 2(b), https://perma.cc/3SR7-G5DK.
57 *See* Abdullahi Mire, *"I Wish I Was a Boy": The Kenyan Girls Fighting Period Poverty*, AL JAZEERA (Feb. 24, 2020), https://perma.cc/MD9D-U7Q2.
58 *See* Sylvania Ambani, *Crooks Caught Repackaging 300,000 Expired GoK Sanitary Towels for Sale*, NAIROBI NEWS (Jan. 17, 2020), https://perma.cc/P5WD-7EWN.
59 *See* Mire, *supra* note 57 (quoting Emmie Eronanga, director of the NGO Miss Koch, which provides menstrual products to girls and raises awareness of women's issues in the country).
60 *Id.*
61 *See* Kevin Mwanza, *Kenya Paves the Way for Menstruators: The Government Approves a Policy Exclusively on Menstrual Health and Hygiene*, WATER SUPPLY & SANITATION COLLABORATIVE COUNCIL (Nov. 26, 2019), https://perma.cc/W3WU-62C8 (quoting a statement issued by the Kenyan President's Strategic Communications Unit about the newly approved policy).
62 *Id.*
63 *Id.*
64 *See* Claire Fialkov & David Haddad, Menstrual Hygiene Management for Girls in Kenya: An Evaluation of the Always School Program (unpublished manuscript), https://perma.cc/H868-Z48W (expressing hope for national curriculum).
65 *See* Maggie Fick, *Kenya Partially Reopens Schools, Six Months After COVID Closed Them*, REUTERS (Oct. 12, 2020), https://perma.cc/LJ7P-EHX3.
66 *See Coronavirus: Kenyan Schools to Remain Closed Until 2021*, BBC NEWS (July 7, 2020), https://perma.cc/7U2Z-W73D.
67 JANE GARDNER ET AL., PLAN INT'L, PERIODS IN A PANDEMIC: MENSTRUAL HYGIENE MANAGEMENT IN THE TIME OF COVID-19, at 12 (2020), https://perma.cc/J32R-5SM3.
68 *See* SARAH HOUSE ET AL., MENSTRUAL HYGIENE MATTERS: A RESOURCE FOR IMPROVING MENSTRUAL HYGIENE AROUND THE WORLD 31 (2012), https://perma.cc/J9QN-WPMW (contrasting attitudes of girls in different countries about sources of information about menstruation).

69 See Damaris Seleina Parsitau & Evelyn Jepkemei, *How School Closures During COVID-19 Further Marginalize Vulnerable Children in Kenya*, BROOKINGS (May 6, 2020), https://perma.cc/JVC3-TKQ4.
70 See Linda Mason et al., *"We Keep It Secret So No One Should Know"—A Qualitative Study to Explore Young Schoolgirls' Attitudes and Experiences with Menstruation in Rural Western Kenya*, 8 PLOS ONE e79132, at 6 (2013), https://perma.cc/QK54-FA55; Matthew Jukes et al., *Education and Vulnerability: The Role of Schools in Protecting Young Women and Girls from HIV in Southern Africa*, 22 AIDS S41 (2008), https://perma.cc/QV7J-LTCN (explaining ways that expanding primary and secondary education for girls reduces risk of HIV infection).
71 Mason et al., *supra* note 70.
72 *Id.*
73 *Id.* at 3.
74 *Id.* at 4.
75 *Id.*
76 Penelope A. Phillips-Howard et al., *Menstrual Needs and Associations with Sexual and Reproductive Risks in Rural Kenyan Females: A Cross-Sectional Behavioral Survey Linked with HIV Prevalence*, 24 J. WOMEN'S HEALTH 801, 804 (2015), https://perma.cc/7GCW-K25A.
77 *See, e.g.*, Ginger Hervey, *Kenyan Schoolgirl, 14, Kills Herself After Alleged Period Shaming by Teacher*, GUARDIAN (U.K.) (Sept. 13, 2019, 3:00 PM), https://perma.cc/X7B3-H6FU.
78 See Vitalis Kimutai, *School Receives Seven-Months Supply of Sanitary Towels*, NATION (Nov. 6, 2020), https://perma.cc/W6HE-E2CG.
79 *Id.*; see also Hon. Esther M Passaris (@EstherPassaris), TWITTER (Sept. 11, 2019, 7:44 AM), https://twitter.com/EstherPassaris/status/1171796692997431297 ("Together with fellow Women MPs, we've laid siege at the Ministry of Education in protest of the 14 year old girl who committed suicide after a female teacher publicly ridiculed her for soiling her clothes with her periods. #EndPeriodShame").
80 See *Dandora Sewage Treatment Plant*, SMEC, https://perma.cc/9XFH-XQCH.
81 Hilary Kimuyu, *Condoms, Sanitary Pads Behind Nairobi's Clogged Sewer System*, NAIROBI NEWS (Aug. 22, 2019), https://perma.cc/9F27-WYD6.
82 Marni Sommer et al., *Girls' and Women's Unmet Needs for Menstrual Hygiene Management (MHM): The Interactions Between MHM and Sanitation Systems in Low-Income Countries*, 3 J. WATER, SANITATION & HYGIENE FOR DEV. 283, 291 (2013), https://perma.cc/TEX8-BTJE.
83 *Id.* at 283–84.
84 *Id.* at 287 (discussing menstruation-related secrecy and the association of menstruation with curses).
85 INTERMEDIATE TECH. DEV. GRP., LIVELIHOODS & GENDER . . . IN SANITATION, HYGIENE AND WATER SERVICES AMONG THE URBAN POOR (2005), https://perma.cc/3DBA-89NX.
86 Sommer et al., *supra* note 82, at 290.

87 Damaris Mbui, *I Looked at How Polluted Nairobi River Is. What I Found*, CON-VERSATION (Oct. 7, 2019, 9:45 AM), https://perma.cc/5XCX-3YSZ.
88 *Id.*
89 *See, e.g., GST (Goods and Services Tax)*, INLAND REVENUE, N. Z. GOV'T, https://perma.cc/RST8-UQPN.
90 *See, e.g.,* Eli Meixler, *Australia Ditches "Tampon Tax" After 18 Years of Outrage from Women's Rights Groups*, TIME (Oct. 2, 2018), https://perma.cc/D6LV-JRHM (quoting Josh Frydenberg).
91 *See, e.g., "Tampon Tax": Australia Decides Not to Remove Controversial Levy*, BBC NEWS (Aug. 21, 2015), https://perma.cc/QC7D-YSTD.
92 *See* Miranda Stewart, *Seeking Sanity on GST Sanitary Tax Debate*, TAX & TRANSFER POL'Y INST.: AUSTAXPOLICY (Oct. 9, 2019), https://perma.cc/3S6B-ECNZ; Jennifer Hewett, *Tampering with the Tampon Tax Is Peak Silliness*, FIN. REV. (Aug. 5, 2018, 5:18 PM).
93 *See* Melanie Wilcock, *GST Removed from Female Sanitary Products*, CHANGE.ORG, https://perma.cc/US9M-BEBC (petition to Minister for Women Paula Bennett).
94 *See* Tom Pullar-Strecker & SMH, *NZ Unlikely to Follow Australia in Axing "Tampon Tax," Says Expert*, STUFF (Oct. 3, 2018, 4:08 PM), https://perma.cc/B4UN-L2Y6 (quoting Allan Bullot).
95 *Id.*
96 Press Release, Prime Minister Jacinda Ardern & Hon. Julie Anne Genter, New Zealand Gov't, Free Period Products in Schools to Combat Poverty (June 3, 2020), https://perma.cc/2P5B-T5XD; Press Release, Prime Minister Jacinda Ardern & Hon. Jan Tinetti, New Zealand Gov't, Free Period Products to Be Available in All Schools and Kura (Feb. 18, 2021) [hereinafter Press Release, Free Period Products in Schools and Kura], https://perma.cc/5HD5-TQ9L.
97 *See* YOUTH19, YOUTH19—PERIOD POVERTY FACT SHEET, https://perma.cc/A5AB-9D6U; *see also Ministry Funding Deciles*, EDUCATION.GOVT.NZ (Jan. 27, 2020), https://perma.cc/E6R9-FKQ6.
98 Press Release, Free Period Products in Schools and Kura, *supra* note 96.
99 Press Release, Victoria State Gov't, Free Sanitary Pads and Tampons in All Government Schools (Aug. 5, 2020), https://perma.cc/4JTH-3ACN.
100 *See South Australian Schools Tackle "Period Poverty" with Free Pads and Tampons for Students*, ABC NEWS (Austl.) (Feb. 11, 2021, 3:42 AM), https://perma.cc/3N2T-BD6X.
101 *See* Madeleine Keck, *This Australian State Will Experiment with Free Pads and Tampons in All Public Schools*, GLOB. CITIZEN (Mar. 5, 2021), https://perma.cc/9N4B-HSKW.
102 *Almost a Quarter of New Zealand Women Who Responded to a KidsCan Survey Have Missed School or Work Because They Have Been Unable to Afford Sanitary Items*, KIDSCAN (Nov. 1, 2018), https://perma.cc/TR3W-SB5J.

103 *See* Anastasia Santoreneos, *The Demeaning Truth of What It Means to Be Poor in Australia*, YAHOO FIN. AU (Nov. 13, 2019), https://perma.cc/B5VL-8YE4.

104 HOMELESSNESS AUSTL., HOMELESSNESS AND WOMEN (2013), https://perma.cc/P2MM-96PT.

105 Craig Quartermaine, *WA Police Criticised for Fining Woman Who Stole Tampons*, NITV (Oct. 19, 2015, 8:47 PM), https://perma.cc/83JR-N47H; Calla Wahlquist, *Aboriginal Woman in WA Fined $500 for Stealing $6.75 Box of Tampons*, GUARDIAN (U.K.) (Oct. 14, 2015, 11:26 PM), https://perma.cc/YJW5-STRG.

106 *Homelessness*, AUSTRALIAN GOV'T DEP'T OF SOC. SERVS. (Oct. 3, 2019, 9:44 AM), https://perma.cc/9RU4-VLXQ.

107 Press Release, Countdown, Lower Prices on Sanitary Products Aim to Help Reduce Period Poverty (July 24, 2018), https://perma.cc/55TJ-H29K.

108 *See, e.g.*, Adele Merson, *Aberdeen Hosts £42,500 Trial Providing Free Sanitary Products*, EVENING EXPRESS (July 12, 2017, 10:29 AM), https://perma.cc/S8ML-KDNR.

109 *See* Jill Foster, *The MP Praised for Speaking About Her Period in Parliament on Why We All Need to Address Period Poverty*, GLAMOUR (July 16, 2018), https://perma.cc/5NUN-858P (quoting Danielle Rowley).

110 Danielle Rowley, *I Told the House of Commons I Was on My Period, but I Shouldn't Have Had To*, INEWS (U.K.) (June 29, 2018, 5:11 PM), https://perma.cc/XB7P-93B3.

111 *See* Ceylan Yeginsu, *Scotland to Provide Free Sanitary Products to Students*, N.Y. TIMES (Aug. 29, 2018), https://perma.cc/JVA2-52A3.

112 *See* Laurel Wamsley, *Scotland Becomes 1st Country to Make Period Products Free*, NPR (Nov. 25, 2020, 12:29 PM), https://perma.cc/47EK-XR9L.

113 SCOTTISH GOV'T, ACCESS TO FREE SANITARY PRODUCTS PROGRAMME FOR GOVERNMENT COMMITMENT: BUSINESS AND REGULATORY IMPACT ASSESSMENT 1 (2018) [hereinafter ACCESS TO FREE SANITARY PRODUCTS IMPACT ASSESSMENT], https://perma.cc/HMC4-SWRV.

114 *See* Wamsley, *supra* note 112.

115 *Students to Get Free Access to Sanitary Products*, SCOTTISH GOV'T (Aug. 24, 2018, 12:00 PM), https://perma.cc/8XRF-TRYQ.

116 ACCESS TO FREE SANITARY PRODUCTS IMPACT ASSESSMENT, *supra* note 113, at 2–3.

117 *See* Libby Brooks, *Scottish Council to Provide Free Sanitary Products in Toilets*, GUARDIAN (U.K.) (Aug. 17, 2018, 9:47 AM), https://perma.cc/WC6J-UH59.

118 *Id.* (quoting Joe Cullinane).

119 Specia, *supra* note 7 (quoting Monica Lennon).

120 *See* Gina Davidson, *Scotland Becomes First Country to Have Universal Free Period Products*, SCOTSMAN (Nov. 24, 2020, 6:52 PM), https://perma.cc/8WC5-HUMG.

121 *Id.*

122 *See* Wamsley, *supra* note 112.
123 *See* Laurel Wamsley, *Scotland Poised to Become 1st Country to Make Period Products Free*, NPR (Feb. 27, 2020, 1:23 PM), https://perma.cc/TZN7-5DAQ (quoting Neil Findlay).
124 Specia, *supra* note 7 (quoting Monica Lennon).
125 *Id.* (quoting Aileen Campbell).
126 *Id.* (quoting Nicola Sturgeon).

CONCLUSION

1 *See* Press Release, Nippon TV, Global Hit Format Dragon's Den Reaches Milestone 40th Adaptation (Jan. 14, 2020), https://perma.cc/J2WJ-M6RC.
2 *See* Katie Jgln, *And the Most Sexist Invention Award Goes to This German Startup*, MEDIUM (Apr. 21, 2021), https://perma.cc/NV8B-FXV5.
3 *Produktdetails*, PINKY GLOVES, https://perma.cc/NP87-PA78 (translation by authors).
4 *See, e.g.*, Jennifer Gunter (@DrJenGunter), TWITTER (Apr. 13, 2021, 9:01 PM), https://twitter.com/DrJenGunter/status/1382182119670124544; Gabriela Greilinger (@ggreilinger), TWITTER (Apr. 14, 2021, 11:46 AM), https://twitter.com/ggreilinger/status/1382404866350387210; Nik Still Staying Home (@longtimetohere), TWITTER (Apr. 13, 2021, 11:02 PM), https://twitter.com/longtimetohere/status/1382212552482979840; Luna (@Lunalore), TWITTER (Apr. 13, 2021, 9:41 PM), https://twitter.com/Lunalore/status/1382192155301658624; Schwarz-Roter Henno (@realHenno), TWITTER (Apr. 14, 2021, 1:32 AM), https://twitter.com/realHenno/status/1382250383393882113.
5 *See* Mustafa Gatollari, *People Are Roasting the Men Who Made These Pink "Period Gloves" for Women*, DISTRACTIFY (Apr. 22, 2021, 7:58 AM), https://perma.cc/YS9K-5PAS.
6 *See* Kristine Cannon, *3 Dudes Create Pink Glove to Dispose of Tampons & Just . . . WTF*, SCARY MOMMY (Apr. 15, 2021), https://perma.cc/4EZB-VHF7 (quoting Instagram posts from the Pinky Gloves account); *Statement*, PINKY GLOVES, https://perma.cc/HR69-HC5V (translation by authors).
7 *See, e.g.*, Gail (@_AngelLady_), TWITTER (Apr. 24, 2021, 2:31 AM), https://twitter.com/_AngelLady_/status/1385889056433876993; melissa beutler (@melissagoin), TWITTER (Apr. 13, 2021, 9:35 PM), https://twitter.com/melissagoin/status/1382190725262098433; Kristine Tarbert, *"Disappointed": Pink "Tampon Gloves" Spark Outrage Online*, YAHOO LIFESTYLE (Apr. 19, 2021), https://perma.cc/6DKV-N43A.
8 *See, e.g.*, Alice Hearing, *Tampon Tax: How Laura Coryton Started the "Stop Taxing Periods" Campaign While a Student*, INDEP. (U.K.) (Feb. 23, 2016, 3:28 PM), https://perma.cc/3T9J-TNC9.
9 Sarah Groustra, *Stigma Around Periods Produces Undue Shame*, SAGAMORE (Apr. 26, 2018), https://perma.cc/G6N8-9HHE.

10 Shannon Barbour, *Middle Schoolers Protest After Their Principal Said They'd "Abuse the Privilege" of Free Tampons*, COSMOPOLITAN (Oct. 30, 2019), https://perma.cc/KCM9-RC8F.
11 *See* CARES Act, Pub. L. No. 116–136, 134 Stat. 281 (2020); Press Release, Congresswoman Grace Meng, FEMA to Permit Homeless Assistance Providers to Purchase Feminine Hygiene Products—Such as Tampons and Pads—With Federal Grant Funds (Mar. 1, 2016), https://perma.cc/J9VQ-3TCA.
12 Press Release, Congresswoman Grace Meng, Meng Renews Effort to Make Menstrual Hygiene Products More Accessible and Affordable to Women (Feb. 13, 2017), https://perma.cc/8NXA-XW7L.
13 *See, e.g.*, ALA. CODE §§ 14-3-44, 14-6-19 (2019); Press Release, Office of the Mayor, Mayor de Blasio Signs Legislation Increasing Access to Feminine Hygiene Products for Students, Shelter Residents and Inmates (July 13, 2016), https://perma.cc/R7NJ-Y7TS.
14 *See, e.g.*, Eleanor Goldberg, *Women Often Can't Afford Tampons, Pads in Federal Prisons. That's About to Change*, HUFFPOST (Dec. 20, 2018, 11:12 AM), https://perma.cc/HX22-EXGB.
15 *Sabarimala: India's Kerala Paralysed amid Protests over Temple Entry*, BBC NEWS (Jan. 3, 2019), https://perma.cc/TWR6-58WB.
16 Eliza Collins, *This Lawmaker Pushed the Trump Administration to Put Tampons in Prisons. She Isn't Stopping There*, USA TODAY (May. 28, 2019, 11:23 AM), https://perma.cc/K9BX-NDLS (quoting Grace Meng).
17 *See* Ema Sagner, *More States Move to End "Tampon Tax" That's Seen as Discriminating Against Women*, NPR (Mar. 25, 2018, 7:01 AM), https://perma.cc/25L2-VWL5.

INDEX

absenteeism, 14–15, 69–70. *See also* attendance at school
access to menstrual products: affordability barring, 69, 198–99; constitutionality of, 99; in India, 192; law ensuring, 86–87; Maloney, S., on, 104–5; Meng highlighting, 103; menstrual capitalism addressing, 181; in prisons, 91–93; in public, 104–5; Salt Lake City encouraging, 106; students impacted by, 69, 71; tampon tax contrasted with, 64; women impacted by, 200–201
accommodations, 51–57, 79–80, 113, 116–20, 123–24
ACLU. *See* American Civil Liberties Union
activism, 208; bleaching changed by, 153; for disclosure, 163–67; law and, 3–7, 25–31, 163–67; against tampon tax, 3–4; in twenty-first century, 4; of Weiss-Wolf, 5
advertisements: empowerment in, 175; feminism embraced by, 173–75; inclusivity in, 140–41; for menstrual products generally, 24–25; by Procter & Gamble, 175; public awareness, 163; for Thinx, 175–76
advocacy: discrimination situating, 143; global, 10; inclusivity in, 142–45; international, 49; leaders in, 6; for menstruation, 144; "naming and shaming" in, 164; by student, 66; against tampon tax, 48–49; third-wave feminism drawn on by, 4. *See also* menstrual advocacy movement

affordability: access barred by, 69, 198–99; in homeless shelters, 13; in Kenya, 194; of menstrual products, 14–16, 31, 36, 194; shame and, 70; students impacted by, 70–71, 200, 202–3
Aisle, 176–77
Ajello, Edith, 49
Akinyi, Dorothy, 194
Always (menstrual products), 154, 157, 174
American Civil Liberties Union (ACLU), 96, 101, 134
Americans with Disabilities Act, 51, 119
Aotearoa. *See* New Zealand
applicators, 147, 158, 159, 160, 161, 163, 164
apps, 173, 183–84
Ardern, Jacinda, 199–200
Are You There God? It's Me Margaret (Blume), 1, 23–24
Arizona, 32, 50, 91–92, 163
Arkles, Gabriel, 143
Arnold, Stephanie, 86–87
attendance at school, 14–15, 69–70, 191–92, 194–95
attitude: on menstrual equity, 126; toward menstrual leaves, 124; on menstruation, 135–36; as negative, 124–25; politicians and, 49, 92, 210–11; as positive, 124. *See also* stigma
Australia, 16, 26, 28, 198; environmental issues, 159; menstrual products provided in, 107, 189; New Zealand relationship with, 198–99; period poverty in, 200–201; tampon tax eliminated in, 37, 49, 199

availability of menstrual products, 28–29, 60–61, 63–64, 168–69, 188–89, 198, 203–4
awareness: Johnson, J., on, 88; law compared with, 78; menstrual equity with, 17; of menstruation, 210; of period poverty, 15–17, 33, 87–88; of trans experience, 133–34

Bangladesh, 20
bar exam, 32
Barzilay, Arianne, 123
Basic Education Amendment Act, 195
bathrooms, 28, 66–67, 69–70, 72–80, 105–6, 116–17, 129, 137–38, 159, 255n28; disparate impact imposed by, 78, 118; in factories, 117; OSHA on, 117–18
Baxter, Bex, 127
B-corporation, 176–78
Berman, Jennifer, 31
Biden administration, 75, 82
Bill Emerson Good Samaritan Food Donations Act, 89
B Lab, 176
bleaching, 153
Bluetooth, 178–79
Blume, Judy, 1, 23–24
Blumenfield, Bob, 107
Bobel, Chris, 3, 4
Bonds, Anita, 49
Bostock v. Clayton County, 74–75
Boston Women's Health Book Collective, 2–3
Bozelko, Chandra, 93–94
Brief, Amanda, 178
Brown, Elizabeth, 106
Brunner, Jennifer, 41–42
Bullot, Allan, 199
Bush, Sophia, 175

California, 93, 102, 107, 162; menstrual products in schools, 62–63, 73; Menstrual Products Right to Know Act in, 165–66; pink tax prohibited by, 141; tampon tax in, 41, 48–49, 55, 63
California Federal Savings and Loan Association v. Guerra, 123
Cameron, David, 35
Campbell, Aileen, 203, 205
Canada, 36–37, 153
Canadian Medical Association Journal, 153
Canny, Paula, 93
carcinogens, probable in menstrual products, 154, 161, 167
CARES. *See* Coronavirus Aid, Relief, and Economic Security
C-corporation, 176
CDC. *See* Centers for Disease Control and Prevention
celebrities, 18, 24, 174–75
Centers for Disease Control and Prevention (CDC), 150–51
Chamallas, Martha, 122, 137
Chambers-Saini, Carinne, 176–77
Champion, Sharron, 86–87
Chavarriaga, Alexandra, 100
Chicago, Judy, 4
Chiddix, Posey, 66
China, 122
Chopra, Parineeti, 190
Clemmer, Cass, 11
coaches, 77, 185
Coexist, 127
Coleman, Alisha, 110–17
Columbus, Ohio, 106
comparison: complexity of, 50–56; discrimination and, 51, 56; in law, 56, 67–68; limits of, 56–57; menstruation requiring, 113–14
complexity, 12, 50–56, 131–33
compliance, 6, 117; law limited by, 30, 209; within prisons, 90–91; procurement laws incentivizing, 168–69; Proposition 65 enforcing, 167; *Washington Post* on, 91

constitutionality: against abuse, 99–100; of access, 99; in *Geduldig v. Aiello*, 44; of menstrual products, 99–102; of tampon tax, 42–49; women protected by, 190
consumer: health of, 156–58; manufacturer changed by, 177–78; procurement laws influencing, 170; public intervening on, 162–63
control, 93–96
Copps, Sheila, 36
Coronavirus Aid, Relief, and Economic Security (CARES), 31–32
Coryton, Laura, 34, 208
cosmetics, 155
Cosmopolitan (magazine), 4, 38
cost, 16, 36, 65, 158–61, 201
Cotropia, Christopher, 15, 69–71
cotton, 147, 153, 158–61, 169
Countdown, 140–41, 201, 241n39
COVID-19 pandemic: education in, 195; healthcare delivery during, 29–31; hygiene disrupted in, 29; law revealed by, 30; menstrual products during, 31–32; menstruation in, 25–31; period poverty in, 27; schools impacted by, 29; toilet access during, 28; water access during, 28
Cox, Courtney, 24
"Creating a More Equal Post-COVID-19 World for People Who Menstruate" (Sommer), 130
Croft, Annabel, 186
Cullinane, Joe, 203
culture, 18, 19, 20, 23–24, 50, 57–58, 83–84, 134, 197
Cuomo, Andrew, 40, 57, 63–64, 72, 141, 165

Dame, 160
Darnell v. Piniero, 100
Davis v. Monroe County School Board of Education, 81–82
de Blasio, Bill, 62
delivery, 26–27

detainees, 103–4
Dev, Sushmita, 192
Dillon, Caroline, 66
dioxins, 151–53, 154, 155, 161
disclosure: activism for, 163–67; of contents, 153–54, 163–64; laws on, 163–67; in legislation, 164; in New York, 164–65; on packaging, 165; procurement laws met by, 168–70; Women's Voices for the Earth demanding, 164
discrimination: comparison and, 51, 56; EEOC and, 115; Equal Protection Clause violated by, 40, 44; firing as, 110–16; Flores opinion determining, 113–14; in *McDonnell Douglas Corp. v. Green*, 53–54; menstrual leaves reduced by, 121; menstruation basing, 7–9, 40, 44–45, 99, 110–15, 145; self-reporting impacted by, 133–34; sex, 7–9, 40, 44–45, 99, 110–15, 143–45; significant burden contrasted with, 55; tampon tax as, 37–38, 42; Title IX prohibiting, 68–69, 74, 110
disparate impact, 78–79, 118
disposability, 29, 158
Diva International, Inc., 176
double standard, 39–40
Due Process Clause, 100
Dümmel, Ralf, 207
dysphoria, 136

education, 196; in COVID-19 pandemic, 195; culture supplementing, 18; on environment, 160; Lennon prioritizing, 204; on menstruation, 83–85; in schools, 200; stigma fought by, 83–84; taboo and, 190; teasing and, 84
EEOC. *See* Equal Employment Opportunity Commission
employees, 8, 110–18, 125–26
employer, 111–12, 115, 126–29
employment discrimination, 52–54, 109–29

empowerment, 174; in advertisements, 175; halo effect and, 172–73; menstrual capitalism selling, 187; period subscription boxes emphasizing, 179–80; with philanthropy, 175–76
endometriosis, 29–30, 238n27
environment, 146–71, 254n6
Environmental Protection Agency (EPA), 152–53
Equal Employment Opportunity Commission (EEOC), 115
Equal Protection Clause, 1, 40, 42, 44, 102
Eronanga, Emmie, 257n59
essentialism, 12
Ethiopia, 20
euphemism, 21, 105, 140, 182

facial neutrality, 43–47
factories, 117
Fair Packaging and Labeling Act, 155
FDA. *See* Food and Drug Administration
Federal Bureau of Prisons, 90
Federal Emergency Management Agency (FEMA), 87–88
feminine hygiene products. *See* menstrual products
feminism, 173–75
FemTech, 184
Ferreras-Copeland, Julissa, 60–61, 68, 72, 86
Findlay, Neil, 204
Fingerson, Laura, 80
First Step Act, 8, 89, 91, 209
FitrWoman, 185
Flo Health, Inc., 184
Flores, Alba Quinones, 104, 113–15, 118
Flores, Jennifer, 98–99
Flores, Joyce, 109–10
Flores v. Va. Dep't of Corr., 113–14, 144–45
Florida, 40–41, 48, 50, 54, 91, 93
Food and Drug Administration (FDA), 3, 148–49, 151
Ford, Gerald, 148

Frank, Sarah, 136–38
Free the Tampons, 128–29
Frydenberg, Josh, 199
Fugate, W. Craig, 88
Fu Yuanhui, 186

Gandhi, Kiran, 61
Garcia, Cristina, 62–63
Geary v. Dominick's Finer Foods, Inc., 3–4
Geduldig v. Aiello, 44–45, 51–52
gender: GLAAD-Harris poll on, 133–34; language and, 134–35; marketing and, 138–40; menstrual products highlighting, 138–39; menstruation and, 9, 11, 131–32, 139–40, 196–97, 211; profit and, 177; in schools, 73; of students, 72–73; tampon tax framed by, 49; Title IX protecting, 74–75; Williams Institute study on, 133–34
gender nonbinary individuals, 11; menstruation and, 9, 11, 132–139, 145
General Electric v. Gilbert, 44
Georgia, 50, 64–65
Gilman, Michele, 184
Ginsburg, Ruth Bader, 47, 123
Girl Scouts, 6
Girls in Power (Fingerson), 80
GLAAD-Harris poll, 133–34
Good Samaritan Menstrual Products Act, 88–89
Gottlieb, Alma, 21
Goyal, Deepinder, 127–28
Green, Robert, 91
Grillo, Trina, 12
Grimm, Gavin, 74–75
Groustra, Sarah, 105
Gunter, Jen, 179
Gurowitz, Margaret, 24

Hakim, Jamal, 107
halo effect, 170, 172–73
Haneman, Victoria, 175, 178
Hannifin, Kiri, 241n39

harassment, 8, 17, 80–83, 96, 121
Harry Potter (Rowling), 130
health, 9, 146–71. *See also* toxic shock syndrome
healthcare, 29–31, 137
Hernandez, Barbara, 73
High School for Arts and Business, 60–61
hoarding, 26
Die Höhle der Löwen (television show), 207
Homeless Period Ireland, 181
homeless shelters, 13, 61–62, 86–87, 181, 188
Houglin, Melissa, 99
humiliation, 95, 103, 117
hygiene, 27–30, 140

identity, 134–35
"If Men Could Menstruate" (Steinem), 21–22
Illinois, 3, 36, 48, 63, 73
immigration, 103–4
inclusivity: in advocacy, 142–45; of Countdown, 140–41; of language, 12, 134, 142; within menstrual advocacy movement, 142; reductionism contrasted with, 135; trans people and, 130–31
India, 190; access to menstrual products in, 192; environmental issues in, 162; menstrual leave in, 127–28; pandemic in, 26–27; taboos in, 20, 188–90; tampon tax repealed in, 49, 57, 192–93; toilet access in, 28, 255n28
intermediate scrutiny, 42, 47
Ireland, 15, 181
I Support the Girls, 26, 86, 87, 176
Italy, 122, 188

Jaising, Indira, 189
Jankovic, Jelena, 186
Jenner, Caitlyn, 131
Johnson, Jeh, 88
Johnson, Margaret, 16–17, 111

Johnson, Patti, 100–101
Jones, Jan, 64

Kagan, Elena, 59, 85
Kannan, Bharti, 190
Karlan, Pamela, 75
Kelly, Brigid, 49, 57, 210–11
Kelly, Megyn, 22
Kenya, 10, 20, 29, 30, 193, 195, 198; affordability in, 194; availability in, 188–89; consumer backlash against Procter & Gamble in, 156–58, 194; environmental issues in, 198; Sanitary Towels programme providing, 194–95; schools in, 194–97; social media in, 157; taboos in, 188, 197; tampon tax, 36, 37, 188, 193–94
Kenyatta, Uhuru, 195
Khan, Zarmina Israr, 192–93
Kory, Kaye, 96–97
Kotz, Deborah, 164
Kramer, Nancy, 128–29
Krengel, Rachel, 13

language, 9, 11–12, 73, 139–42; complexity of, 132–35; inclusivity and, 130–32, 134, 142
Lau, Holning, 45
Lavelle, Rose, 185
law: access ensured by, 86–87; activism and, 3–7, 25–31, 163–67; apps and, 183; awareness compared with, 78; comparison in, 56; compliance limiting, 209; COVID-19 pandemic revealing, 30; on disclosure, 163–67; enforcement officials in, 95; gender specified by, 85, 122–23; on harassment, 81–82; menstrual equity and, 25, 85, 89, 209; on menstrual products, 67–68; menstruation and, ix, 7, 10–11, 205, 209; schools impacted by, 67–68; silence from, 25; sustainability through, 161–62; with third-wave feminism, 5
Lawrence, Jay, 92

Learn with Dignity Act, 63, 73
Lee, Joo-young, 156
legislation, 40, 48–50, 62, 65, 72, 86, 89, 91, 104, 120, 122–28, 151, 164–65, 202, 210
Lennon, Monica, 33, 202, 204–5
Levy, Karen, 183
Li, Hillary, 45
Lidl Ireland, 181–82
Lilian (menstrual products), 156
litigation, 6–7, 36, 39–42, 48, 93–94, 98–99, 101–2, 156, 189–90
LOONCUP, 179
Lord Ayyappa Temple, 189–90, 209
Los Angeles, 107
luxury items, 34–36, 39–40, 47, 50, 56, 106, 192

Maloney, Carolyn, 151–52, 169
Maloney, Sean Patrick, 104–5
manufacturer, 162–63, 169–70, 177–78, 242n1
market, 172–73, 176–78, 194
marketing: gender and, 138–40; of menstrual products, 138–40; packaging displaying, 138–39; rhetoric in, 172–73; trans people ignored by, 138
Marlowe, Dana, 26, 89
McCormick, Emily Bell, 49
McCray, Chirlane, 62
McDonnell Douglas Corp. v. Green, 53–54
McHugh, Maureen C., 21
Medenhall, Erin, 106
media, 4–5, 23–25, 34, 72, 78, 87, 134, 174. *See also* social media
Melbourne, 107
men, 21–22, 43, 46–47, 51, 73, 80–81, 84, 114, 123, 125–26, 130–45, 207–8
Meng, Grace, 31, 72, 107, 210; access highlighted by, 103; with FEMA, 87–88; Menstrual Equity for All Act proposed by, 64, 90, 98, 128, 152, 209; menstrual equity prioritized by, 88–89

menstrual advocacy movement, 1, 16–17; history of, 2–3; inclusivity within, 142; language of, 142; on social media, 208; women's health movement with, 2–3
menstrual capitalism, 172–87
menstrual cup, 35, 96–97, 140, 146–48, 154, 160, 165, 169, 172, 175, 178
menstrual equity, 37, 67, 125; attitude on, 126; with awareness, 17; Ferreras-Copeland championing, 61; law and, 25, 85, 89, 209; Meng prioritizing, 88–89; in New York, 86–87; safety contrasted with, 157–58; tampon tax beginning, 57–58; Weiss-Wolf coining, 16; Women's Voices for the Earth explaining, 16
Menstrual Equity for All Act, 72, 104; Meng proposing, 64, 90, 98, 128, 152, 209
menstrual justice, 16–17
menstrual leaves, 123; attitude toward, 124; decline in, 121; discrimination reducing, 121; for employees, 125–26; employer adopting, 126–27; Italy considering, 122; menstrual products compared with, 128; women debating, 122
menstrual products, 13; absenteeism influenced by, 14–15; advertisements for, 24–25; affordability of, 14–16, 31, 36, 194; alternative, 154, 160; Australia providing, 189; availability of, 60–61, 63–64, 168–69; bar exam excluding, 32; Bluetooth in, 178–79; buildings providing, 105; in California, 62–63; categories of, 147–48; constitutionality of, 99–102; cost of, 65; during COVID-19 pandemic, 31–32; delivery of, 26–27; for detainees, 104; disposability of, 29, 158; employer providing, 128–29; environment damaged by, 158, 161; Equal Protection Clause and, 102; Federal Bureau of Prisons

on, 90; gender highlighted by, 138–39; hoarding of, 26; in Kenya, 156–58; law on, 67–68; Lidl Ireland distributing, 181; in Los Angeles, 107; luxury items compared with, 34–36, 39, 50; market for, 172; marketing of, 138–40; in Melbourne, 107; menstrual leaves compared with, 128; Muskegon County Jail withholding, 101; in New York, 63–64; in North Ayrshire, 203; in Ohio, 106; plastic in, 158–59; price of, 27; in prisons, 8, 89–102; private governance for, 170–71; in public, 104–8; Reading on, 138; regulation of, 148–51; in restroom, 70, 129; safety of, 154; Sanitary Towels programme (Kenya) providing, 194–95; scarcity of, 103; in schools, 59–66, 68–71; Scotland providing, 72–73, 202–3; social media seeking, 87; in South Korea, 156–58; stigma reduced by, 66–67; sustainability of, 146; as tax exemption, 54–55, 193; technology and, 178–79; terminology of, 140; toilets broken by, 159; toxicants in, 152; uniform and, 77; use of, 147–48; women with, 140, 256n30, 257n59; at work, 128–29; yarmulkes compared with, 40, 43, 47
Menstrual Products Right to Know Act, 165–66
menstrual surveillance, 185–87
menstruation: accommodation concerns, 79, 119; advocacy for, 144; Ardern concerned with, 199–200; attendance impacted by, 191–95; attitude on, 135–36; awareness of, 210; bathrooms and, 117; business of, 9–10; in China, 122; coaches focusing on, 185; comparison required for, 113; complexity in, 131; *Cosmopolitan* highlighting, 4; in COVID-19 pandemic, 25–31; discrimination based on, 7–9, 40, 44–45, 99, 110–15, 145; education on, 83–85; of employees, 8, 110–16; employer and, 115; environment influenced by, 146–71; gender and, 9, 11, 131–32, 139–40, 196–97, 211; around globe, 188–207; health and, 9, 146–71; with hygiene, 140; in identity, 134–35; in language, 130; law and, ix, 7, 10–11, 205, 209; in media, 23–25; by men, 130–45; misunderstandings on, 17; in New Zealand, 189; in PDA, 115–16; performance impacted by, 185–86; pregnancy contrasted with, 45–46; preparedness for, 70–71; in public, 86–108; in schools, 59–85; separation caused by, 20; shame of, 13–33, 76–77; Shanley on, 23; silence on, 1, 15–16, 20–23; stigma of, 13–33, 70, 77, 210; of students, 72–75; students impacted by, 8; technology and, 187; termination and, 110–16; for trans people, 135–38; at work, 109–29
"Menstruation Bathroom," 4
menstruators, 17, 130–31, 134–35, 142
Mexico City, 163
Mikkelsen, Sarah, 140–41
Mirvis, Tova, 19–20
Modess (menstrual products), 24
Modi, Narendra, 26–27
Morrisons, 182
most-favored-nation argument, 53–54, 68
Mother Jones (magazine), 104
Muller v. Oregon, 123
Murphy, Megan, 131
Muruganantham, Arunachalam, 192
Muskegon County Jail, 101
my.Flow, 178

Nader, Ralph, 3, 151
Nairobi River, 198
nanosilver, 153, 154
National Family Health Survey, 191–92
Nebel, Rebecca, 69

New York: consumer product disclosure laws in, 164–65; menstrual equity in, 86–87; menstrual products in, 63–64; pink tax banned in, 141–42; schools in, 59–62; tampon tax in, 39–40, 62
New York State Green Cleaning Law, 168
New Zealand, 189, 198–202
Nguyen, Viet, 66
Nike, 126–27
Nilson, Jorie, 13
North Ayrshire, 203
Northern Tanzania, 81, 84
"No Water, No Toilet Paper, No Tampons" (Redden), 104

Obama, Barack, 47
Obama administration, 74–75
Obergefell v. Hodges, 45, 57
Occupational Safety and Health Administration (OSHA), 117–18
ocean, 159
Ocean Conservancy, 159
Office of Civil Rights (OCR), 71–72, 79–80, 82
Ohio, 41–42, 57, 106
Okore, Scheaffe, 188–89
Orthodox Judaism, 19–20
OSHA. *See* Occupational Safety and Health Administration
Our Bodies, Ourselves, 2–3

packaging, 138–39, 141, 165
Pad Man, 192
pads. *See* menstrual products
Pandora's Box, 177
Patriot (newspaper), 149–50
PDA. *See* Pregnancy Discrimination Act
perfluoroalkyl and polyfluoroalkyl substances (PFAS), 154–55
period. *See* menstruation
period blanket, 180
Period. End of Sentence, 192
Period Equity, 5, 8, 16, 169

period leave. *See* menstrual leaves
period poverty, ix, 7, 182; in Australia, 200–201; awareness of, 33, 87–88; Campbell addressing, 203; in COVID-19 pandemic, 27; Homeless Period Ireland addressing, 181; in homeless shelters, 86–87; in New Zealand, 200–201; New Zealand addressing, 199–200; in *Pandora's Box* exploring, 177; private actors addressing, 201; in Scotland, 189, 202; shame of, 13–33; stigma with, 13–33, 15
Period Products Bill, 2, 33, 203–4
period subscription boxes, 179–80
Personnel Administrator v. Feeney, 43
petition, 34, 36
PFAs. *See* perfluoroalkyl and polyfluoroalkyl substances
philanthropy, 175–76
phtalic acid esters, 153
Piebiak, Jill, 36–37
pink tax, 141–42
Pinky Gloves, 207–8
pit latrines, 198
Planned Parenthood, 131
plastic: environment hurt by, 163; in menstrual products, 158–59; with polyethylene, 161; sustainability reducing, 162
Polsky, Claudia, 158–59
polyethylene, 161
pregnancy: in *Geduldig v. Aiello*, 51–52; menstruation contrasted with, 45–46; OCR supporting, 71–72; in *UPS v. Young*, 52
Pregnancy Discrimination Act (PDA), 44, 51–52, 79; accommodation within, 119; limitations of, 119–20; menstruation in, 115–16; PWFA compared with, 120; Title IX amending, 112
Pregnant Workers Fairness Act (PWFA), 51–52, 57, 120
price, 27, 180, 201. *See also* affordability

prisons: abuse in, 94, 101; access in, 91–93; compliance within, 90–91; litigation challenging, 98; menstrual products in, 8, 89; visitors to, 96–98
privacy, 184
private actors, 201
private governance, 170–71
Procter & Gamble, 139; advertisements by, 175; celebrities with, 174; in Kenya, 156–57; within market, 173; market developed by, 194; Rely by, 149–51; social media used by, 174–75; taboo utilized by, 190
procurement laws, 168–70, 250n144. *See also* Sustainable Menstrual Products Procurement Policy
production, 160–61
profit, 177
Proposition 65. *See* Safe Drinking Water and Toxic Enforcement Act of 1986
protest, 6, 67, 190, 209
public: access in, 104–5; buildings in, 104–8; consumer intervened on by, 162–63; manufacturer intervened on by, 162–63; menstrual products in, 107–8; menstruation in, 86–108. *See also* bathrooms; homeless shelters; prisons; schools
Public Citizen Health Research Group, 3, 151
PWFA. *See* Pregnant Workers Fairness Act

Radcliffe, Daniel, 130
rational basis, 41, 42, 43, 48
rayon, 147, 153, 160–61
Reading, Wiley, 136–37, 138
Redden, Molly, 104
"Red Flag," 4
reductionism, 135
regulation, 115–16, 148–51
Rely, 149–51
rhetoric, 172–73. *See also* language

Rigby, Cathy, 24
Rodríguez, Anahí, 163
Rodriguez, Gina, 174
Rose, Elizabeth, 62
Rosenthal, Linda, 38, 40, 164–65
Rowley, Danielle, 202
Rowling, J. K., 130–31, 134
Rydström, Klara, 137–38

Sabarimala decision, 189–90, 209
Sachimi Mochizuki, 121
Safe Drinking Water and Toxic Enforcement Act of 1986 (Proposition 65), 166–67
safety, 151–52, 154, 157–58, 197–98
sales tax, 39
Salman, Athena, 92
Salt Lake City, 106
Sanghera, Jyoti, 17
Sanitary Towels programme (Kenya), 194–95
Scalia, Antonin, 40, 43, 47
scarcity, 103. *See also* COVID-19 pandemic
Schofield, Kim, 64
schools: bathrooms at, 75–76; COVID-19 pandemic impacting, 29; education in, 200; gender in, 73; in Illinois, 63; law impacting, 67–68; menstrual products in, 59–66, 68–71; menstruation in, 59–85; in New York, 59–62; stigma in, 20, 61; teasing impairing, 82–83. *See also* absenteeism; attendance at school
Schumer, Amy, 173–74
Scotland, 204–5; menstrual products provided by, 72–73, 202–3; period poverty in, 189, 202; Period Products Bill passed in, 2, 33
Scott, Dawn, 10, 185
Sebert Kuhlmann, Anne, 14
Serino, Sue, 38
sewer and wastewater systems, 28, 159, 197–98

shame: affordability and, 70; control with, 93–96; euphemisms signaling, 21; in Kenya, 197; of menstruation, 13–33, 76–77; Modess signaling, 24; of period poverty, 13–33; State of the Period reporting, 18; with stigma, 13–33; for trans people, 136
Shanley, Laura, 23
Shetty Women Welfare Foundation, 193
silence: culture of, 50; from law, 25; on menstruation, 1, 15–16, 20–23; Pinky Gloves contrasted with, 208; social media defying, 23; stigma reflected by, 13; tampon tax and, ix, 49
Simms, Natalie, 95
soap, 27–28
social media, 258n79; #bloodybarpocalypse on, 32; #EndPeriod Poverty, 174; in Kenya, 157; menstrual advocacy movement on, 208; menstrual products sought on, 87; #MyAlwaysExperience, 157; #periodsarenotaninsult on, 22; Piebiak crediting, 36–37; Procter & Gamble using, 174–75; silence defied on, 23; students using, 67; Trump on, 22
Sommer, Marni, 130
South Korea, 156–58
Spendlove, Robert, 49–50
sports, 185–87, 189
Srinivasan, Divya, 190
State of the Period, 14–15, 18, 69
statutory amendment, 115–16
Steinem, Gloria, 21–22, 23
Stewart, Miranda, 199
stigma: Countdown removing, 241n39; in culture, 19; education fighting, 83–84; Garcia fighting, 63; Lawrence reinforcing, 92; menstrual products reducing, 66–67; of menstruation, 13–33, 70, 77, 210; with period poverty, 13–33; Pinky Gloves reinforcing, 207–8; in schools, 20, 61; shame with, 13–33; silence reflecting, 13; UN on, 102

Stone, Rebecca, 105
Strausfeld, Laura, 5, 38–39, 169
students: access impacting, 69, 71; advocacy by, 66; affordability impacting, 70–71, 200, 202–3; gender of, 72–73; menstruation impacting, 8; menstruation of, 72–75; social media used by, 67; teachers limiting, 76
Sturgeon, Nicola, 205
styrene, 154
Sununu, Chris, 72
superabsorbent tampons, 149–51
Supreme Court, of United States, 42, 53–56, 68
sustainability: through law, 161–62; of menstrual products, 146; New York State Green Cleaning Law exemplifying, 168; plastic reduced with, 162; private governance for, 170–71; profit and, 177
Sustainable Menstrual Products Procurement Policy, 169

taboo, 13, 17, 19–21, 63, 68, 70, 121, 127, 188–91, 197–98, 210; athletics and, 186; education and, 190; Procter & Gamble utilizing, 190; Rowley on, 202; waste and, 198. *See also* shame; stigma
Táin Bó Cúailng, 19
Tampax Period Education Survey, 17
tampon. *See* menstrual products
Tampon Safety and Research Act, introduced, 151–52
"Tampons for ALL" (McCray), 62
tampon tax, 7–8, 52–53, 56; access contrasted with, 64; activism against, 3–4; advocacy against, 48–49; in Australia, 10, 16, 35, 37, 49, 57, 188, 199; in California, 41, 48, 55, 63; in Canada, 36–37; in Colombia, 49, 57; comparison dismantling, 67–68; in Connecticut, 48, 91; constitutionality of, 42–49; in culture, 57–58; as discrimination,

37–38, 42; facial neutrality arguments and, 43–47; in Florida, 7, 40–41, 48, 50, 54, 91, 93; gender framing, 49; in Georgia, 50, 64–65; in Illinois, 3–4, 36, 63; in India, 10, 35, 49, 57, 188, 192–93; intermediate scrutiny analysis, 46–47; in Kenya, 10, 34, 37, 188, 193–94; in legislation, 48–50, 188; menstrual equity efforts beginning with, 57–58; in New York, 39–40, 48, 62; in New Zealand, 199; in Ohio, 41–42, 48, 49, 57; petitions against, 34, 36–37, 56, 208; silence and, ix, 49; similarity influencing, 54–55; in UK, 10, 34–35, 49, 57, 64–65, 188, 208; variations on, 34–35; Washington, DC, 48; Washington State, 49, 57
TANF. *See* Temporary Assistance to Needy Families
tax exemption, 34–35, 39, 50, 54–56, 193
teachers, 20, 76–77, 174
teasing, 80–84
technology, 178–79, 183, 187
Temporary Assistance to Needy Families (TANF), 14
Tennessee, 91, 92–93, 97–98
termination from employment, 110–16
terminology, 134–35, 140
Thinx, 15, 154–55, 175–76, 180
third-wave feminism, 4–6
Tinetti, Jan, 200
Title IX, 1, 71–72; discrimination prohibited by, 68–69, 74, 110; disparate impact embraced by, 78–79; employer violating, 111–12; gender protected by, 74–75; OCR compared with, 79–80; PDA amended by, 112; termination violating, 112–13
toilets, 1, 25, 27, 28, 32, 59, 63–67, 70–75, 82, 85, 97–100, 105–8, 109, 116–18, 128–29, 159, 191, 203–5, 207, 255n28
Torah, 19

toxicants, 3, 152, 154, 169
toxic shock syndrome (TSS), 3, 92; CDC on, 150; with menstrual cup, 154; superabsorbent tampons and, 149–51; in women, 150–51
trans individuals: awareness of, 133–34, 136; discrimination contrasted with, 143; *Flores* opinion, 145; GLAAD-Harris poll on, 133–34; inclusivity and, 130–31; marketing, 138; menstruation for, 135–38; Williams Institute study, 133–34
Trump, Donald, 22
Trump administration, 22, 74–75, 82
TSS. *See* toxic shock syndrome
Turano, Cynthia, 102

UK. *See* United Kingdom
UN. *See* United Nations
uniforms, 76, 77, 78, 79
United Kingdom (UK), 35, 64–65
United Nations (UN), 102
United States Department of Agriculture v. Moreno, 48
United States v. Virginia, 47
United States v. Windsor, 57
UPS v. Young, 52, 68
US Women's National Soccer Team, 10

VDOC. *See* Virginia Department of Corrections
Vernose, Vienna, 66–67
Vimalarajah, Subeta, 37
Virginia Department of Corrections (VDOC), 109–10
visitors to prisons, 96–98

Washington Post (newspaper), 91
waste, 155, 158–63, 197–98
water, 15, 17, 19, 26, 28, 30, 100, 155, 159, 190, 197–98
Watson, Emma, 130

Watson, Heather, 186
Weiss-Wolf, Jennifer, 4, 31, 38, 60, 105, 143; activism of, 5; Ferreras-Copeland coalition with, 86; menstrual equity coined by, 16; third-wave feminism and, 5–6
Whaley, Betty Ann, 94
Widiss, Deborah, 115
Williams Institute study, 133–34
women's health movement, 2–3

Women's Voices for the Earth, 16, 154, 164–66
Wood, Jill, 70
work, 109–29

yarmulkes, 40, 43, 47
Yumiko Murakami, 121

Zambrano-Byrakov, Ana, 61
Zomato, 127–28

ABOUT THE AUTHORS

BRIDGET J. CRAWFORD is Professor of Law and a University Distinguished Professor at the Elisabeth Haub School of Law at Pace University.

EMILY GOLD WALDMAN is Professor of Law and the Associate Dean for Faculty Development & Operations at the Elisabeth Haub School of Law at Pace University.

Lightning Source UK Ltd.
Milton Keynes UK
UKHW011829150622
404479UK00003B/63/J